Dead Men Still Snore

A WOMAN'S TRUE STORY OF LOVE, LOSS AND CHANNELING HER HUSBAND'S MESSAGES FROM THE OTHER SIDE

TAMMY TYREE

Shale Empire Press

Dead Men Still Snore: A Woman's True Story of Love,
Loss & Channeling Her Husband's Messages from the Other Side
A memoir by Tammy Tyree, BCCHt
Copyright© 2022 Tammy Tyree
https://tammytyree.com

Published by: Shale Empire Press
Division of Shale Empire Properties Ltd.
830 Brian Road, Kelowna, BC, V1X 1H4

Cover by: Tammy Tyree & Larch Gallagher

Editing: Kenzie Templeton

ISBN:
EBook: 978-1-7780658-1-1
Paperback: 978-1-7780658-0-4
Hardcover: 978-1-7780658-2-8
Large Print: 978-1-7780658-4-2
Audio: 978-1-7780658-3-5

A Note About the Cover Design

I am what I would call an "Aspiring Artist." Teetering somewhere on the
edge of "okay" and "pretty good," I like to dabble and dribble paint on the
canvas when time allows. Where I don't think any artistic talent lies, hidden
or otherwise, I was encouraged by a friend who is a "retired" graphic artist to
meditate on this book, then create a painting of my own to be used in the
cover design. With many thanks to Christy Brennand for her input,
feedback and creativity, the cover was painted and then improved upon by
the talented Larch Gallagher.

The meaning of the Canary will soon become apparent, as will the cigarette.
The eye of the Canary, however, may not seem as obvious as the beak on his

face. This is a cutout of the headlight of our Jeep, whose role in our drama will unfold before you in the first chapter.

The skull in the cigarette smoke, well... that was *not* intended. Believe it or not (and it was quite unbelievable), it simply *appeared* there when I was blending the whites and grays into the curl of the smoke.

My husband would have been the first person to say he didn't carry a lick of creative talent in the nail of his pinky finger, but based on my knowledge of his input in all aspects of this memoir, I'd say he finally had his Picasso moment.

Contents

"Do you think the universe fights for souls to be together? Some things are too strange and strong to be coincidences."
—— Emery Allen

"Coincidence is the language of the stars. For something to happen, so many forces have to be put into action."
—— Paulo Coelho

Donna —

Thank you so much for your support, feedback & sharing your story with me! Appreciate you so much & look forward to a new friendship!

Much love,
Tammy
xo

This book is dedicated to my incredible children, without whom my life would have no meaning, no purpose, no plan. Also to K.K. We are forever grateful you're part of our family.

Introduction

It's difficult to have loved and lost, especially when the person we've lost has left us for reasons beyond our control. For many, the pain of losing a child, a spouse or a parent to an unforeseen event lays a shocking burden upon our hearts for what feels like an eternity. Well-meaning friends and their condolences may punctuate that pain repeatedly, or, perhaps through certain, personal beliefs to which we cling, we hold those we've lost in the endless depths of mourning. Those who have traveled the path of losing a loved one in an accident or some other senseless occurrence know very well this universal truth: there are many jagged rocks along the milestones of healing, some which can easily be tossed aside, while others are boulders, impossible to budge.

For those who remain in the land of the living, we are left with so many questions unanswered. How could it be that our beloved was hit by the only other car on the road within miles, the driver falling asleep at the wheel in the moment just before impact? What do we call it when the circumstances leading to our loved one's departure happen in the same, small fragment of time as the events that ultimately claim their life? To what degree is our loss either the hand of God manipulating destiny as it's always been written, or the influence of the Devil, hell-bent on disrupting and corrupting the grand Divine Plan? We may find ourselves able to easily answer some of these questions, or we may choose to ignore them, leaving them to the disparaging argument of Fate v. Coincidence.

Let me be clear. This is a book about "coincidence." Or, more to the point – that *there are none*. Growing up, I was raised in the Christian tradition, and so my understanding of "coincidence" was based on the belief that every eventuality was either "God's Will" or the "Devil's Work" being done. For example, if someone died from a drug overdose, then clearly, the Devil had run amok in that person's life and took the poor soul to the depths of Hell to join Satan's Legion. On the other hand, a child running into the road to retrieve her ball, only to be met with the bumper of an SUV, was clearly an act of God's Will, and the child – thankfully – would now reside at the Lord's side in Heaven and become an angel. Provided, of course, she had been baptized within the first few weeks of birth. If not, then who knew?

When we believe that the reason for any eventuality is either the result of God's hand or the Devil's, we thereby give ourselves someone or something to *blame.* The same goes for the all-powerful notion of "coincidence." Nonetheless, if you hold firm to the belief in Heaven or Hell, I can respect that. I was, after all, indoctrinated into the same belief throughout my childhood, and I have tasted that particular brand of Kool-Aid. However, the bitter, limiting flavor never sat right with me, and I now adhere to a far different story, which you will learn... later. And that brings me to an important point I must note before our story begins. The word "later" may seem a bit repetitive throughout this book, but I had no choice. You see, this story starts at a place in my life *after* making mud pies was fun, but *before* getting off the couch was difficult, and, as with any story, there is required background to provide to make the foreground of the full picture clear... later. So please, bear with me, snuggle up and keep turning the page.

It all starts with the passing of my second husband in February 2019. This is where the "truth" of our existence, in our human "skin suits" and beyond, is proven to me beyond reasonable doubt, as relayed to me by the spirit of my late husband for the benefit of all humankind. In writing this book, I am making an attempt to share this truth with you, as it has been tasked upon me. This book was written for each and every one of us, and, in particular, those who find themselves facing the "accidental" death of a loved one, or their own certain demise through an incurable malady. This book is *especially* for those in search of the truth, those who know in their hearts that there is much more to our existence than just *to exist*. This is for those who've experienced far too many synchronistic events in their lives that a belief in "coincidence" is no longer possible. My story, I hope, will provide you with proof.

Know that this story is genuine. The events within these pages really happened to me, to the best of my shaky, concussed recollection, and this is my life as I know it to be. I have changed the names of friends and family involved, or mentioned no name at all. Not to belittle their existence, but merely to protect and respect the privacy of those individuals. Thank you for allowing me to share my story and the messages from Source encoded within these pages.

Now, let us begin.

CHAPTER 1

The End

February 28, 2019, Mexico

Slowly, like moving through thick sludge, I opened my left eye. The view was hazy, tinted red, but I saw him. His golden-blonde head leaning against the steering wheel, the Jeep's powdery white driver's side airbag now deflated and tinged red, resting under his head. A useless pillow. Splatters and smudges of blood lay under his left cheek, dribbling down the once-white airbag.

I looked at his face. *That's not right,* I thought.

His upper jaw appeared to be dislodged from his mouth; his beautiful, large white teeth broken in the center spacing, almost crumpled in half. His face was hollow. Cheeks sunken, eyes closed. His silky mane of blonde hair smeared with red, and his long, proud German nose, broken repeatedly in bar fights and logging accidents, was now shifted and busted yet again for the final time. My strong, indestructible husband leaned against the steering wheel, broken. His body was limp, arms resting between rubbery legs. In the single moment my left eye opened, viewed the *not right* and then closed again... I knew.

Michael was gone.

VORTEX

After seeing the "not right" and knowing in my heart that Michael had passed, I closed my eye and entered The Vortex. I could feel my body *whooshing* backward and felt for certain I had just exited my dimension for a new reality, one without Michael in it. I felt no hands and wasn't aware of any voices, just the feeling of being pulled back, as if through thick, dark water.

This is it, I'm alternating my universe. Wait, am I dying? I can't leave my children! I want to see my grand baby grow up!

I peered into the darkness, looking for the opening to the black hole that had just swallowed me, but I found nothing. Frozen in terror, I called on Archangels Michael, Raphael, Gabriel, Uriel, Haniel and Jesus Christ to wrap me in a healing blanket of protection, love and light, then hung on for dear life. My children's faces flashed before me, gripping my heart. I said a silent goodbye in the event this was, indeed, my ending, and I promised to watch over them from my new place in the cosmos.

In retrospect, I realized I was physically feeling the pull of a person – or persons – dragging me out of the vehicle and placing me on the shoulder of the highway. But in my mind, I was being pulled from my current universe into another, anticipating whatever was next. Somewhere, very far in the distance, I heard the faint wail of sirens, then... nothing.

SCENE

I'm sitting on the side of the highway, blood streaming down my face, saying, "I don't know what happened, I don't know what happened," over and over again. My mind refuses to register the trauma. I'm in a state of unconsciousness, only my mouth hasn't gotten the memo. My white T-shirt and black and white flowered skirt, both particular favorites, are now completely soaked with blood. Michael's upper body, limp and broken, rests on the side of the highway as far as they could pull him; his lower body, legs and feet still resting inside the back of the Jeep, which is turned on its side, how it had landed after an endless roll. None of this scene I can recall, but all of it will be described to me... later.

Michael's beloved Jeep – dubbed the "Canary" for its bright yellow bird color – is completely obliterated: roll bars ripped off, the front windscreen, the hood of the engine and the entire driver's side are all gone. Shards and chunks of the apparently destructible hardtop roof are spewed about the highway, along with all of our luggage – the first things to exit the stage and the first things to be picked clean by the Federales and heartless observers. Michael's once-shiny, beautiful pride, his toy and his joy, is now completely mangled, taking its owner with it in a similar fashion. Its final resting place will be some Mexican Auto Wreckers to be recycled for what few parts can be salvaged, but that must be nearly impossible. Likely, it will be crushed into a smaller, denser version of what lay on the road-side. Besides, if Michael could no longer have his toy, then nobody could.

Debris is everywhere, scattered far and all across the highway. A boat trailer lays behind the obliterated Jeep, mysteriously devoid of an owner, marking its place in our macabre play. A line-up of vehicles pull in behind the Canary and the on-coming lane as vehicles approach, slow down and then stop. Onlookers exit their vehicles, gawking and shouting, then someone calls the local police, who arrive within minutes yet far too late for my beloved. Someone I don't know covers Michael's body with a towel, and other people, speaking Spanish, try to help me, wash my face and offer water, but I'm oblivious, trapped in my own world of confusion. My malfunctioning brain is in a tremendous state of shock, a broken record on repeat, "I don't know what happened."

Mexican paparazzi – locals with cell phones – snap picture after picture that will later be spread around the web, splashed across television screens in between tragic Mexican soap operas as the latest breaking headline. And others, being as obvious as shoppers at a blue light sale, rifle through our bags and belongings thrown across the highway, stealing any piece of our lives they deem valuable; jewelry, money, laptops, iPads, iPhones and passports to be gifted or sold later. The ambulance arrives, and paramedics move me from my seated position beside Michael's limp body to a spinal board, a loathsome neck brace then strapped around me, holding my neck loosely in its too-large grip.

I feel nothing, am aware of nothing. I'm not in my body at all. As they lay me on the board, my arms – elbows bent at a 45-degree angle, hands bloody and fingers curled into tight fists – are unmovable if anyone even tries. Rigor mortis of the living, but why? Something I will soon be wracking my tortured, concussed, uncooperative mind about. The paramedics hoist me, unconscious, into the back of the ambulance and head for the nearest hospital, sirens wailing. Assessing my injuries and finding them to be "minor," they alter their route, taking me to the local clinic where my new life, born of chaos and tragedy, will begin... later.

THE BEGINNING

April 1990, Canada

The first time I met Michael, I was a fresh-faced-23-year-old, married to another man and about nine months pregnant. It was a beautiful April morning in 1990, just a few days before the arrival of our first-born daughter, Nicole. My husband Wayne and I were sitting in our 1977 white Corvette Stingray, parked near a local cafe, T-roof off, as the day was a bright and warm one in our small, Canadian mountain town. The Corvette was replete with red leather interior; super classy if you were a bell-bottomed-pants-wearing-flower-child of the 70s, or a hairy-chested-porn-star of any era. We were neither, so it was a ridiculous expenditure that proved to be a less-than-perfect vehicle and a soon-to-be impractical one.

Michael was strolling to his own vehicle, a refurbished, lifted Chevy, approximate year, 1970. For most men with a lifted vehicle, I'd find myself wondering which body part he was compensating for, but I made an exception with Michael. He was tall, probably 6'2", thickly-muscled with a long torso, so a smaller vehicle just wouldn't fit his frame, and it was quite likely all of his body parts were proportionate. (Not that I gave any thought to said parts at that time – that juicy tidbit is reserved for later.) He was sporting a freshly-shaved head and those delightfully large gold-rimmed, aviator-style glasses, a fashion win of the time that would later become iconic when an ironically cool dude named Napoleon Dynamite would bring them back into a weirdly acceptable style. His glasses were perched upon a rather prominent, proud nose. I noted a slight deviation to the right and briefly wondered what stories that nose could tell.

Despite the shaved head, or maybe because of it, I thought

he was incredibly handsome. He had a brilliant smile, with very large white teeth that fit his mouth perfectly. His thin upper lip was cleverly disguised behind a burnt auburn roguish mustache, not quite the Magnum P.I. chop he was likely going for, but I noted the effort. His eyes were an intense denim blue, softened by feathery blonde lashes and – to this day – still the most gorgeous eyes I've ever seen, apart from my children. He was wearing jeans, heavy work boots and a simple T-shirt. A thin gold chain and small gold cross lay over the shirt fabric, glinting in the sun. I briefly mused what wearing the cross meant to him, whether it was a testament to his personal beliefs or simply a gift bestowed upon him by a friend or relative. I did note that there was an absence of curly chest hair peeking above the collar of his T-shirt. This was a fairly rare condition in most men, in my personal opinion of such things. Michael, as I would discover much, much later, was nothing like most men.

"Hey there, how are you doing?" Holy hell, the voice! An incredibly melodic, deeply resonant, sexy vibration came from the House of Beautiful Teeth. I could tell that he was fairly lean and muscular, but not to the extent of supplementation or steroid use, and he didn't strike me as the kind of guy who would need it, so this voice – this resonant, deep dive into the baritone end of the band – this was *all* him.

"Awesome! How are you?" Wayne replied. "This is my wife, Tammy." He remembered to introduce me. Brownie points for him.

"Hello," I smiled and gave a brief wave. My shoulder-length dirty-blonde hair, curly from a recent permanent, bobbed in its ponytail as I nodded toward him. I was wearing a short skirt and T-shirt to beat the heat of the glorious spring day. The outfit complimented my best feature – "Legs for Days" – and my burgeoning belly nicely.

"Hello, and congratulations," the baritone nodded toward

my basketball. I hadn't quite reached watermelon status yet, but despite the 60 pounds I gained during that pregnancy, my belly stayed well out in front, giving nothing away from the backside view, should one be looking at my backside.

"Thanks," I replied, and that was the extent of our first conversation. I wasn't naïve to the glint in his deep blue eyes as he swiftly glanced over my long, tanned legs and ready-to-breastfeed chest. Both were impressive (if I may be so audacious), and unlike other characters who may have made the same notation, Michael didn't creep me out. Rather, I felt comfortable being so admired by this Zeus of a man.

The guys chatted for a bit, during which I discovered they had met at the shooting range and had spent a little time together "plinking" (the term used for driving on forestry roads and "shooting at stuff"), and they'd partnered up on occasion for target practice at the local rifle range. As their conversation unfolded, that smile and voice, both Leonard Cohen-worthy (which, as I found out – again much, much later – was his favorite singer and Canadian poet), totally and completely dazzled me. During this brief encounter, I had no indication that this voice would one day be whispering exciting, naughty things into my ear during long, intense love-making sessions and lulling me into a deliciously deep sleep in the moments after.

As Michael remembers it, this was the moment he first met the sexiest and most beautiful woman he could never forget. He said, on numerous occasions during our life together, that he had taken one look at my long, tanned legs, beautifully blossoming belly and swelling breasts, and was completely and utterly smitten. He also pondered life's cruelty.

"Why was a woman like that married to an elf like him?" It was a question he often asked, once life bowed to his favor. Wayne was shorter than me, not that I really ever noticed or cared. He was super fun, a little crazy, and he could make me laugh gut-wrenching, tear-streaming laughter. He's also a wonderful father to our four children. I believe it was that specific reason – the creation of our children – that the Universe, in its infinite wisdom, brought us together, and that served as an abundant reason for me to appreciate and be thankful for our relationship, no matter the outcome.

Our short meeting that sunny spring day ended with Michael walking his tall, muscular body over to his lifted Chevy and deftly hopping into it as we drove by. I gave a brief wave once again and quietly contemplated my new acquaintance. Was meeting him that day a matter of coincidence, fate or what I was raised to believe – God's Will? I never gave it a thought at the time of our first meeting, but it was definitely something that had to be considered and quantified... later.

CHAPTER 2

Segue

B efore we go any further, it's necessary to fill you in on some of the more, shall we say, "controversial" details of my early life. In the introduction of this book, I mentioned that I no longer subscribe to the same spiritual beliefs and dogma I was raised to follow as a child. One of the primary intentions for writing and publishing this book is to provide proof for the universal truth of the undeniably non-coincidental nature of our existence and life's experiences. In order for you to understand how I was able to finally arrive at this truth after a lifetime of searching and inquiry, as well as the role the nightmare of losing my second husband played in this journey, I must first take you back to my spiritual origins.

I met Michael about five years after busting out of the Christian-indoctrinated home I was raised in and ventured out on my own in search for true meaning. Growing up, I was raised in a stable household with two loving parents and four siblings (all much older than me), two sisters and two brothers. One very devout older brother scared the living daylights out of me, constantly spouting the "burn in Hell" doctrine when I was merely an impressionable child. Up until that time, I had my own set of beliefs – if a child could form a belief or even understand what that was. I suppose it was more of a *knowing* of the power within myself and my connection with the Universe and world around me. I had many supernatural experiences that many children at a young age can only later remember as adults. At night, I would come out of my body and travel across the world. I had seen the pyramids and had been to the top of the Eiffel Tower before I ever even learned what these incredible landmarks were called. I would lay in the tall grasses on our family's acreage and breathe with the Earth, hear the hum of the 2nd-dimensional vibrations and listen to her – Gaia – tell me what she needed. I understood that crop circles (which fascinated me immensely) were communications from the beyond to Gaia, and my childhood play involved moving small objects using *only my mind*.

I learned very quickly that I couldn't share these wonderful explorations with my family, after a particularly cool event occurred while "messing around with nature" with my childhood friend Andrea. She and I were around the age of 8 years old, while we were still able to live in Theta state, or "waking hypnosis," which all children do until that age. Or until the adults who run society tell them they're wrong. We had spent the afternoon trying to levitate her little brother, Gavin, just for fun. (Don't all little kids try to do that, or was it just us?) With Gavin sitting on the edge of their short porch deck, legs dangling below the knees, we placed our fingers under either side of his thighs, Andrea on one side, me on his other. All three of us closed our eyes, concentrated, and focused on raising Gavin up above the wooden deck. After a short time, we realized our fingers could no longer feel the fabric of his jeans. We both opened our eyes to see Gavin hovering in the air, slightly above our hands.

Squealing and giggling, Gavin dropped back to the deck, the spell broken. Their mother came out to the deck to see what all the fuss was about. I was so excited and ready to burst, but Andrea spoke up first, "Nothing, Mum. Just having a laugh." I knew from the look she shot me that our discovery was not to be discussed with her incredibly religious, Anglican parents. When I went home that day, I attempted to tell my own mother what fun we had, but she just passed it off like it was nothing more than silly child's play. Adults – especially church-going ones – wouldn't believe the stories we could tell, and they'd likely consider a punishment for the attempt. Message received.

If I couldn't share my Earth-given talents with my mom, I definitely couldn't with my Holy Roller brother. Despite the 11-year age difference, my brother and I had been best friends, and we did everything together. Some of my happiest childhood memories were the times we spent together. He was a willing chauffeur for every Halloween, driving me around in his blue VW Bug, hitting up as many neighborhoods as it took until we had two or three pillowcases absolutely packed with treats. We'd play games at home, or watch movies, go to the beach and do all the fun stuff close siblings would do.

It ended when he went to University to study Theology. I would anxiously await our time together when he would come home for summer breaks, only to win second place to his Bible studies. That, coupled with the emotional abuse I suffered at his threats of Hell and damnation if I didn't accept the Lord Jesus, left a mark on my childish heart that has taken me years of hypnotherapy and disassociation to heal from. On top of that, I was constantly ridiculed for my family's beliefs and called the "Good Christian Girl," something I probably should have been proud of, but – taken in context – it was incredibly embarrassing. However, I didn't rebel or convert to a "Bad Girl," both out of respect for my parents and fear of my brother's wrath. His emotional abuse continued on and off in our tumultuous relationship, but the early childhood wounds from his threats in the name of God ran deep and held strong for most of my life.

My parents were far less extreme; my mother, borderline. They raised me in the faith, and we "religiously" attended the United Church every Sunday. I had attended Sunday School since I was a wee one, and in my early teens, I attended either Christian or Ukrainian summer camps. My mother, proud of her Ukrainian heritage (and likely disappointed that I had inherited my father's Dutch, tall, blonde-haired, blue-eyed genes) insisted I go to an immersive Ukrainian camp and learn how to make Easter bread, pierogies, learn the language and, you guessed it – Ukrainian dance. I was the tall blonde Dutch girl in the dance troupe – quite the spectacle. I was often asked to perform as one of the men if the troupe was short on male dancers – being that I was as tall, if not taller, than most of the boys at camp. The best part about camp was that I attended with my cousins. They made it far more tolerable, even fun.

Around the age of 15, I completed Christian Evangelical Catechism and received my baptism, subsequently accepting the Lord Jesus Christ as my Savior. As I stepped into the cool lake waters at my baptism and was held by our pastor, his one hand on my upper back, another on my forehead, I felt nothing. Not the love of Christ, nor the relief of being blessed with eternal life in Heaven. My body obeyed the command that my heart never truly followed, as he dipped me, fully dressed, into the cool, baptismal waters. I followed the procedure as it was expected by my parents, particularly my mother. By then, I had forgotten about my childhood experiences and relationship with Mother Earth. Instead, I learned about free will and that we could decide on the road more or less traveled, but it always came with a price; and we (humanity) were the recipients of either a wonderful or dreaded prize – eternal love beside God on his throne, or burning in the pits of Hell. So what choice did I have?

The Kool-Aid wasn't sitting right with me, however, and there were too many things about Christian faith to be fearful of. For instance, fearing God himself. This made no sense to me whatsoever. How could God be loving *and* spiteful at the same time? It was drummed into me that if I didn't abide by God's command, I would be struck down and sent to Hell, or whatever other mentally and emotionally abusive rhetoric was flung at me like a monkey throwing its own feces. Take that shit and shove it right back where it came from, thank-you-very-much.

Also, why did everyone consider God to be separate from us, like a wise old sage that you visit every night when you kneel by your bedside and pray, yet he lived within each of us at the same time? What was the truth? Are we all one, or are we all separate from each other and God? My brother would always tout, "Jesus is the answer," but wasn't Jesus a mere mortal such as I? And if he could be born with such incredible powers, such as the ability to walk on water or turn the water into wine, couldn't we all? Was there never to be another "chosen one" to walk upon the Earth? I understood that the world was waiting for his return, but I could never get past the feeling in the deepest part of my being that said Jesus was simply a mortal man whose message of love and peace had been twisted, turned and misconstrued to the benefit of man's quest for power.

I searched, but I could never find a clear answer in "The Good Book" (mine was white with gold edging, and it was one of the first things I "lost" when moving away from home). The teachings of the Bible as a whole disturbed me. It was written by mortals, and I felt deeply that much of the "truth" was actually lost in translation, and I couldn't – *shouldn't* – trust it. There was just something about Christianity that never, ever felt true to me. As a child, I knew there was more to the limiting, power-guided beliefs I was told to obey. I was at once in love with nature but confused by the hate, wars and evils in the world that were carried out "in God's name." Talk about a bullshit excuse for the greed, power and control that man desired. It was just all wrong.

COMRADES

I met my first husband Wayne when I was 16. He was the son of a Pentecostal pastor, and I frequently attended church service with his family, ignoring the warning of my mother. She knew the Pentecostals for their "holy roller in the aisle" style of worship and beliefs that were largely fear-based. (As if ours weren't?) My mother fretted that they would be a dangerous influence on me, that I would become exposed to their "cultish" ways. My boyfriend's father, on the other hand, found the United Church to which we belong to be "wishy-washy" in their structure and beliefs, and he didn't want his son attending. So, either church I went to, I felt damned.

Being the son of a Preacher Man was no picnic for Wayne. He had his own set of dis-beliefs in what they touted as "truth" coming from his father, and he would receive a back-lash or the switch if he didn't conform. The fear in me matched the fear in him. He no more felt God's love than he felt love from his own father. He was always placed second to the church, and I experienced the same with my devoutly religious older brother. My instinct was to keep silent through the family dinners I was invited to. To argue passages in the Bible or venture to make a point in the Spirituality v. Christianity debate would be like trying to move Mohammad off his mountain.

I remember one particular conversation we were having over a home-cooked meal at Wayne's home. His mother had made her specialty: lasagne with overcooked tomato sauce, topped with Kraft Singles cheese slices. We often struggled through dinner with either political or religious conversation, and the conversation, just as often, would become rather heated between Wayne and his father. This evening, it was about the Universe as a whole. Wayne's mother stated that "the Universe only extends as far as we can see, and we, Earth and its people, are at the center of it. There is no existence beyond the planets we can see with a telescope; it says so in the Bible."

My mouth dropped open, melted, gooey cheese slices threatening to fall out. To think that there was nothing and no one beyond, to me, was profoundly arrogant. Wayne agreed and ventured to say as much. The dinner promptly ended with him storming off and slamming his bedroom door and me excusing myself quietly to talk things over with him in his room. Despite the struggles with our families, it was nice to have someone in my life who was as confused about Christianity as I was. Our discussions on the subject were deep, meaningful and cathartic, solidifying the bond between us.

FREEDOM

After graduation and moving out on my own, I never attended another church service. Growing up in guilt, fear and shame, I feared my brother's wrath if I questioned God or did anything against my brother's beliefs. Although I had lost the ability to connect fully with the Earth or move small objects with my mind, I could feel the itch of spirituality crawling up my spine. I needed to break free of the ties that bound me to the Christian indoctrination and remember *who I really was*.

Wayne and I set out to find our own truth, in our own way. The day we moved in together caused significant issues with him and his parents. He had been in a motorcycle accident and preferred to heal at my apartment downtown, rather than at his parents, who lived much farther away. We were officially "living in sin," and this cataclysmic event warranted a visit from his father and mother. We were both lectured on God's word, and the colossal sin that we were committing was surely our ticket to Hell and damnation. There was no mention of the love that we shared between us, no mention of our utter joy from being together as the adults we were, experiencing adulthood as one. Just damned. My parents eventually learned of our new living arrangement, although it was easier to hide, as they lived in another town over an hour away. They weren't too pleased but fully expected a wedding to follow sooner than later.

We married less than a month after I turned 20, in a United Church, much to the dismay of Wayne's family. As my parents were footing the bill, it made sense that they should choose the venue. We conceded to our guilt and pressure from his father, however, and asked him to be the minister to marry us, so there was some reprieve there. This caused quite the stir between our United Church minister and my future father-in-law, but once we married and were on our own, we were free to explore our own beliefs. What put me back on my spiritual path and introduced me to hypnotherapy were the books and case studies of Dr. Brian Weiss and Dr. Michael Newton. These two doctors blew open the doors to my spirituality once again. Through their work and the thousands of case studies of clients they each worked with in hypnosis, particularly the "life between lives" work Dr. Newton had accomplished, I felt a realignment with the Universe and the understanding of it I'd had as a child.

Realigned and, to a certain extent, reconnected, I was now free to continue my search for deeper meaning, not satisfied with the belief that we have no purpose in being here other than merely existing, or that there is no choice but Heaven, Hell or sleep when we die. As I dived deeper, I could finally let go of the Kool-Aid belief that our lives are in the hands of

God, and not our own, that we are separate from God, he being the creator and ultimate "decision maker" of our lives. I no longer had to live with fear, judgment or guilt. I could finally open myself up to pure love and respect for all of God's creatures, the world and everything in it, as my belief that we are all one was etched in the deepest parts of my soul. I could finally create my own path and my own existence, following my intuition and what I simply knew to be the "truth," at least for me. My studies soon gave way to raising a family, and I had to be thankful for the lessons I learned as a child, raised in fear. This was something I vowed not to do to my own children.

Married life has its ups and downs, as any marriage does. During the ups, I gave birth to four children – all before I turned 30. I thought this was an exceptional achievement, until my father reminded me that my mother had four kids by the time she was 23! They had one set of twins in that mix and then waited 11 years to have little ol' me, the "baby," or the "Centennial Kid," as my father would introduce me, proud to have a child in the 100th year of Canada's birth. To my father, Canada was the land of God, having immigrated from Holland with his family to the fruitful promise of God's unused land when he was only 4 years old. We raised our children to determine their own faith, much to my mother's dismay.

"How are they going to know anything about God or Christianity if you don't teach them?" She asked.

"We will introduce them to God and the various forms of religion, but we won't indoctrinate them," I replied, my husband chiming in. "They can do so of their own free will, something we did not have."

My mother did her best to bring my children up as Christian as I would allow. Once my parents retired and moved to the mountain town where we lived so they could be closer to our little clan and help me out by babysitting, they often brought the kids to Sunday School at the United Church, but only those who truly wanted to go attended. I was fine with it; my husband, not so much, but he would allow the kids to go just the same. We homeschooled our children until it was necessary for me to go back to work, as supporting a family of six in a large home was far too burdensome on my husband's salary at the local sawmill. The only homeschooling group in our town was, naturally, a Christian one. We joined, bracing for guilt and judgment from the other parents for our lack of commitment to the Christian faith, but we received none. Our kids played with their kids, and we all took turns hosting family gatherings and events. It was a wonderful time, as much as it was a trying one, but eventually, the stress of raising a large family, along with the expense of our large home and the purchase of a new vehicle, was too great. We sold the home for what we paid for it, sold the vehicle at a loss and moved our large family into a smaller home.

The pressure and stress, coupled with my husband's unhappiness in his career (not chosen, but forced, as it was all that was available in our small town), was far too great for us to handle. After 14 years of marriage, I found myself in the awkward and unfortunate situation of being a single mother to four absolutely incredible young children. My marriage had fallen apart, but I believe we created the relationship to bring those four beautiful lights into the world, and for that, I'll be forever grateful for the experience, no matter how difficult it ultimately became. My ex-husband remained an amazing dad to our children, and, mostly, we were amicable throughout the separation and divorce. When we parted, Wayne told me, "Keep studying, keep learning and find the truth." I knew he meant to continue the spiritual journey we had started together. I was on to something, and he knew it; he just didn't have the resolve within himself to continue the quest.

I picked up my pursuit to learn the truth about our existence and who we really are once my children were older. I learned meditation and tarot and began automatic writing (a form of channeling). Gaining ground on my communication with the Divine, I dove further into healing my past through self-hypnosis, and my heart felt lighter, releasing the buried traumas of my "hellfire and brimstone" past. I started courses in hypnotherapy – a sinful adjunct that created the final rift between myself and my Holy Roller brother. That age old story had to cease for my sanity and personal healing.

TRAJECTORY

During the first year of wearing my new, single skin, I had myself a wee bit of fun. I played a lot of slow-pitch, drank far too much wine and partied pretty hard for the two weeks a month that my kids were with their father. In the two weeks they remained with me, I was an ultra-mom. Struggling to make ends meet on a part-time bank teller's income, but still managing, at times with help from the local food bank or my parents, to put a solid meal on the table. Not the best situation, but we endured, and they grew into healthy, brilliant adults.

The kids played human ping-pong for a short period until they each decided whose home they would permanently live in. My oldest two girls stayed with me, while my son and youngest daughter, somewhat of a tomboy who idolized her older brother, moved in with daddy. They remained at their stations until leaving home some years later, each around the age of 18. I worked as a bank teller for several years, enjoying my job and my life as a mom. I had settled into the groove of single motherhood but wasn't terribly interested in dating again, not for real or for life, not yet anyway.

Then one day, I got the thrilling opportunity to see Michael again, as he and his crew of surveyors came into the bank to receive their pay, cabled to the branch from their head office in Calgary. It turned out this was going to be a bi-weekly occurrence, hoorah! It had been at least 14 years since I had seen him last, and so much of my life, and his, had changed! I was so delighted to see his brilliant smile once again, and we spent several minutes "catching up" on almost everything. I couldn't help but notice little butterfly movements shifting through my belly throughout our conversation, and I couldn't stop staring at his smile.

When the bi-weekly cable was received at our branch, I was more than happy to organize the funds into the specified bundles for each of the guys and had the pay ready for their imminent arrival, late afternoon every other Friday. When Michael would walk in the south door of the branch, I admittedly got a little winded. He often wore his hair a little long, the blonde curly tendrils hanging out from under the back of his battered baseball cap. Michael's face was often scruffy with a wiry, 5-day-old beard, tinged a rusty red, as he never had the time or energy for a daily shave. His deep denim eyes sparkled and danced when he would see me, his smile lighting up his entire face. Occasionally, he would still wear a high-visibility vest and a dusty pair of work boots, causing his already tall frame to be that much taller.

His dazzling smile was always ready for me once he'd caught my eye. He would wait in line, usually allowing his workers to go ahead of him to gather their pay from their choice of tellers. Michael would wait until I was available, then take his turn in line and appear at my wicket. This secretly thrilled me, knowing he was waiting to see me, and I enjoyed making him smile, sharing a little laugh or mundane small talk about his work or the weather. His deep, resonant voice, the one I'd been so taken with from the moment I first heard him speak, was comforting and thrilling. A gritty baritone, I could listen to his voice for hours and enjoy the swirl of deliciousness it churned within me.

I never considered myself to be brave. I couldn't even muster up the courage to give him my phone number, and he, the lion that he was, couldn't summon any more courage than me. Therefore, every other Friday, we danced around each other with our eyes, our smiles and flirty comments. One day, however, I thought I'd take the step and offered my banking help anytime he was "going to be late coming for their pay or had questions of any kind... relating to absolutely anything." I gave him my business card, which had my name, the usual banking information, phone and fax, address and so on, and on the back I wrote my personal extension, 224. Oh, how much courage that took, and it wasn't even my personal phone number! Feeling the part of a fool, or at the very least, the equivalent to an awkward teenager who just tripped over her two left feet, I passed the card across my wicket. He took it, smiling, and thanked me for the offer. If there were 50 shades of red, I was wearing 49 of them. Flushed and excited, I had to excuse myself and head to the ladies to take a chill pill. I was so excited by this large lion of a man, and I couldn't get him off my mind.

I never heard from him on my extension, but whenever the phone rang for the next couple of weeks until I saw him again, I was always jumping to answer it. Of course he wouldn't call! It was so lame that I gave him my card in the first place! Why didn't I just give him my personal number? The bi-weekly Friday procession of surveyors only lasted a couple more months, until the company they worked for finally got their poop in a group and started paying the guys by direct deposit. I never saw Michael in the branch after that, as he was a member of a different bank, so there wasn't any reason for him to drop by, and he never called my extension. I often thought, "well, I guess that's that," assuming he wasn't even remotely interested in me. I went about my life, living my day-to-day, working and spending time with my children.

I didn't see him again until a couple of years later, when I was out in my backyard planting some flowers. A tennis ball rolled onto my side of the yard between myself and the neighbor. A sweet, medium-size fuzzy black lab followed. As soon as she saw me, she loped in my direction and covered me in fervent kisses with her shiny pink tongue. I heard her owner approaching. Assuming it was my neighbor, it pleasantly surprised me when Michael appeared, calling his pup over.

"Hi!" I exclaimed, gathering myself to stand and brushing off the dirt.

"Well, hello there! I didn't know you lived here!" He replied, just as stunned as I was to see him standing there. He had apparently just finished work and was at the neighbor's, who, as it turns out, was a co-worker, sitting in the backyard for a beer. There was an obvious skunk scent of weed wafting over to my yard, so I assumed he was partaking in more than an after work cold one.

I willed the butterflies in my stomach to settle as we chatted niceties, him petting his dog, who was madly chewing on the fuzzy green tennis ball he rolled into my yard for her, and me wishing I'd taken the time to do my hair and makeup before working in the garden with my grubby jeans and T-shirt. Not that Michael was dressed in his Sunday best. He was wearing his work clothes, ratty jeans, scuffed work boots and a work shirt. His blonde silky locks were in need of a trim and poked out beneath an equally ratty ballcap. He was also wearing a surveyor's vest; a big red safety vest with a fluorescent "X" on the backside and large pockets with more fluorescent safety reflectors on the front. There is just something about a man in work clothes that really sends rockets running through my spine and severs the communication wires between my brain and my mouth. I was afraid to speak for fear of the drool. We ended our conversation with the same niceties we'd started with, and he and his little black dog retreated to the neighbor's yard. I never mentioned him not calling me at the bank or suggested we get a coffee, still assuming he wasn't interested.

I couldn't have been more wrong, as I would find out... later.

CHAPTER 3
Awake

February 28, 2019, Mexico

Out of the blackness, the thick, dark, heavy feeling behind my eyes, I could hear the voices of several people, assumedly gathered around me. I had no clue how to open my eyes. It was like I'd forgotten how eyes functioned. I could hear my own breathing – short, empty bursts – and I could feel some sort of vice that an unseemly, horrifying stranger must have placed my head in. *Where was I?* I lay there, silent, as the voices became clearer. It wasn't English; it was – *oh my God* – Spanish! The realization swept over me, coating me like a blanket of jellyfish, stinging me with their electric tendrils.

I was in a hospital, somewhere in Mexico...

Oh. Shit.

I briefly imagined a scene from a war movie; laying in a single-sized cot, white iron bed frame, a small table beside the bed, in a room full of other single-sized cots, and in each cot lay a broken soldier, bandaged from head to toe. The nurses, of course, would be wearing traditional, starched white hats and crisp white dresses. Or perhaps they were all nuns? I listened harder to the multiplex of voices mingling around me. There must have been at least five or six hospital staff. I tried to relax. The layering of chatter meant there were several hens at the party. *Oh great.*

"Manuel dijo que el accidente fue horrible. Piezas de automóviles en todas partes."

Manuel said the accident was horrible. Car parts everywhere.

"Me pregunto que paso?"

I wonder what happened?

"Conducen demasiado rápido y perdieron el control?"

Were they driving too fast and lost control?

"Si, ese es probablemente el caso. Estaban en un Jeep deportivo."

Yes, that is likely the case. They were in a sports Jeep.

The chatter continued for several minutes, each hen clucking her "tsk-tsk" and leaving two cents on the subject. It took me either one or several moments – time had absolutely no meaning behind the blackness of my eyelids – to realize that they were speaking fluent Spanish, *and I was understanding,* just as fluently. This wouldn't have been a spectacular realization, aside from the fact that I couldn't understand much Spanish at all. At least, not to the extent and the speed at which it was currently being spoken. As my brain was no longer communicating with my eyes, I couldn't fling them open upon this heady realization.

Was this one of those miraculous situations where, after a traumatic experience, I could not only understand the language, but suddenly had the ability to speak it as well? And what other fantastic miracles would develop from this? Were there other languages that I could speak and understand beyond English and Spanish? I strained to listen for someone, anyone, speaking Italian or Latin or French, but I heard nothing.

My mind raced with possibility. Would I be able to play Chopin or Beethoven just as fluently as I understood Spanish? Would I suddenly become a masterful artist, the caliber of a Van Gogh or Matisse? I felt a small giddy feeling welling up inside of me as I wondered how quickly I could find a baby grand piano to test my new skills. Surely there would be a spot on Oprah for me, once she found out, or, at the very least, Ellen.

Mental recall returning, I *knew* in my heart and soul that Michael had died, but someone had yet to confirm this in the hen party chatter. I listened to the layering voices as they made their opinions as to the how and why I was in the bed before them. I felt like I was in a bad Mexican soap opera, the recipient of a recent brain transplant, a gift from my identical twin who sacrificed her own life to save mine. Praise be, look at the miracle before us!

I moved my tongue slowly, conjuring up the saliva necessary to open my mouth, then speak. I wasn't even sure if I *could* open my mouth, the motor function for my eyes currently on pause, but my tongue appeared to be operational, so I would give it a go. "Mi esposo, está muerto?" I managed in a raspy whisper. *My husband, is he dead?* Until that moment, I hadn't known the Spanish word for "dead." At least, I didn't think it was previously in my limited dictionary of Spanish words, and it wasn't something that I had needed to use until now. Yet, there it was.

Someone replied, "Si, lo es. Lo siento mucho." *Yes, he is. I am so sorry.*

I slowly nodded my understanding, or rather, tried to nod,

and felt so incredibly... *empty.* With the confirmation firmly in my grasp, I felt the indelible mark on my heart. *He's gone. He's really, truly gone.* I wanted to cry, but my eyes had not only forgotten how to open, they also couldn't release tears. I wanted to scream, but my throat was incapable of an expulsion worthy of my heart's feelings. So, I just laid there, letting the emptiness wash over me and the sweet comfort of darkness take me once again.

Regaining consciousness sometime later (it could have been seconds or hours – I was without the benefit of a clock, watch or the ability to check such a device), I was certain of two things. First, that I was in a hospital somewhere in Mexico; and second, I had lost my husband in an accident. As I lay there, eyes somehow glued shut, listening to the sounds of the hospital hustle and bustle, I forced myself to think and asked myself a series of questions.

What was my full name? That I remembered with easy recall; Tammy Tyree.

What is your birthdate? This I also found easy to remember; July 11, 1967.

Where do you live? Ok, a little trickier, but still appeared from nowhere; British Columbia, Canada, and in Cayo District, Belize. I briefly celebrated the minor victory of recalling these first three facts. Now for something a little harder.

Do you know what happened? This one stumped me, but I persisted until the fog slowly lifted. Had I been more aware, I surely would have heard the "Jeopardy" theme song strumming through my head.

We were traveling in our Jeep? Yes, the bright yellow Jeep we called the Canary.

Where were we traveling from? And where were we traveling to? Hmm, this one was tricky and took a while to summon. Oh yes! From our property in Belize, and we were traveling to our timeshare in Cancun, Mexico!

Wait, had we even crossed the border into Mexico? Am I still in Belize? This one also took a while, or perhaps it didn't. Then I remembered – yes, we had! Bit by bit, I pieced together fragmented memories of our first-ever Belize to Mexico border crossing by car. We had crossed and then were herded like sheep without a shepherd through an immigration check-point. I focused on that brief memory of the immigration terminal and realized I had absolutely *no memory* of leaving that area.

Did the accident happen right there? Am I in a hospital in Chetumal? Or did we make it all the way to Cancun? Am I in Cancun? But what happened? Was there an explosion? Did the Mexican Cartel blow up the border crossing, and catch us in the middle?

I tried harder to bring the facts into focus, but to no avail. There was just nothing but a dark abyss where my memory should have been. Fragmented pictures would pop into my mind, like the elusive puzzle pieces you can never find, despite hours of scanning over the scattered pieces. Then the one you've been looking for pops out at you like a flash bulb. I remembered coming *through* immigration and felt a joyous victory of remembering that we had passed Chetumal, deciding not to explore the duty-free shopping area, Michael saying he would do so on his way back to Belize, once I had left Cancun for Canada after our holiday to visit family back home. After that, completely blank. So, I *must* be in Chetu-mal. Feeling both bittersweet satisfaction at recalling at least *that* much of our journey and, at the same time, resigned yet grateful for not remembering the accident itself, I turned my focus to my body.

How badly was I hurt? Eyes still refusing to open, I relaxed and scanned myself from head to toe, something I ask my hypnotherapy clients to do while under hypnosis to find the body part(s) associated with a past trauma or event. I was aware of a great deal of pressure around my temples and neck and surmised that I probably had whiplash from the accident and, likely, a concussion. I let my focus drift into my shoulders, arms, central body, legs, feet, and toes; all felt completely normal.

Wait, did I lose limbs? Is that why I can't feel any pain? No, that made no sense. If I had lost limbs, I would feel *a **lot*** of pain, wouldn't I? Oh my God... *am I just waking from surgery to **remove** body parts?* Having no point of reference, due to never losing a limb previous to this current predicament, I concentrated on my toes.

Can I wriggle them? My brain fired up the damaged circuits and carried the question down the length of my body, and my toes responded with slight movement. Hurrah! Within what may have been a few brief minutes or a few long hours, I had remembered my personal details and felt my body for the first time since arriving; small victories in what was the most excruciating circumstance of my life thus far.

Doing my best impression of an MRI, I scanned my body once again, this time trying to focus my attention on my arms and hands. I tried to signal my fingers to wriggle but received no response. I tried again, and this time, I could feel a slight twitching in a couple of fingers, but more so, I had a feeling that my hands were curled into fists. I could feel my fingertips resting on the base of my palms, so I tried stretching them out, elongating my fingers, but again, no response other than the feeling of being very shaky. Something was clearly damaged there, and as of yet, I could not open my eyes, too afraid to look anyway. I faded in and out of sleep, listening to the hustle and bustle of the hospital and aware of my bladder needing relief. I was so grateful when the nurses would consistently hoist my ass up and slide a bedpan under my butt so I could relieve myself. Eventually, my mind's Sight Department decided to get back to work, and I was able to peer through my eyelids and view the room through a dim, red haze.

It was a rather typical hospital room, although the walls were painted white (not the usual hospital green), and it had no door leading to the hallway, just a large, arched entryway. I was in one of three beds; the one beside me lay unoccupied as far as I could tell, while the one across from me was occupied by a woman moaning in the rhythmic patterns of someone in the early stages of labor. My bed and hers were closest to the doorway. There was a bathroom beside her in the far corner but no clocks on the wall, just one, small window, blinds drawn, near the bathroom. The brief time it took to peer through my eye slits exhausted me.

I had faded in and out of consciousness many times since arriving. It could have been days – or weeks, for that matter – since I'd arrived. I wondered if they even knew who I was? Where were all of my things? My cell phone to call home? And where exactly was I? I assumed I was in Chetumal, as that was where my memory of our trip had ended. But perhaps they had transported me as far as Cancun? I silently hoped that was the case, as I'd be one step closer to an airport and a flight home to Canada. When approached by one of the staff for a check-in, I readied my tongue to ask. The nurse, noticing my slight movement, came closer to my head and leaned in to listen.

I asked, slowly and at a mere whisper, "Dónde estoy? Estoy en Cancún?" *Where am I? Am I in Cancun?*

"Estás en el hospital de Bacalar, Quintana Roo." *You are in the hospital in Bacalar, Quintana Roo.*

Bacalar? Where was that?

Then I remembered. A tiny light switch went off in my brain, illuminating another piece of the puzzle for me to find. We had actually gone much further than the Belize/Mexico border. We had traveled at least an hour outside of Chetumal, maybe more. Our destination was approximately five hours from the border, so we had only gone part way.

I asked about my phone, hoping to call my family. The nurse said she didn't think they brought me with any of my things but would check for me. I drifted back to sleep once again. My eyes felt gritty and heavy. My contacts! Were they still in my eyes? I'd worn contacts for years but never usually during sleep, and I wasn't sure how long I had been out. Were they around the side or above the eye? The thought of this possibility gave me the creeps, thinking of anything floating around my eye that shouldn't otherwise be there. As difficult as it was, I had to ask, "Mis contactos. Están en mis ojos?" I whispered to the nurse who was still bustling about my bed if my contacts were still on my eyes.

"Oh, no lo sé. Llamaré al doctor." She retrieved the doctor assigned to me. Lucky him, or lucky me, depending on his ability to find my floating prescription lenses. He gently opened one eye at a time and shined a light in. I instantly regretted asking. My eyelid wanted to close tight, my eyes wishing they could recoil to the back of my brain. The intrusive light burned an unwelcome hole in my concussed head. It was all too much to face, but I needed to know if the contacts were still there or if they needed to be peeled off the top or side of my eyeball. The thought of them floating around my periphery was truly disturbing. Realizing this likely wouldn't be the only time I'd have to brace myself for poking and prodding, I relaxed. One thing to face at a time.

"No hay nada. Sin contactos. Es posible que los asistentes de ambulancia los hayan retirado." He found nothing. The emergency crew at the accident scene may have removed them, but I thought it was more likely that they simply blew off of my eyes when they squeezed shut on impact. I thanked the doctor and drifted back to sleep, exhausted from whispering, and a throbbing headache ensued from the spotlight fiasco. Time passed, or maybe it didn't. A couple of nurses and a beautiful young woman wearing brown slacks and a beige top woke me. I couldn't yet open my eyes fully, but I could peer through my lids long enough to get a picture of my surroundings and the people around my bed. Both the nurses and the young lady spoke only Spanish, and I replied, whispering in Spanish, still able to understand the language. This bit of amazement at my astounding new ability didn't escape me, and I was tempted to share my good fortune, but I shelved it for now.

"I am Johanna, your social worker. Do you remember what happened?" The young lady asked. *My social worker? Am I a lost child? Did they think I was in a domestic disturbance? Why would I need a social worker?* Johanna must have noticed my quizzical brow, assuming my brow was capable of being quizzical, so she explained, "We assign people a social worker after an accident to get them the help they need." *How lovely.*

I attempted to shake my head, "No, I don't remember what happened."

She replied, "I regret to inform you that your husband perished in the accident."

I simply said "yes," and at that moment, tears sprang forth from my upset eyes and trickled down my temples, pooling into my ears. The two nurses who accompanied her purred their sympathies, one massaging my legs and the other tenderly wiping away the gathering pools of water in my ears. I was grateful for the care and the mothering. Then a prickly heat ran through me. Terror. I was alone, Michael was gone, and my family didn't know what had happened.

"Do you remember your name?" Johanna asked.

This I knew! If I could have patted myself on the back for playing my mind game earlier, I would have, and I made a mental note to do so later. As I would soon discover, mental notes came and went like wisps of dandelion fluff. I gave her my name and that of my late husband. She asked who she could call and what the number was. For a moment, I panicked. It's just too easy to forget people's phone numbers in our digital age, *if* you even knew the number in the first place, yet I could rattle off my oldest daughter's name and phone number easily – and in Spanish! Praise be! Prickly heat flooded through me again, this time from relief. I explained she was in Canada – "long distance" – so Johanna would know to add the required digits for an international call.

She punched the number into her phone and placed it to my ear. I could hear the distinctive rings, then the automated voicemail greeting picked up and told me Nicole was not available and to leave a message. My heart sank, disappointed. I figured she likely didn't pick up because she wouldn't have recognized the "unknown" number. I didn't want to leave a message. What would I say? And how would I tell her to get back to me? I had no phone of my own that I knew of. I could speak slowly and quietly, my voice thick with pain and fear, but I was desperate enough to get in touch with my family, so I would try my best.

The message I left went like this: "Nicole… it's Mom… we are in Mexico, and there's been an accident. I'm in the hospital… I have a neck brace… and I don't know what's happening, but they tell me that Dad is dead…" Then there was a flutter of activity and garbled voices; I believe I was asking for a number for her to call back, then… nothing. I don't remember leaving that message, but Nicole kept it for me to listen to at a later date, and it was purely awful to hear.

Johanna and the nurses left me for a bit, and I drifted to sleep again. A short time later, Johanna woke me up, explaining that she had my daughter on the phone. She placed her cell phone in my ear, and I whispered.

"Nicole?"

"Mom!" Nicole's voice broke. She was sobbing, trying to speak.

"I'm ok," was all I could manage, tears trickling down my temples again. The relief I felt speaking to a family member was indescribable. "We were in an accident."

"Yes, they told me," she said through her tears.

"They keep telling me that Dad has passed. I haven't seen him, but they keep telling me Dad died." Saying the words out loud sounded so incredibly foreign and unreal. I knew Michael had passed the moment I'd opened one eye and saw him right after the accident, but, as the old adage goes, I couldn't believe my eye, and I didn't want to admit or accept the truth.

"Yes, he's gone, Mum." Nicole was crying harder now. My poor girl! I wanted so badly to reach out and hug her, to give her some sort of comfort. Nicole had a 3-month-old baby at home, my first granddaughter, and I could only imagine the difficulty she was having coping with this news and an infant at the same time.

I kept telling her I was ok, imagining the absolute hell my children must be going through. As difficult as it was for me to be the accident victim, it had to be 100 times worse for my loved ones. Nicole asked me where I was so that she could make plans to come get me. Even though I was told earlier, I couldn't remember, so I had to ask Johanna, again in Spanish. They passed the phone over to my doctor, the only person in the hospital who spoke fluent English, albeit with a heavy Spanish accent. He gave Nicole the name of the hospital in Bacalar, Quantara Roo, Mexico. She said she was going to come and get me, and we hung up the phone.

NICOLE

I was having coffee with a family friend when my phone rang. It was a foreign number, so I didn't answer it, thinking it was a telemarketer or crank caller. I got home, and a call came from that number again, and again I didn't answer. This time, the caller left a message. It was Mom, telling me they had been in an accident and that my step-dad was dead. I didn't know how to call Mom back on that number, as it was a foreign number, so there were at least five minutes of crying and sheer panic, my daughter also crying and needing my attention. I finally figured out how to call the number back, and a Spanish-speaking woman answered the phone.

I told her who I was and asked to speak to my mother, Tammy Tyree. She brought the phone to Mom. She kept saying she was in a neck brace and how much pain she felt, how uncomfortable. I asked if she knew where she was – what the name of the hospital was – but she couldn't even understand what I was asking, so she turned the phone back to the woman who had answered it. It took a while to get the information, as the woman on the other end had to find the only other person in the hospital who could understand and speak fluent English, my mother's doctor.

The doctor, somewhat rushed, told me the name of the hospital, town and state in Mexico. Even though he was fluent, with the heavy accent it was very difficult to comprehend what he was saying. He told me that someone had to come get my mother and sign for the body of my step-dad. I could only agree, as I furiously scribbled notes during our conversation, writing the names and places the best I could. They let me speak to Mom again. She kept saying, "I think Dad is dead," and I kept repeating that yes, he was indeed gone. There was a lot of crying on both of our parts and repeating the same information. She was clearly in shock and concussed, not fully aware of her condition, and likely scared as hell.

After hanging up, I called my cousin Andrea, who was in Belize on my parents' property. They had been visiting for a week and had stayed an extra day, even though Mom and Dad had left for their Cancun trip the day before. I told Andrea what had happened, the names of the hospital and town that were given to me, as accurately as I could. We did some Googling together while on the phone. I told Andrea a family member had to go get Mom and help bring her home to Canada, but she was hesitant to assist in that manner, afraid of traveling into Mexico with their young daughter. They were the closest people in distance to Mom, but they had to discuss whether it was possible for them to fulfill the vast request.

While I was on the phone with Andrea, my partner Shawn came home from work and took the crying infant from my arms. Andrea said she would call back; they would research the possible locations Mom may be at and whether or not they could assist in retrieving her. During this entire time, I was on the floor near the wood stove in our home. I hung up and Shawn asked, "What the heck is happening?" He had walked into an actual nightmare of tears and sheer panic, to which he had now joined. When I told him the devastating news, all he could manage was "No, no, no, no, no..." The three of us sat on the floor and bawled. Michael had been a father to Shawn, who had lost his own father to cancer several years previous. The news of Michael's passing devastated us all. Our daughter had met her "Opa" only once when she was 2 months old, and she would never have the benefit of growing up with his love and wisdom.

The next person I called was my sister Casey. She was with our brother in the middle of a move to their new, shared apartment two hours away. I told her they should pull over, that I had something difficult to tell them. When they did, I let them know about the accident, that Mom was ok but that Mike had passed. They reacted as I would expect, with a lot of tears, grief and anxiousness to get to Mom and bring her home. I had to tell them I didn't have enough information to enable us to go, but I would let them know more as I found out.

Next, I called my youngest sister, Carrie. She was at work and took the news very calmly. However, ten minutes later she called me back, letting me know she left work in tears and immediately went to Michael's mom's house ("Oma" to me and my siblings). The RCMP had already been to see Oma a little earlier to give her the news, and she was home alone, making calls to family. I didn't know it then, but my brother had contacted Michael's son and broke the news to him.

Andrea called again. They had found the hospital and discussed traveling into Mexico to assist, but they decided it wasn't the best idea, correctly assuming the time it would involve. They had a business back in Canada that required their attendance, vacation now over. My passport had recently expired, and I also had a newborn to contend with, so it wasn't really an option for me either.

In the meantime, Mom's doctor had called again, requesting a copy of her identification and asking when someone was coming to claim her. This confused me. It was as if he did not know the travel time from Canada to Mexico. He also said the authorities would require identification for the release of Michael's body. Thankfully, only five months earlier (rather synchronistic, it would seem), Mom had given me a binder and flash drive full of personal and estate information, copies of their passports, IDs, banking information and everything that was now required. I even had copies of their Wills that they had recently updated.

I asked Casey to go with our youngest sister to Mexico to represent the family. Casey was eager to go, of course; however, we were both in such shock and confusion that we couldn't conceptualize the steps needed first, next and last. A family member was required to be in attendance for Mom's release from the hospital, but I felt it was too momentous a task for Casey and Carrie to undertake alone, so I called our long-time family friend Katrina and asked for her help.

Katrina jumped into action asking, "What do you need, what do you need?" And when I told her, "I need you to go to Mexico with Casey and bring Mom home," she said she'd call me back in ten minutes, and she did. She had immediately called her travel agent friend and already had the tickets to leave early the next day, a car booked to take them from the Cancun airport to Bacalar and a place to stay. I was instantly relieved. Our family desperately needed Katrina's take-charge attitude and capabilities right now. I couldn't have asked a better person to take on the momentous task that lay before us.

Katrina encouraged me to start a Go-Fund-Me campaign with our next call to each other. Hearing from Mom and her social worker that there was no evidence of their existence – no wallets, passports or anything found in or around the Jeep, everything presumably stolen – meant I would have to cancel credit cards, debit cards and so on, and I did not know how we would handle the upcoming expenses. I was again thankful Mom had left me all of their estate and banking information. When I logged on to her online banking to check their credit cards and accounts, sure enough, suspicious charges had already been made. Because of this, I alerted the credit card companies and the banks, who froze everything immediately. We were most definitely stumped for a way to pay for the expenses we were about to face. The Go-Fund-Me was now absolutely necessary.

I had originally set the funding goal at $5,000, but potentially, we were facing a far greater expense than that, not knowing the cost of hospitalization, hotel rooms, flights, funeral home expenses and bringing Michael's body or ashes back to Canada, let alone the care Mom would require once back home. The Go-Fund-Me turned out to be one of the greatest blessings during this time. I shared the news with friends on Facebook, which, unfortunately, was the first time many of them found out about Michael's death. A co-worker of Michael's spread the news via email chain to the entire company that Michael contracted to, and it went viral.

With hours, the Go-Fund-Me quickly rose to $10,000, and then $34,000 within a couple of days. This just had to be enough to cover the international expenses, as well as months of Mom's recovery care and Michael's Celebration of Life. Words will never express the gratitude we all feel toward those individuals responsible for bringing Mom home to our family. We are forever in your debt, and we thank you from the bottom of our hearts.

I spoke to Mom as much as possible during this time, usually every two to four hours, and I had to continually reiterate the plans, as she wasn't able to retain the information from one call to another. I spent the rest of my time fielding calls from friends, family, their contacts in Belize and organizing the information that the Canadian Consulate in Mexico would require to facilitate Mom and Mike's return.

SNORING

Back at the hospital in Bacalar, Nicole called once again. Johanna held the phone to my ear. "Katrina and Casey are coming to get you and bring you home," Nicole said. I felt tremendous relief hearing this but couldn't speak. The tears were flowing now, clearing my eyes and washing away all the dirt, blood and junk that caked them.

"Ok, I love you. I'm ok." And with that, I was finally able to fully relax and slip into a relieved, restful sleep. My family was coming to get me. I had been there for what seemed like an eternity but was actually less than 24 hours. I would only have to wait one or two more days before seeing Katrina and Casey, then my journey home to Canada and a full recovery could begin.

That night, the sound of Michael's snoring startled me awake. He had an unmistakable, epic snore. For the entirety of our relationship, I had to wear earplugs when he was home after a long stint at work and we were sleeping together again. If I didn't, I wouldn't get a wink of sleep. I had previously recorded one particularly epic event and would find it later, stored on the Cloud, many months into my recovery. His coffee-percolating-locomotive snore was just too unreal not to record. I don't recall if I ever played that recording for him. I likely did, as he didn't always believe me when I said his snoring was enough to scare the howler monkeys. If there was a Guinness Book of World Record category for "Snoring," Michael would have taken the prize annually.

My eyes, for the very first time since the accident, flew open. The snoring ceased. I noticed through an unstable peripheral view they had placed a new patient in the bed beside me and briefly wondered when that had happened. I listened for the sound of snoring, while the occupants of the two other beds slept soundly, their own breathing rhythmic and silent. I was so confused. They told me he had passed, didn't they? I mean, I *knew* this to be true, didn't I? Disbelieving, the best I could do was close my eyes and try to fall back asleep, only to be woken, perhaps moments or hours later, to the sound of his snoring once again.

I froze, keeping my eyes closed, lest opening them would end the insufferable snore, and listening to the familiar percolating. I breathed and listened for the direction of the locomotive. Perhaps it was someone in another room down the hall, or *in* the hall? Not knowing how big the hospital actually was or if there were gurneys with patients lined up in the hallway, I slowly opened my eyes once again. The snoring stopped. Again, I strained to hear through the silent halls into the other rooms. There was nothing, only the footfalls of the night nurses as they made their rounds to check on their patients.

Confused, I lay silent, trying hard to think. They *did* tell me Michael had passed, didn't they? The snore I heard was definitely *his* snore, wasn't it? There couldn't possibly be a single person on earth with a snore to match, so it just *had* to be him. Scared, and very uncomfortable, I felt all the aches and pains in my body. My neck was very sore, and I could feel the hard, plastic, way-too-large neck brace attempting to support it. My back was very uncomfortable, and for the first time since my arrival, I realized there was no pillow beneath my head. I tried shifting a little but could barely move. My hands felt cramped and uncomfortable, and I couldn't move my arms to see what shape they were in. I could only tell that they were un-bandaged, so that was a good sign.

I fell into a restless sleep, then deeper, and for the first time ever, wished the sounds of Michael's snoring would manifest, hinting to his location. I could sense that it was nighttime because of the stillness of the ward. There were no lights on in the hallways, nor any coming through the blinds of the small window in the room, so there was no point to laying awake, feeling lost and confused. Sometime later, in what may have been the "wee hours," my mind stirred. Eyes closed, I could feel a shift in the air, the room and the ward falling into a deep silence. I was in a vacuum. I could hear only one heartbeat, as if the other patient's hearts were in sync with mine, all of us breathing in unison.

Then, I heard a voice.

Not just any voice – Michael's voice!

Low and rhythmic, unmistakably his. He had one of the deepest voices I've ever heard in my life, then or since.

He spoke.

"*It's so incredible here.*"

Our collective hearts skipped a beat. A rush of fear washed over me, swiftly followed by comfort; the warmth of an unseen blanket covered me. I was surprised to hear his voice, but I kept my eyes closed, afraid to break the spell, allowing his words to flow through me.

"*I wish you could experience this with me,*" he said. "*I am surrounded by pure love.*"

An indescribable feeling flooded me. I *felt* what he must have been feeling. It is so unlike the love we feel for even our own children. It is deeper, wider, more abundant and beautiful, and so very intoxicatingly *pure*. In this feeling, there is no pain, fear, or loss; only sheer joy and love. I wanted to stay with him, to bask in that feeling forever. Knowing that this was where he was, that this is what we feel when we pass, filled me with reassurance. I was so comforted and grateful for this moment, floating in a luxurious pool of comfort, ease and love. Nothing else existed, nothing else mattered. The world simply fell away. I could no longer feel my body, the pain I had experienced moments before hearing Michael's voice had simply vanished.

"*I'm ok,*" he continued. "*What happened was part of a plan. The Plan.*" His voice was so clear and concise, not like he was talking *in* my ear, but talking *through* me. His words permeated my entire body. "*You are going to be ok.*"

I wept, relieved.

His words flowed for what felt like hours. He became more excited, more animated in his speech, and the messages started layering themselves, one overtop of the other, as if there were a multitude of Michaels, all talking fast with messages of what he saw and felt, then moving into messages for friends and family.

"*I'm so joyful...*"

"I am celebrating, everything has gone as planned..."

"The light and love is so powerful here..."

"Oh, wow! I'm such a beautiful color!"

"There is so much peace, love and light..."

"There is so much more to do, and I will guide you..."

"It had to be this way..."

"You must continue to do the work..."

"Tell my mother she is going to join me soon, and there is nothing to fear... I cannot wait for her to see this..."

"Tell Paul that his dad is so happy... Oh! Give him all of my Jamie Oliver cookbooks! He'll love that." Michael laughed a hearty, deep laugh. He and his friend Paul had a love/hate competition between Jamie Oliver (Michael's favorite chef) and Gordon Ramsay (Paul's favorite). Gifting Paul (himself being an *actual* brilliant chef) with Michael's complete collection of Jamie Oliver cookbooks would be such a funny "slap in the face," just the sort of joke only the two of them would appreciate. I started giggling too, as a steady stream of tears slid down my temples.

"Tell the kids, I'm ok. They're all going to be ok. They have to stay where they are and do great things..."

"I see my dad. I feel such love and forgiveness for him..." This also got to me, and I wept harder. Michael and his father didn't have a good relationship, estranged when his father passed many years previous. The messages and thoughts continued to flow through me, along with the explicit "knowing" that I was to make a record of it all.

Michael confirmed the same when he said, *"You will write a book! In this book, you will write about our life and this experience, and the experience of death and dying. You will show people the other side, what truly happens when we die, and show them they must not fear death. It is the threshold into their true existence. You will also show them how to release their own fears, anxiety and depression so that they can live a full life of meaning and purpose."*

He gave me the entire synopsis of the book, and it is what I've written from the moment I started this memoir. He also explained that I have many tasks before me, outside of writing this book. He told me it is my journey – my *responsibility* – to bring an awareness and understanding to the people of Earth of their limitless power, their truth and their purpose, that I was to join with millions of others to teach and open minds to the truth of who we really are and what we can become. Everything he was saying made so much sense, I wondered why I hadn't seen it before. So simple, yet so incredibly helpful and decisive. My mind, working hard to process everything Michael was telling me, was all at once thinking tremendously clear and firing on all cylinders. Realization of universal truth, conception of man and the formula to tackle our human fears, depression and anxiety flooded me, then dissipated like sparks that flashed hot and bright, vanishing just as quickly.

The information was so great and powerful, coming in at such speed and flow, that I finally had to ask him to stop. I had been silent until now, simply absorbing as much as I could. I hadn't even asked one question until now. I didn't have pen or paper, or the use of my hands to write anything down! I asked Michael to help me remember and tell me again later, when my mind was clear of the concussion cobwebs and I could make a record of it all. The messages slowed, fading into whispers, then ceased.

The moment they stopped, I felt the pressure of someone sitting at the foot of the bed. I opened one eye, just a crack, assuming that a nurse was there watching over me. There was no one. I closed my eyes, and the pressure shifted, moving across the entire left side of the bed, as if someone was lying beside me. I kept my eyes closed, completely in awe. It just had to be Michael. He was curled up on my left, the side he slept on our entire married life. I wanted to reach out and feel for him or the indentation in the mattress, but I couldn't move a muscle. I could smell his cologne, the unmistakable woodsy, sporty scent I loved so much and would breathe so deeply, nuzzling his neck whenever he'd wear it. I wasn't afraid, just comforted, and I fell into a deep, restful sleep once again, Michael by my side.

CHAPTER 4

Visitors

March 1, 2019, Mexico

I t had been days since arriving at the hospital in Bacalar. At least, it felt like it had been days, when actually, I had only just woken up from my first night there. One night seemed like several, as I faded in and out of restless sleep throughout the previous day and night. I was exhausted and overwhelmed; from being woken by Michael's snoring and receiving his messages and the responsibility of what was tasked on me to create, to the hospital noise and general activity of the nurses, each moment felt like an eternity had passed. Michael had been quiet for the rest of the night. He'd listened to my request for shelving the messages until I could write again. Instead, I felt him curled up beside me, comforting me in my deepest, albeit intermittent sleep cycle. I didn't even hear him snore. That alone was blissful, and I was grateful.

When daylight was no longer a rumor, I awoke, the heavy

impression on the bed now gone. The hospital was bright and bustling. I laid there for a few long minutes, eyes closed, reliving what I could from Michael's visit. I sensed people approaching. When I opened my eyes, I saw a plain-clothed man and a woman standing at the foot of my bed. I thought perhaps he was a doctor; however, he wore no scrubs or white coat, as I had assumed doctors at a Mexican hospital would, just as they do in Canada.

The man and woman were clearly Mexican and about the same height, each approximately 5-and-a-half feet tall. She wore classic, dark slacks and a blouse, with a pretty, colorful silk scarf wrapped around her neck. Her hair was shoulder-length and very dark. She had lovely wide-set brown eyes and a beautiful, sweet smile, her generous lips shellacked in a colorful shade of lipstick. He wore a dark pair of slacks and a crisp, clean, short-sleeved beige shirt, with an emblem embroidered on the right breast. I couldn't make out what it said, my eyes not used to focusing or even being open for any length of time. His face and narrow-set dark eyes were solemn. His dark, close-cropped hair matched his equally close-cropped beard and mustache.

The lovely young lady spoke first, in halted English. "Hello Miss Tammy. We are from the Campestre Recinto Exequial. The funeral home in Chetumal."

Oh wow. It was really happening. Michael *had* passed. The voice in my head was truly him, and we *were* in an accident. This wasn't a dream. The very small piece of me that was still wishing, hoping that he had survived the accident, was doused in the gasoline of these people's presence and ignited. My world came crashing to a halt with one simple confirmation, and I suddenly forgot how to breathe.

"We are very sorry to tell you that your husband passed away in the accident."

This I knew, no matter how much I didn't want it to be

true, and there was no end to the people who could confirm this for me. However, coming from these two, it was abundantly clear, and somehow, more believable.

"Thank you," I managed, fighting the explosion of tears that stung my eyes.

"This is Adam Vergara," she continued, "and I am his interpreter, Vera Kamul."

They apparently didn't know that I no longer needed an interpreter, with my newfound ability to understand and speak Spanish fluently, but it was a lovely gesture. In the next moments, however, I would find that I had lost that ability when I heard Adam speak in fluent, rapid Spanish, his face half turned to Vera. His words were completely foreign to me now. Feeling a crushing disappointment, I looked at Vera for her interpretation.

"We are going to be taking care of you from now on." *Oh? What did that mean, exactly?* "We will ensure you receive the proper treatment and assist your family in taking you back to Canada." *Oh, very good.* That was a tremendous relief.

"Does my family know? Are they on their way?" I rasped. My voice sounded like I had gravel and thick sludge lodged in my throat. I had already forgotten that I had spoken with my daughter several times the day before and that travel plans for Kat and Casey had been arranged.

"Yes, but we do not know if they are on their way," Vera explained. "We will have to discuss this with your social worker; however, she is not at the hospital until later today." In fact, they were already on their way, but it would take two or three more calls with Nicole for me to retain that bit of knowledge. I felt satisfied with this answer, for now.

That was the extent of their visit. Vera said they would be back to see me again tomorrow and every day after that, until they knew I was safely on my way home to Canada. The gratitude and appreciation I felt for these kind folks was indescribable. So far, I'd felt very well cared for since my arrival. The times that I was conscious I watched the nurses tend to me, provide me with the bedpan and tuck me in under my thin sheet, all while cooing kindness in soothing Spanish. I was also very grateful for their care. I never saw a doctor, forgetting about the ridiculous contact lens incident, but assumed one had checked in on me at some point. Apparently, my short-term memory cleared the data banks on a moment-by-moment basis.

After that, I felt I could rest some more and awoke sometime later to see Johanna bearing sustenance! She had a bowl of broth and a spoon and settled onto the chair beside my bed to feed me. It surprised me that this was her job and not that of the nurses. How differently things worked outside of Canada! She attempted to bring the spoon to my lips, then thought better of it, as I was in a full lying position. She placed the bowl on a table beside me, moved to the end of the bed and grasped a hand crank that elevated the head of the bed into a slight sitting position, then she returned to my side to take up the task of feeding me once again. I could only manage a few spoonfuls through tight lips. My jaw, incredibly jammed up and sore, would only open a fraction, allowing me small sips of broth or speech in a mere whisper. I couldn't finish the bowl.

Johanna didn't speak a word of English. However, since I could speak and understand her previously, she assumed I still could and rattled off in Spanish to me. I grimaced and shook my head slightly. I could no longer understand, but I could whisper "non comprendo." She looked momentarily confused, then took out her phone and punched a finger over an app. She dictated a sentence into the phone, and the phone responded with the translation in English.

"Would you like to call your daughter now?"

A slight nod – yes, please! I was soon connected with

Nicole once again, Johanna holding the phone to my ear. "Nicole?" I tersely whispered.

"Oh Mom, how are you, are you ok?" She was relieved to hear my voice, almost as relieved as I was to hear hers. Forgetting about the previous night's events – hearing my husband and receiving his messages – I asked, for the umpteenth time, if she was coming to get me.

"Oh Mummy!" Nicole sobbed. "Katrina and Casey are on their way to get you." Katrina, our long-time family friend, had been in our lives since Nicole was 10 years old and started babysitting Katrina's first son, prior to her second son's imminent arrival. Casey is my mini-me, tall and lithe, with long blonde hair and beautiful, large blue eyes. Ever since she was little, our favorite saying to one another was, "Love you to the moon!" Casey is a gentle yet fierce soul. It didn't surprise me that she would be the child to come "to the rescue." If Nicole had told her she had to stay in Canada and let someone else handle it, Casey would have found a way to be on the plane anyway. No one's the boss of that girl. Besides, she had the most flexible work schedule of all of my children, and at the time of this event – a valid passport.

"They are?" Joy bubbled up from beneath the depths of sorrow at this news. "When? Today?"

"They are on their way now but probably won't get to you until later today, or maybe tomorrow." My joy bubbles burst. As much as I appreciated the care here, I was desperate to hold my kids and grandbaby again. "Oh Mom," Nicole continued. "I don't know how you survived the accident. It's all over the news. The pictures of the Jeep... oh Mom, I just don't know how you survived." Nicole was sobbing again.

All over the news? She had seen pictures of the accident? How did that happen so quickly? I had no indication, other than the clucking of the hospital hens, of the celebrity status I had on the Mexican news until my release days later.

"In the pictures... you can see yours and Dad's bodies at the side of the road..." she sobbed. Oh. My. God. How awful. If I could protect my children and Mike's son and mother from that image, I would do everything in my power to do so, but I feared it was already too late.

"Has anyone told Oma? And Mike's son?"

Nicole assured me they knew. I found out later that it was my son who had called Michael's son, and, naturally, he took the news incredibly hard. I could only guess that he would spend the next few months or more in a deep depression with a great sense of loss. Those thoughts were brief, however, as most thoughts were. Every moment felt like hours, even more so now that I knew my family were on their way. I closed my eyes and tried to rest once again, willing the day to pass quickly.

Upon awakening from intermittent naps, I grew increasingly more uncomfortable. It was a good sign, I suppose, that I could even recognize discomfort. It meant my body was waking up, just as I was. I could feel my bed, the sheet over my body and whether the air was warm or cold. It was cold. Air-conditioned, of course. I also felt an incredible barb of pain in my neck and head area. It felt like there was a knife lodged deeply in the top of my head, the pain swooped down into my neck and jaw. Whiplash and a concussion, most likely.

I could move my toes, feet and legs. I also tried moving my arms, and to my sheer delight, I could! This was a miraculous achievement! My neck still wouldn't move, but I could feel the too-large brace in its pathetic attempt to support it. When I was in a full lying position, the neck brace was more like a cage than a source of support. My head and neck rested on the bottom half of the brace, the top half supporting nothing but my chin. I wondered how bad my neck was, or if it was worse because of the lack of support. All I knew is it hurt, badly, especially in a full lying position. Thankfully, the hospital staff had elevated the head of the bed, so I wasn't lying flat on my back, and if a nurse asked by indicating laying the bed flat, I firmly said "no," as this only shifted the brace to support absolutely nothing. It floated over my chin, not under it. I wondered why no one noticed or provided me with a better-fitting one.

But my hands! They were the only thing I couldn't wriggle. I had no sensation of having hands at all, and this terrified me. Spinning back to my original assumption that I had lost my hands in the accident, I closed my eyes and tried to focus on the feeling of fingers. I felt a slight twitch but had little faith that it wasn't the ghostly twitch of hands that were no more. With some trepidation, I brought my hands up to eye view. *Oh, thank goodness.* There they were, still attached. Feeling rather ridiculous for being so fearful, I inspected my hands, squinting as I did so.

My hands shook slightly, the strain of being lifted to my view was clearly an arduous task on my fingers and arms. My fingers were curled into loose fists. I tried to stretch them open but could not. I briefly wondered what happened that had made them so. There was no bandaging, just several scrapes and large scabs of dried blood on the back of both hands. An IV needle was embedded into my left hand and securely fastened with white tape, attached to a drip line that trailed past my peripheral view. I couldn't feel the scrapes and cuts, nor could I feel the IV needle. I was only slightly aware of the cool, steady stream of IV fluid as it flowed into the veins of my hand.

My wedding ring, bloodied and dirty, was still on my left hand where it had been for the last 11 years and 362 days. There were no other rings. I knew I had been wearing a ring on my right hand, a favorite of mine that Michael had bought for me in Mazatlan on our second honeymoon, but it was missing. I made a mental note to ask the staff if they had retrieved our jewelry and where it was, but that mental note disappeared as quickly as it came.

As I studied my hands further, I was able to uncurl my fingers slightly. I could see the divots my nails had made into my palm from making a tight fist. I couldn't understand why my hands were curled in such a fashion, and I had absolutely no memory of the accident itself, so I was at a loss. The rest of my body seemed perfectly ok. I wouldn't be able to see my legs or torso until the nurse would remove my bedsheets, but they felt fine.

I noticed that the wedding ring finger was swollen and a deep purple color. My fingers are long, my knuckles bony, and my hands are the perfect mix of my mother's (Ukrainian round-knuckled) and my father's (Dutch long-fingered and "mannish"). My hands are slightly disproportionate to my small wrists and long arms, but wearing my nails a little long "girl's them up" somewhat, so I've learned to live with them. Rings usually rolled around and floated between my middle and lower knuckles. Not this one. It had swollen so much that my wedding ring was now cutting into my deep purple skin. *Shouldn't someone pop my finger and let the blood out?* That rather silly surgical procedure seemed as logical as any other, and again I made a mental note to ask the nurse to do so later, and again, the mental note left as quickly as it came. My hands fluttered with tension and exhaustion from their elevated position, so I let them rest by my side.

The discomfort in my neck area was a concern. I couldn't move anything but my eyes, and even that was a stretch. They were still sore and I couldn't see very well out of the left one. It was cloudy and tinted red, perhaps swollen or burst capillaries? I didn't know how bad the accident really was, or what type of injuries I had sustained to my noggin; I could only guess, and my guesses, up to this point, weren't exactly good ones. The charge nurse came in, and seeing I was awake, immediately brought me the bedpan and tucked it under my tush. They had done so a few times the day before, but I couldn't remember the feeling of relieving myself. Now that I was coming back into my body, I could feel the urine trickling down between my butt cheeks and heard the tinkling in the metal pan. The feeling was just wrong, like peeing the bed as an adult. Nonetheless, the feeling of relief surpassed the feeling of "wrongness," and I sighed.

"Gracias," was all I could manage in a whisper as the nurse removed the full pan and walked it over to the corner bathroom to flush it.

Next, she busied herself with straightening my sheet. As she pulled the top sheet away from my body, I could see my legs for the first time: long and tanned from the hot Belizean sun, and without a single scratch. Incredible. I quickly wiggled my toes and watched them wave back at me before the nurse could toss the sheet over my legs once again. This was my opportunity to mention how cold I was, having only a thin sheet on top of me. The air conditioning blew its frigid frost full blast through the hospital air vents, my body feeling the chill as it "came to," and I shivered.

"Frio," I managed. I definitely had the word for *cold* in my permanent Spanish vocabulary.

"Ahhh! Si, esta frio!" The nurse replied and rubbed my arms and legs lightly before scuttling off to find a thin flannel sheet. It wasn't exactly the comforter I was hoping for, but it was better than the cool cotton one, and I had no energy to argue. I could look around a little better now, my eyes adjusting to the midday light and opening slightly wider than they had the day before. Tempted to ask for a mirror, I quickly thought better of it, for as much as I was curious, the thought of actually seeing myself horrified me. I wasn't ready to go there yet. I was just grateful that, other than the neck and head discomfort and weird fingers, I appeared to have survived the accident virtually unscathed. I wouldn't know the extent of this miracle until after seeing the accident pictures.

Sometime later, Johanna arrived with my lunch. It was, again, a simple bowl of broth, and I sipped it from the spoon held out for me as best I could without turning my neck or head toward her. I was becoming more and more uncomfortable and asked by gesturing if there was a way to elevate the upper bed a little more so I could sit. The bed was nowhere near Canadian standards; no button to push to elevate the torso section up or down. No, it was more of a gurney with a hand crank at the bottom of the bed. Johanna turned the crank until I was sitting up a little more. My head felt very heavy, and the more the bed elevated, the more the neck brace crept up onto my chin. I kept my head back against the bed, but that too was very uncomfortable. With no pillow under my head, I felt unsupported and uncomfortable. I gestured toward Johanna, pointing a knuckle at my neck and crinkling my brow, and she lowered the bed down again. I sighed. I couldn't find the words in Spanish to articulate what I wanted, so I just let it slide.

"Mi familia?" I asked. *When were they coming?* I wondered, a giddy anticipation rolling through me.

"Ellas llegan hoy, pero tarde," she replied, but I couldn't understand. I silently wished I had kept the gift of fluent Spanish and felt disheartened that I'd lost that ability as quickly as it came. She could see my confusion and the slight shake of my head, so she dug out her phone, punched at it, and held it up to her mouth. She repeated her last statement into the phone. The translation app answered my question.

"They arrive today, but later."

My heart sank. I was truly hoping they would be here as soon as I woke up, but that, apparently, wasn't the case. Johanna dialed Nicole and held the phone to my ear.

"Hi, Momma! How are you feeling?" Nicole was chirpy, and it made my heart feel lighter.

"I'm ok, honey," I managed. "When are you coming to get me?" I hoped she would say she would walk in the door any second, but no.

"I'm not able to come, Mom, but Katrina and Casey are on their way." I could not recall our conversations from the day before, in which Nicole had repeated the plan. Every single call – and apparently we spoke every two to four hours – she had to answer the same questions, over and over. My mind, unbeknownst to me, was in a severely concussed state.

"They are?" I was a record player, skipping through the same questions and receiving the same answers.

"They left early this morning. I think their flight arrives in the middle of the afternoon?" Oh! That wasn't so bad!

"So they should be here soon?" Clearly, I was desperate. I was clinging to the thought of my saviors taking me home to safety and to my family. That was all I wanted in the entire world, just to see my family, to hold my precious grand-baby and smother her in kisses.

"Well, no, their flight comes into Cancun around 3:00 p.m., and a hired car will bring them to where you are, but it's a long drive," she explained. "I don't think they'll get there until very late, and then I'm not sure they'll be allowed to see you at the hospital until tomorrow."

My heart sank to the bottom of my chest as tears trickled down my cheeks. "Oh," was all I could manage. I don't recall the rest of that conversation. Nicole and I spoke a few more times during the day, and again she had to listen to the same questions and repeat the same answers. At one point, she told me she had started a Go-Fund-Me and that it was up to $10,000! I felt immense relief pour over me with this news. I had given no thought to my financial situation; it wasn't the priority, and any thoughts outside the world of my hospital bed and my desperation to leave it didn't exist. But she made an excellent point; just how was I planning to pay for all of this care? I was in a hospital in a foreign country! Surely that would be expensive? Did we have insurance to cover this? I couldn't remember what insurance we had to buy to cross the border in the first place, and I could barely even remember crossing the border, so there was no point in thinking about it now. I said a prayer of gratitude to the kindness of our friends, family and – I was guessing – complete strangers. The relief was exponential.

The entire day was a blur of napping, sipping broth and whining in discomfort. Using very lame hand signals, I showed my charge nurse that my neck was severely uncomfortable and asked if I could have a pillow. I got a few blank stares and rapid-fire Spanish, but as I could no longer understand or communicate my request, the result was no pillow. I imagine they were just as confused as I was that I could no longer speak as I had the day before. (Or was it earlier today? Or two days ago?) Nor could I understand their questions. The confusion was obvious in one nurse's face when she came to greet me, fresh on her shift, and rattled off something in Spanish, to which I could only reply "non comprende." She raised a quizzical brow and eyed me, confused. I did the best I could to shrug. She merely fussed with my sheets and then carried on to the next patient, who *could* understand and even answer just as rapidly. I was intruding on their secret clubhouse activities and was thus regarded as "some white lady" in the corner bed. I had never felt so alone.

Vera and Adam returned, taking their stance at the foot of my bed, just as they had done on their first visit. At that time, I couldn't recall who they were or their names, but I knew they had something to do with me returning home, so I was elated to see their lovely faces. They could request a pillow for me, but as Vera was told, there were none to be had. Somewhat appalled, I asked how a hospital could have no pillows? Vera explained I wasn't in an *actual* hospital; it was more of a clinic, and it was the closest medical facility to the location of the accident. The doctors deemed my injuries to be noncritical, so it wasn't necessary to transport me to the hospital in Chetumal or Cancun. I was happy knowing my injuries were minor, yet also unhappy that they would not transfer me. Surely one of the bigger hospitals would supply simple luxury items such as a pillow.

Apparently, the clinic had a "bring your own things" policy, to which I was ill-informed and thus, ill-prepared. I knew I had just been through what was the most devastating event of my life, lost my love, stranded and alone, but the minor details shadowed the larger ones, which I couldn't fully comprehend, nor was I willing to face them in my current state. The truth hurt, and small things mattered. A simple pillow would have softened the pain. Vera and Adam's visit was brief, friendly and – I'm guessing – informative. I don't think they gave me any real details, knowing it would be too difficult for me to understand at this point. I recall little of anything they may have said to me on their brief visits, but having them there was comforting, and I was grateful to have a supportive team. It was they who mentioned that Katrina and Casey – "mia familia" – would arrive around 10:00 p.m. that evening.

That was so late! The car ride from the Cancun airport to Bacalar is approximately five hours. *Really?* I thought. *I was that far from Cancun?* I knew it had been the last destination of our anniversary trip before the accident changed that plan forever, but I thought we were much closer than that! I tried my best to have patience. I slept, peed, sipped broth, spoke to Nicole a couple more times, again asking the same questions and getting the same answers, and fussed in discomfort throughout the day, all the while saying silent prayers for my family to arrive safely and for time to speed past.

Darkness arrives early every evening in the Caribbean nations. Being so close to the Equator, dawn and dusk arrive at the same time every day, day after day. So, around 6:00 p.m., the light through the single window grew dark, and hall lights filtered into the room. Not understanding time with no clocks on the walls and completely forgetting about the early sunsets, I assumed it was past 10:00 p.m., therefore Katrina and Casey weren't able to make it to the hospital that night. Visiting hours would have long since been over, so I figured I would see them in the morning and slipped into a deep, disappointed sleep. Sometime later, I awoke to the sound of rapid chatter coming from the hallway. It was still very dark, the hallway lights dimmed or turned off. I heard elevated voices, one in Spanish and one in... English! I strained to hear. Was that Casey? Katrina? I could only make out a few words.

"We're her family, and we've come a long way; we just want to see her."

That just *had* to be Katrina! Unless there was another English-speaking lady somewhere in the clinic that they had come for? The thought that someone else from the States or Canada could be down the hall from me was, at once, intriguing and disappointing. Who were the people in the hallway looking for? My heart didn't know whether to leap or sink. The chatter and voices turned to shouting and loud foot falls. Suddenly, Casey appeared through the doorway!

"Mumma!" She cried, quickly striding over to my bedside. She embraced me the best she could, laying her head on my chest, her hands on my shoulders. Katrina appeared and came around the other side of the bed and did the same. It was a pile of family, tears and relief.

"I can't believe you came!" I said to Kat. It absolutely amazed me she would drop everything to make this trip to save me. She had been a long-time friend, but in that moment, she surpassed being a "friend" and solidified herself as a true and forever part of our family.

"Of course I did! There was no other choice for me! I had to be here," she said through her own tears. The three of us cried and cried. I just couldn't get enough of them. Casey had tried so hard to be strong and not cry, intending to be a rock for me, but she couldn't help herself. We let the tears fall, hugged, held and thanked, grateful for the comfort of being together, and allowed the devastation of the real reason for their visit to sink in.

CASEY AND KATRINA

Casey: Nicole called as my brother and I were moving our last load of furniture from our old apartment to a new one. Needless to say, we were shocked and horrified to hear of the accident, and the rest of the day was a blur. We unloaded the truck, and as we were connecting with another family member (my brother immediately called Michael's son to give him the news), I attempted to pack for the trip to Mexico I knew I was going to make, even before my sister asked me to go. Something that should have been so simple as packing a suitcase was suddenly monumental. I couldn't figure out what I would need, and in between waves of grief, wailing, crying and hugging my brother for comfort, Katrina called and gave me a list of what to pack. That helped immensely.

Katrina: I got the call from Nicole while I was at work. My immediate response was to jump into action and get moving! There was no time for allowing the news to fully sink in, I just felt the need to act – now. I ran into my boss's office and quickly explained the situation. She got to work moving my scheduled appointments to other staff members, and I called my friend, a travel agent, to secure plane tickets for myself and

Casey. I called Nicole back within about ten minutes, one of several calls made to her over the next few hours. We talked about starting a Go-Fund-Me for the potential expenses that we would incur. Thankfully, I had just received a brand new Mastercard with a high limit, so I could purchase the tickets and book hotels right away. I grabbed my things and left work. It was only then that I let go of some of the emotions that were brimming at the surface.

Casey: Very early the next morning, Katrina and I took a cab to the airport and boarded the plane to Cancun. We were seated across the aisle from each other, me beside a couple on their honeymoon. Throughout the flight, I was an absolute mess, sobbing, snot running down my nose and wiping my eyes behind dark glasses. The happy couple beside me had to put up with my grief through the entire trip. The flight attendants were wonderful, once Katrina explained that we weren't heading out for holiday – after all, no one is usually sobbing when on their way to Cancun – but that we were, in fact, living a nightmare. They were gracious enough to keep the tea, water and drinks coming.

Katrina: "Drinks" being the word here! Not because we were celebrating a trip to Mexico, but because our nerves were so shot, we both needed something to calm us down. Couldn't the plane go any faster?

Casey: Once we arrived in Cancun, we collected our baggage and found the hired transportation to take us to Bacalar. It was the longest car ride of my life, taking almost five hours. When we arrived in Bacalar, it was 10:00 p.m. We had the hired car take us directly to the hotel so we could unload our things, then walk to the small hospital only a few hundred feet from our hotel. We knew that seeing Mom may have been impossible, but I needed to hold her and kiss her, so we decided we wouldn't let the staff stop us. They tried, but I busted past them, peering into doorways until I found her. I tried so hard to stay strong, and I honestly thought I had shed all of my tears on the trip down, but apparently not. Seeing her was such a relief. I had lost my step-dad and almost lost my mom; the simultaneous grief and relief was overwhelming.

Katrina: There was no way I'd let anyone stop us from seeing her. We were both a mess by this time; exhausted, red-faced from all the crying on the plane ride over, but determined.

GRATITUDE

The hospital charge nurse bustled in, silencing us and requesting they leave. It was very late, and the other members of my clubhouse were trying to sleep, the lady across from me, previously in labour, now snuggling her newborn. (When did *that* happen?) I could finally rest easy, as they promised they would be back first thing in the morning. Over 15 hours of travel had exhausted them, and they still had to unpack and settle into their hotel. I asked if they could take me home the next day, but they explained that they would have to talk to the doctor in the morning. Likely, I would have to stay in hospital for a few more days, but they would be there to keep me company as much as the staff would allow.

As they left I breathed a tremendous sigh of relief and settled into a grateful sleep. My heart was full. My tears, which had fallen from a very full and deep well, were finally dry. Soon, I would be well enough to be released from the hospital and travel back to Canada – easy peasy. I just had to be a good girl, rest and get better. For the first time in my life, I experienced a tragic accident in a foreign country (in *any* country, for that matter) and had lived to tell about it. I would bring my husband home with me and would allow myself to grieve the loss once the plane wheels hit the Canadian tarmac.

Nicole kept everyone updated back home, her Facebook and Go-Fund-Me post for that evening reading:

Our family members have made it to my mother in the hospital. We are beyond

relieved to have people there with her now. Everyone is completely exhausted and

will be trying to get a bit of a rest for tonight. Tomorrow is another very busy day of things we need to get accomplished, so thank you again to everyone for showing your support but still allowing us space to breathe and deal with things we need to deal with.

In my concussed state, I had the benefit of naïveté, oblivious to the massive amount of paperwork, political hoops and criminal activity that were waiting for us over the next few days, which I will share with you... later.

CHAPTER 5

You've Got Mail

July - August, 2005, Canada

After 35 years of service, the financial institution that employed me had retired our lovely manager. The new manager turned out to be the biggest, misogynistic asshole I had ever encountered in my five years with the company, which propelled me into taking a permanent hiatus from the riveting life of a bank teller. I moved onwards and upwards to my next adventure and full-time work as a receptionist at a local non-profit in my small hometown. Full-time employment was just what this single mom of four kids needed, and, ever the organizational fiend and master typist (thanks, in part, to the many turned-over egg cartons I pretended were typewriters as a child), I was grateful for the opportunity to work with a large group of lovely individuals, counselors and therapists. I ruled my new roost with precision, professionalism and a natural talent for making everyone around me smile, laugh and feel better, just by breezing through my open reception area.

I continued my spiritual studies at home and had developed a deeper sense of "knowing" who I really was, as well as a belief in how the Universe works. I didn't have any interest in God as my brother knew him, separate from our individual selves, but I could agree that there was something – a higher power, perhaps – that somehow participated in our creation and was fully and completely part of us all, all of us being "One." My quest for truth pulled me toward a meditation group that was really more of an initiation into the deeper side of my spiritual self. There, I learned psychometry (reading the energy on objects), seeing auras and psychic attainment. It was all so fascinating, loving and peaceful. I journaled my studies and experiences and compiled them into an upcoming program and book; *All Women Are Psychic*.

Fear of persecution never left me, however, but the reason why I had this fear was so far outside the scope of my understanding, other than the obvious (my brother and the way I would often be reprimanded by him for my beliefs). I was envious of other women whose husbands either supported or believed in the same spiritualism that their wives did, and I longed for a relationship where I could be completely open with the person I loved the most in the world. That person would surely be "the one" that my heart was longing for. At this point in my life, however, I only had myself and family members, many of whom would only preach and reprimand, rather than listen and understand, so I kept my spiritual self a highly-guarded secret. The only people I felt safe enough to open my heart to were my children and the ladies of my writing group, "The 4th Tuesday," and my meditation group. The women in these groups allowed me to express my childhood hurt, anger and emotions through my writing, and they bore no judgment, regardless of their own beliefs.

I enjoyed my day job, as I structured my work much like life in our home. However, being organized meant I would complete tasks quickly and often had idle time on my hands. I would then poke around on the good ol' internet, reading recipes or parenting and spirituality articles. On one such occasion, I noticed a well-placed ad on the right side of a single mom parenting article I was reading. The banner ad was from a dating site, denoting a possibility for people of the opposite in my area sex available to chat.

Momentarily hesitating – thinking, *what were the chances that I could find "the one" from a dating site?* – I decided "what the hell," and clicked on the ad. All you had to do was input your postal code to find a match. Maybe there would be someone around these parts who would fit the bill! I was dreaming a little, as "these parts" were small, and I likely knew everyone in them, but, according to my previous indoctrination, "boredom and idle hands do the Devil's work." Clearly, in this case, he was rooting for my team.

I wasn't exactly new to internet dating, although it had been a couple of years since I had originally posted my personal dating curriculum vitae on any site of this nature, only to take it down a mere six weeks and 40 weirdos later. Admittedly, I was kind of "asking for it," as I had planted the seed of Wanton Lustful Sex Goddess to the masses by head-lining my bio with "Cougar Seeking Stud." Weirdo numero uno? Me.

As with the previous dating site, this one took me through a series of not-so-tricky life questions and required a personal headshot. I answered vaguely and didn't upload my picture, as I was more interested in finding out who was available in my area. By this time, I had been single long enough to have a better sense of who and what I was seeking in a life mate and had been using the Law of Attraction to solidify that message with the Universe. My daily incantation when something like this... actually, it went *exactly* like this, as I kept the laminated note in my journal and still have it to this day:

I am attracting and allowing all that I need to do, know and have to attract and allow my ideal relationship. My ideal partner is taller than me, lean and fit. I am thrilled that my ideal partner is romantic, surprising and delighting me in public and private, always ready to show his affection and shower me with little gifts, notes and special touches. It brings me joy to watch my ideal partner play with and love my children. My ideal partner sets such an outstanding example for them, and they love him back very much. I'm ecstatic that my ideal partner and I have so much in common, and I love that my ideal partner is so outgoing and excited to travel and play, together and with the kids. I feel so blessed to have an ideal partner who has a great sense of self, who is very cooperative, loving and willing to help. It thrills me how we move through our lives as one, being true partners in every sense of the word in our business, family and personal lives. The Law of Attraction is unfolding and orchestrating all that it needs to bring me my desire.

I learned the language from Michael Losier, author of *The Law of Attraction*, or at least, one of many authors to use the same title before and since. I really enjoyed his teachings and his method and still use the tools he teaches.

I input my postal code into the "find your match" space, and *voila!* Four matches in my area. I easily deleted the first three. I knew them, or knew *of* them, and was not attracted to their brand of "special." The fourth, however, piqued my interest. The picture, small and grainy, was the face of a man I somehow thought I knew, but I couldn't quite tell from the photo. Short blonde hair, thin blonde mustache, no glasses, and it was clearly a cropped picture – *not* a good one. The bio, however, was of greater interest, both for its content and as a match to my Universal Unfolding. It read:

ABOUT ME

kaloogan at ne tsca pe dottnett.

(Was he dyslexic? Couldn't find the correction keys?)

Single dad who is looking for a little more from life than just working and parenting. I love the outdoors and spend a lot of time camping in the summers. Not much of a snow fan though, and would love to find someone to spend time with on those cold winter nights. I live in a small mountain town in BC, but through work and the desire to escape, I spend a lot of time traveling the southern interior of British Columbia. My son is going on 12, so I have a lot more time on my hands and would like to meet someone to spend it with. - kaloogan atne tscape do tnet (Again, what was with the weird language? Assuming he'd been tipping back a few during this writing, I read on, curious.)

I am an easygoing, self-employed, single dad who can't quite remember but thinks there is more to life than just working. I would like to meet someone who knows how to have a good time but doesn't have to see the sunset every night, who knows how to relax and make the most of an evening in the country. My son lives with me full-time, so children must not be a problem, and though I could see myself perhaps having another child, I do not want to be changing diapers when I'm 80, unless it is grandchildren.

BASIC INFO

Username: Kaloogan (Okay, this again. What the heck is a Kaloogan!?)
Gender: Man, seeking Woman
Age: 37
Hair: Blonde
Eyes: Blue
Height: 190 cm
Average/Medium Build; Active; Non-smoker

The rest of the "Basic Info" went into a lot of detail and included personality traits, favorite activities, favorite foods, music, leisure and physical activities and so on, all of it seemingly in line with what I was looking for in a mate as well. Also, the age and height were bonus points for him! Being 6-feet tall and coming from a marriage where my husband was a good deal shorter than myself, height was definitely a deciding factor for my next go round. When it got down to the section titled "My Perception of an Ideal Relationship," I took particular interest. Here he stated his ideal was:

Partnership, each person on equal terms and pulling for the same goals, love and affection, mutual understanding and patience. It is not healthy for one partner to make all the rules and have control over the decisions. (Agreed.)
I guess that, to me, the ideal relationship would be to sit back when you are old,

```
look  at  your  partner,  and  realize  that
there is still no one in the world that you
would  rather  wake  up  with!  Of  course,  it
helps if they feel the same way.
```

The next section read: "What I've learned From My Past Relationships," but his response here was a little less forthcoming:

```
Lots  of  long  stories,  and  I  am  tired  of
these questions! Ask me more if you like!
You  can  reach  me  at  ten.epacsten  ta
nagoolak if you own a mirror! Get the hint?
```

I consider myself a human of reasonable intellect, but I stared and stared at that last line. Surely I could work out this riddle. Then, I remembered I hate riddles, but still gave it a shot, despite myself. After a while, it finally dawned on me what all the weird, dyslexic writing was all about! It was a secret code! He had hidden his email address in the bio, as providing your email address on the dating site profile was prohibited. You had to pay for the privilege of contacting someone through the site, but he had figured out a way to provide his email address so that the lady on the other end wouldn't have to pay to connect. Oh. So. Smart. I liked this guy! I decoded the email address in his bio to be kaloogan@netscape.net – *brilliant* – and immediately set about writing him an email from my Telus account, a tingle of gooseflesh rippling up, down and around my spine as I did so.

Here, I would like to give a nod to Universal Intelligence and point out the first piece of substantial proof that I possess in the coincidence argument: that I had printed out – and kept, *all these years* – Michael's dating bio and the subsequent emails we passed back and forth like naughty school kids in class (as you are about to discover). The "coincidences" just get larger and louder from there. I held on to these emails for over 12 years, and, unbeknownst to me at the time of printing, they provide the perfect content for this chapter, giving you, dear reader, the story of a romantic and meant-to-be Universal Unfolding of our wonderful life together. With the exception of spelling or blatant grammatical errors, the following emails have been transcribed here, exactly as they were originally written.

From: Tammy Tyree [tyree@telus.net]
Sent: July 1, 2005, 3:48 p.m.
To: [kaloogan@netscape.net]
Subject: De-coded your message!

Hi there! I think I have successfully decoded your email address on Date.ca!

I'm a single mom of 4 kids living in the same town as you, so I'm sure we must know each other, as our sons are the same age! I didn't recognize you from your picture online, but I'm attaching one of myself. Maybe you recognize me?

If you'd like to get a cup of coffee sometime, let me know?

Tammy Tyree

His reply came around nine days later. During those nine days, I suffered enormously from anticipation, doubt and a little girlish disappointment. I shouldn't have mentioned the kids! Who would want to hang around a woman with FOUR kids?

I probably could have denied their existence until he was so smitten there was no turning back, couldn't I? No, no, that would be wrong, wouldn't it? I read and re-read his bio until I had it memorized. The paper copy I had printed was dog-eared, as if I could uncover his true identity just by reading it. Perhaps I'd overlooked another hidden clue? One could never be too thorough. I'd already developed eye strain from looking at the small, grainy picture he had for a profile photo and got nothing but a slight recollection of someone I might have known, someone from so far in my past I couldn't pull it forward into my present. Finally, on the morning of July 10, the reply came. I checked my email from work and tripped over my own fingers to open it.

From:Michael Friese [kaloogan@netscape.net]
Sent: July 9, 2005, 11:48 p.m.
To: Tammy Tyree [tyree@telus.net]
Subject: Hello!

Tammy,

I have received your picture and I believe we know each other, though not too closely. It's great that you cracked my email code, and thank you for the message!

Anyhow, a little more about me. I am 37 this year and my son is turning 13. I have lived here off and on, with it being home for the last few years. I work in the highway construction industry as a surveyor, so I spend my summers traveling and visiting some of the remote areas of our province that some people pay dearly to visit. I am working in northern British

Columbia as I write this. I was actually in town for the July long weekend for about 24 hours to pick up my son. He is spending 6 weeks here with me and then going to visit his mother for a few weeks before starting high school. Any of this sounding like someone you know?

Having a better look at your picture, thank you. I definitely recognize the smile. So, tell me a little more about yourself and what makes you tick.

I am sorry that I was slow in responding, but I only recently set my office up in a new location so I will be a lot quicker in putting thoughts to type.

I would really like to have that cup of coffee when I return and get to know each other better through the summer if you are interested. Perhaps even a phone conversation later.

Unfortunately, I do not have any pictures of myself to return right now, but I will take some over the next little while and send them if you like.

Your turn,

Michael

As I finished his message, a different kind of excitement came over me. Surveyor? Could it be the Michael that I met so long ago and had seen off and on all these years? Served him his pay on Fridays? Tall, blonde, blue-eyed stunner with an incredible smile? I didn't hesitate to answer.

From: Tammy Tyree [tyree@telus.net]
Sent: July 10, 2005, 9:33 a.m.
To: Michael Friese [kaloogan@netscape.net]
Subject: Hello!

Hi Michael! Glad you could get your office set up and get back to me!

A surveyor working highway construction named Mike is definitely familiar. I live beside Earl, who manages a survey firm. He usually has a Mike working for him. I used to work at CIBC and dole out bi-weekly pay to Earl's band of surveyors — one of them named Mike. Is that you?

I have four kids, my oldest and my third, both girls, ages 15 and 11, live with me full-time, and my son (13) and my youngest daughter (8) live with their dad full-time. It's a brilliant arrangement. We only live a few blocks from each other, so we get to share the kids regularly. The kids are self reliant, so I have a lot of free time on my hands. But they're also a lot of fun to be around!

My ex-husband and I divorced 3.5 years ago, after being married for 14. Looking at your profile, we definitely have some very similar interests. My personality traits pretty much match yours, as do my "I enjoy going out to" and "My favorite physical activities." How neat is that?

If you're in town for the August long weekend, then we'll have to get together at some point.

I'd love a pic or two when you're able! I'm sure your dating profile picture doesn't do you justice.

Talk soon,

Tammy

I read and re-read the email a few times before hitting "send." The points I made about my kids – their ages, how independent and fun they were – would surely completely reduce or eliminate any anxiety he may have had over meeting a woman with half of a baseball team of young humans around. I was happy to share any other details of my life he might ask me, except for one. It was not yet time for me to introduce my spiritual side. The desire to do so was strong, but the fear of persecution and a repeat of being "burned at the stake" by another man was paramount to my desire. I forwent this introduction to my spiritual life until I felt the moment was right. I was absolutely delighted when his reply came only hours later! From here, the story of our budding romance writes itself.

From: Michael Freise
[kaloogan@netscape.net]
Sent: July 10, 2005, 3:28 p.m.
To: Tammy Tyree [tyree@telus.net]
Subject: It's me; one in the same.

Tammy,

Yes, I am the surveyor that you are thinking of. I recognized your pictures, but the Tyree threw me off. That must be your maiden name? Earl is no longer with the firm, I am managing things these days.

He is actually moving, and we have been
negotiating a rental agreement for his
place. Coincidence? I have not seen you in
the bank for a while when I would stroll
by, so I wondered if you were still working
there.

I am afraid that I will be nowhere near
home on the August long weekend. I made the
trip home in July to pick up my son and
found that after 32 hours of driving on a
3-day weekend, I was more exhausted than I
thought I would have been. I guess I am
getting older as much as I try to deny it.
My son's birthday is in August, so we
usually go camping with friends that weekend, but being so far away, we are planning
a brief trip up here instead; sightseeing
in Alaska. It is a good time to watch the
Grizzlies feeding during the salmon run
there. I have hired a couple of local
fellas for surveying and they are taking us
crab fishing next Sunday. I try to make it
fun for my son during the summer and not
just work, work, work.

Your son and mine are the same age. Is
yours going into Grade 8 in the fall or
grade 9? It is good to hear that you have a
good relationship with your Ex, as it seems
so many people have such bitter feelings
towards theirs. That makes it a lot easier
for the children. I only have one son and
even though his mother and I don't see eye
to eye on a lot of things, we don't have a
hard time working out the differences.

It occurs to me now that my friend Linda had told me you were single and thought that you and I would be compatible, when discussing the dating situation back home. Strange how things come around.

I must make a confession. The picture on the single ad is a few years old, but you have seen me since, so I don't think my looks will surprise you. I will try to send a picture or two, but I must warn you I am sporting a beard for the summer. It is at my son's request, but if it annoys me much more by the time I get around to picking up the camera, I will shave it off.

Well, speaking of distractions, I guess I should get back to my paperwork. It was great to hear from you, and I had to prove that a quick response was in my repertoire.

Enjoy your Sunday,

Michael

From: Tammy Tyree [tyree@telus.net]
Sent: July 10, 2005, 4:33 a.m.
To: Michael Friese [kaloogan@netscape.net]
Subject: RE: It's me; one in the same

Well, hello! Now that we have firmly established that we actually know each other, I'm trying to recall when we first met? There is a vague recollection of seeing you downtown; I think I was pregnant with my oldest daughter? I seem to recall that you had a bald head. It looked good on you!

I know little about Earl, but what I know isn't impressive at all, and I believe he's a bit of a "Bad Monkey." Sorry, I know you worked for the guy, and I'm sure you're nothing like him or partake of his extracurricular "habits"?

My son is entering grade 8 as well, yes. He's quite the character and has a wicked sense of humor. My oldest has no interest in public school; she and my son were originally homeschooled until I got divorced and had to go to work. She went to school for a couple years, now she's home again, completing her high school by correspondence.

I know Linda! She and I are friends and have been since she had her oldest son, the day after I had my oldest daughter! We get out of touch now and then since she moved away, but she makes a point of stopping by whenever she is in town.

Your job and location sound fascinating! When do you think you'll be here next?

Also, what the heck is a "Kaloogan"?

Have a great weekend,

Tammy

From: Michael Friese
[kaloogan@netscape.net]
Sent: July 13, 2005, 1:28 p.m.
To: Tammy Tyree [tyree@telus.net]

Subject: Good morning/afternoon

How I first met you and your Ex, I cannot recall. I know I went to the rifle range with him a few times years ago when I was still a member, but as to first introductions, well, memories fade. I remember being quite mesmerized by the statuesque, beautiful blonde lady though.

I think you are the first person to tell me they thought a bald head looked good on me. I always liked it, but everyone shaves their head these days, so I guess it has lost its shock value. As for who I work with, the job is about the only similarity that I have with Earl. I really like the description "Bad Monkey," though. It fits. I do little in the way of partying these days and was never a pot smoker. It's funny the impressions that we give to others and how different they are from our true nature.

My son is in a different elementary school than yours, obviously. I guess he and your son will both be going to high school next year. He stays with his grandmother while I am away, and he helps her out. She is 73 years old this year, and he is quite the helping hand. They have a very close relationship, but sometimes it is hard to tell which one is the child and which is the adult.

Usually, I am on the road until mid-October, but I am aiming to be finished up and home by Labour Day this year, as I want to be around when my son starts high school. There are a lot of loose ends to tie up this year, as I want to start my own survey firm in the spring. I admire your self discipline and drive to be working outside of your home and homeschooling your daughter at the same time. I get distracted by simply doing paperwork at home. Perhaps because it is my least favorite part of my job.

It sounds like you have found an excellent career choice that makes you happy. I sometimes wonder what it would be like to have a job where you are home for dinner every night. The nature of my work has always involved some travel, but the last few years have been to the extreme. I have worked hard to build up a reputation and respect in the industry that should lend itself well to working in the interior of BC this time around. It is good, honest work and keeps me mentally stimulated.

So I have a few questions I would like to ask you to get a better sense of who you are and your personality. Ask one in return, or two, or whatever.

Today's question: If you find yourself with an entire evening with no kids and no demands on your time, how do you spend it?

Well, as I mentioned earlier, I procrastinate, and I am supposed to be doing paperwork, so I guess I will get to it.

Perhaps we will have to slip in a dinner with that coffee when I return?

Michael

P.S. A "Kaloogan" is a German slang that loosely means "Big, dumb oaf." I thought it was clever and resembles how I often feel about myself!

From: Tammy Tyree [tyree@telus.net]
Sent: July 10, 2005, 4:33 a.m.
To: Michael Friese [kaloogan@netscape.net]
Subject: Good evening

You're funny. Also sweet! "Statuesque beautiful blonde lady"… aw thanks (blush). Keep talking…

I don't mind the bald thing, but I like that you have hair now! Haha. I also appreciate that you're taller than me — you do not know how refreshing THAT is… I'm not kidding when I said that I always thought that you were a really nice guy and I'm glad that, however I got the teeniest impression that YOU were a "Bad Monkey," it was wrong.

My mom is 72 and lives in the mobile home park near my place. She and my dad moved here when my youngest was 1, so she's been here 7 years now. My dad passed away 2 years ago, July 19, 2003 — 8 days after my birthday and 2 days before their 52nd wedding anniversary. I miss him a lot and was a total daddy's girl. Instead of making pierogies with my Ukrainian mom in the kitchen, you would find me out building a house with dad (a contractor). I guess I take after my dad in more ways than his Dutch height gene.

It's awesome that your son stays with your mom, that's really fantastic. Sometime I guess we'll get into details about how it came to be that he is with you full-time and not his mom. I don't like to pry or drudge up what may be a bitter past — the past is just that — the past — and doesn't interest me as much as finding out more about who you are now. It is very obvious to me that your son is extremely important to you, and I really love to see that in a guy.

My oldest is a very mature young lady who mostly schools herself. I prepare the curriculum and "grade" her papers, but she's pretty disciplined, so I don't have to babysit her. Oh, and I don't mind paper-work, so if you ever need an assistant or someone to keep you from being distracted you know who to call. ;-)

I'm really impressed that you take your work so seriously. With the attitude you have, you deserve an excellent reputation and respect. How do you like having a crew working for you? Is that something you're used to? Do you find the guys respect you and are diligent — or a pain in the ass? I am fascinated by surveying. I grew up watching my dad and his construction crew level a lot to build on. He even let me play with the orange level telescope thing (ok, you'll have to educate me as to the "lingo") — so when I'm stopped during highway construction and see the guys in the bushes doing the same, I always wonder what the heck they're looking at! And can you see the moon through that thing?

Ok, to answer your question: this one is pretty easy, as I usually have an entire day and evening to myself once a week. My Ex works Saturdays, so the kids all come to my place for a "family" day, then Sunday they go to his place for a "family" day with him and his girlfriend. I always feel a little "off" at first when they're gone, but then I get busy catching up on stuff around the house, usually going for a nice walk or bike ride, reading a book in the sun or having a hot bubble bath for a couple hours. Maybe later, go to the movies with a girlfriend or rent a couple and stay in. I rarely go to the bars, (and never on a Sunday!) but when I do, I have a good time dancing and enjoying the company of my friends.

Now, that's just me being alone with me. If I am so lucky to have a significant other in the picture, my day/evening would be similar, but with some distinct differences. I could still see catching up on some stuff around the house, since my Sunday is about the only day to do so. Then perhaps going out for dinner and a movie, or renting and staying in. Either way, there is cuddling involved and I would definitely top off the evening — or morning — or mid-afternoon — with some "private time"... ;-) I mean, if there're no kids around, then why not?

So, now it's my turn — ready?

How would you like a "first date" to go?

And...

Where do you see yourself in 5 years?

And...

What made you decide to list your profile on a dating site? I don't knock it — it works! I mean, we're conversing, right? But I think you're a really nice, good-looking guy — and as far as I know you're in good shape, don't have a terrible reputation or a third eye, so why post?

Okay, I realize that's more than one question, so if you take days and days and days to answer, I'll understand. Just remember I'm getting older by the minute here...

Your turn!

Tammy

P.S. Dinner AND coffee? Gee buddy — don't push it! HAHA kidding, it's a date!

From: Michael Friese
[kaloogan@netscape.net]
Sent: July 11, 2005, 5:28 a.m.
To: Tammy Tyree [tyree@telus.net]
Subject: Happy Birthday

I noted from the dating site that today is your birthday, and I wish you a happy one! Have any grand plans for the day? You're older than me, but I don't mind. I quite like cougars!

I really enjoyed your idea of spending a day, especially the reference to cuddling. I am a great cuddler, and a lover of bear hugs. "Bear" would be a good nickname for me actually. As my friends would attest, I am a bit of a bear. What would your friends say about you?

In answer to your questions: my idea for a first date would be to surprise my lady with a romantic dinner, made by me, served on a blanket on a beach or shore, under the moonlight. I'm a bit of a sappy romantic, so sorry if that idea is lame! Does that win me any points?

I admire your relationship with your father. My father passed away a couple of years ago as well, but we were estranged, so I didn't even attend the funeral. He was an abusive alcoholic and never gave me any reason to want to pursue a close relationship after he and my mother separated when I was 12.

Where do I see myself in 5 years? Well, hopefully I'm feeling younger, looking thinner and have my hair! Also, I hope to be with the one I'm with for the rest of my life, living out our days on a lovely piece of property, maybe camping or traveling...

Why did I post on the dating site? With

my career, it can be difficult, if not impossible, to meet people any other way!

Sorry for the quick answers, work has been keeping me busy and I must go! Now, same questions right back at ya!

Michael

From: Tammy Tyree [tyree@telus.net]
Sent: July 15, 2005, 9:40 p.m.
To: Michael Friese [kaloogan@netscape.net]
Subject: More riveting details

Thank you for the birthday wishes. I just turned the ripe young age of 38. I don't really have a problem stating what my age is, as I often happily partake in the game of "guess my age." Well, it's more like people often say to me, "WHAT? You're HOW old? You have HOW many kids?" At which I blush and titter, "How old did you THINK I am?" The "oldest" reply I've gotten lately is 27, and I find the younger the person, the younger I seem to them. Strange, but a darn good boost to my ego! I seem to get along well with people of any age. My closest girlfriends are in their 20s, and I have some great girlfriends who are well into their 40s.

I think Bear is an impressive title for you, however, that is dangerously close to the affectionate "Pooh Bear," and not sure how you'd feel if I called you that in front of your co-workers. Apparently, they are not aware that you're a romantic, so "Pooh Bear" might be a dead giveaway. Oh, and with a name like that, you better be a damn good cuddler and sweet like honey!

I'm sorry to hear about your relationship with your dad (or lack of). I'm afraid that I can't relate. My own parents never drank or smoked. My mom grew up with a dad who liked Rye Whisky and Chewing Tobacco so she wanted a husband who wouldn't touch the stuff.

Your friends are usually the best people to label you, and usually the most accurate. You left out "great sense of humor," so I'm adding that to your list of character traits. Mine would say that I'm fun, have a great sense of humor, am easygoing, a little crazy, a good listener, good shoulders to cry on and everyone's friend. My teenagers and their friends think I'm the coolest mom EVER because I treat them like real people and never rag on them to "study hard, stay in school, don't drink, do drugs," etc. They actually LIKE to hang out with me! Fortunately, my teens seem to be independent enough to know who they are and they don't like to hang out with anyone who is into the "crap."

Your idea of a first date? Well, it's no jet ride off to Paris for pizza, but guess it will have to do. HA — kidding — I was speechless. Five stars on the first date idea. Sappy romantic? Are you reading my mind or my diary? Either will tell you that sappy and romantic is a total MUST. Not a real simple thing to find in a bear, so I'm impressed. I'm big on surprises, notes, little gifts and flowers, and did I mention surprises? Nothing big, I think the littlest things count the most. Guys think that they have to go all out, buy enormous flower arrangements for weeks on end, when most girls (myself included) would be just as happy with a few daisies picked out of the field or a note left on their car window or pillow. It's knowing that he thought about me enough to do something that is the key (and this goes both ways). The TRICK is to continue the affectionate displays for 50 years. Oh, and if you tell me you like to light candles at dinner, I'll faint!

In 5 years... perhaps you NEED a cougar in your life to keep you younger, thinner, and who cares about the hair? I don't plan on wandering around my 5000 sq foot house (that I have the plans for) with a pool in the back on a few acres of property with a couple horses grazing in the field, parked next to my Escalade and 25-foot travel trailer that sleeps 8, which is parked next to my then husband's Dodge crew cab 4 x 4... no. I'll retire by the time I'm 50, romping around checking on the various businesses, properties, apartment buildings and houses me and my husband will own, occasionally touring the countryside or world with my husband, and maybe a couple of our younger kids that haven't left the nest to pursue their dreams.

I dream a little, don't I? Although none of this has come to fruition, I am still taking the steps daily to get me there. Gee, reading this again, I realize my idea of a perfect life may sound a little intimidating! You don't scare easily, do you?

Dating site — OK story time. Bored at work one day and poking around the internet, the date site ad came up. What the hell, I thought, let's see what's around town, so I clicked on it, put my postal code in and got a list of some pretty sorry looking dudes… and one great-looking one. I clicked on that one, read the profile, tried not to get too worked up about how similar he is to my liking, cracked his email code and sent him a message. I then put my profile up, again, for the hell of it, under the name Lang Meisje (meaning "tall blonde one" in dutch) but the good-looking guy replied to my message, so I haven't been back on the site since. End of story. Sounds a bit like a confession.

Sadly, I don't have a third eye, but I have some other interesting body parts to keep as a surprise until the third date, minimum. Charm you have, intelligence definitely, and apparently you're a sappy, romantic Bear, so a third date is likely…

How many days until Labour Day?

Tammy

XOXO

. . .

Reading this email – 15 years after first writing it – gave me pause. The "list" of where I saw myself in five years time, retired by the age of 50, was incredibly similar to the life I was living at the time of Michael's demise. We owned multiple properties, traveled the world, and Michael was planning to retire – at age 50 – the year he passed. Chills tore through me repeatedly at this re-write, the echoes of wishes, dreams and hopes for the future had come true, only to be snatched away without warning, and seemingly, without reason. It was only later, after Michael ramped up his communication with me from the other side, that the reason became clear.

From: Michael Friese
[kaloogan@netscape.net]
Sent: July 19, 2005, 10:18 p.m.
To: Tammy Tyree [tyree@telus.net]
Subject: It sucks to find an empty inbox!

Tammy, I am sorry that I have not answered for a while. It has been absolutely crazy busy here. I took Saturday off to go exploring. Even took some pictures for you. I promise to write to you tomorrow night. I am looking forward to another letter, so I better reply to your last one. If I have time I will install the driver for my new camera and include some pictures.
    Michael

From: Tammy Tyree [tyree@telus.net]

Sent: July 21, 2005, 7:09 a.m.
To: Michael Friese [kaloogan@netscape.net]
Subject: It's ok, I forgive you.

In case you were wondering if I'd ever
forgive you for leaving my inbox empty day
after day, I thought I'd write a quickie
and tell you I do. *sigh* It's okay, I
understand. I imagine you're busier than a
bear up there, but I hope you're taking
some time to have some fun too. The sun's
been shining here this past week. It's
about time the darn thing poked out from
behind the clouds and rain. On Sunday I
spent the day with my little girls out at
the lake working on my tan lines. :-)

Well, I just got back from a jog and
should go shower up. Hope you have a great
day. No pressure — email when you get a
chance. I look forward to it!

Tammy

From: Michael Friese
[kaloogan@netscape.net]
Sent: July 24, 2005, 9:18 p.m.
To: Tammy Tyree [tyree@telus.net]
Subject: RE: It's ok, I forgive you.

I am really sorry about the long delay in
writing. Things have been really busy, and
then to top it off my son has decided that
he wants to visit his mother sooner than
planned so I spent my weekend driving him

into the city to catch a bus. Now I am desperately trying to catch up on my work.

I like your idea for a first date, a little cheesy, but what the heck? I am the guy that owns more candles than CDs. Speaking of dates, what kind of food do you like? Do you like to cook?

I am having problems with my laptop and can't download pictures right now, but I will send you some of the beautiful areas I'm working in as soon as I get it fixed. I even got my son to take a couple of me, in case you wanted one.

I would not have mentioned this before, but I am weak in my tired state. When I had seen you again, working at the bank, I was going to ask you out to dinner, but I asked around first and was told that you were seeing someone. I still can't get over the strangeness of you emailing me from a dating site. Sounds like that fate thing I keep hearing about.

So, I am in your thoughts while you daydream at work, huh? Cool! You have been wandering through my thoughts as well. I am more than a little rusty at dating and relationships, having been single for about 6 years now and haven't done a lot of dating during that time. Sounds sad and more than a little scary, but I can honestly say that I found being a father and work fulfilling. I am not a desperate single man looking for just anyone, if that makes sense. I hope it doesn't scare you away, because I have always found you quite enjoyable to talk to and would love to find out if there is a possibility of more.

Your "other interesting body parts to keep as a surprise until the third date" have got me wondering and smiling. You forgot to throw in some questions for me to answer though, so I guess I will get the advantage here, but you can ask twice as many next time. I guess it is too soon to ask if you have any dirty little secrets you want to share, so I won't, unless you feel so inclined…?

How do you feel about horses? I have one, but he is still in training and too young to ride.

What is the craziest thing that you have ever done on a dare, recreation wise, ie: skydiving, bungee jumping, etc.?

And lastly, would you find it a little weird dating your neighbor? I am looking forward to another reply from you and I will start getting up a little earlier in the morning to write, as the evenings seem to be too short.

Michael

This email absolutely thrilled me. Not only was he talking about pursuing "something more," the man also owned a horse! My favorite animal! The excitement that ripped through me overflowed into actual shrill screeches that brought the girls running into my room. "He owns a horse! HE OWNS A HORSE!!!" They screeched along with me. The girls often shared in the email excitement and would always ask what Michael had to say. This relationship wasn't just for me; it was for my children as well. Every piece of it was exciting to share.

From: Tammy Tyree [tyree@telus.net]
Sent: July 27, 2005, 1:30 p.m.
To: Michael Friese [kaloogan@netscape.net]
Subject: Are you kidding me?

Sorry it's taken me a few days to reply — things have been quite busy both at work and at home.

I have to admit that I just about fell out of my chair when you mentioned having a horse! How do I feel about them? Are you KIDDING ME???? I spent my childhood on horses until I moved here. I could never afford my own again, so I've just been renting one now and then for a nice trail ride. It's been a while since I've ridden; I've been waiting until I have property of my own to buy one again. But now maybe I'll have to look at doing that sooner than later! Oh, and I've always wanted my very own cowboy to go with it! Where is your horse, how old is he, how long have you had him, what breed is he and how many hands high?

Food. I really enjoy cooking and so do my girls. My oldest daughter has been fantastic about getting dinner ready for us when I'm going to be late at work, but I enjoy having the time to cook some superb meals.

Funny story. I was getting my hair done yesterday — my hairdresser happens to be your landlord's daughter — when your name came up. She was absolutely GUSHING with pleasant things to say about you. Mainly how NICE you are and how DEVOTED you are to your son, stuff like that. It's always nice to know when someone has agreeable things to say about you, so I thought I'd share.

I think the dating "thing" is a little like the riding a bike "thing." Once you initially get the hang of it again, it's no problem; especially if you're dating someone likable and easy-going, or a neighbor. I can't think of anything more CONVENIENT than dating my neighbor! You asked me if I thought that would be weird. No, not at all, but were you talking about YOU or the old guy three doors down? Does this mean you're moving in next door?

I think it's fabulous that you have found parenting and your career so fulfilling, I really admire that. I look forward to meeting your son! What does he like to do for fun? Is he a "skater dude"? Does he like school and get good grades? Does he enjoy living with you? Where does your mom live? Is he secretly hoping dad finds a girlfriend or NEVER finds a girlfriend? My kids are constantly pointing out guys to me, insisting I need to find "the one." It's too funny. I love having teenagers!

Ever since my kids were little, I couldn't wait for them to grow up so I could "hang out" with them! My son is a "skater boy" and by the looks of his beat up legs and (recently) sprained ankle, it's obvious he's extreme. Either that or just incredibly clumsy.

If things seem to work out between us, then perhaps somewhere between the 5th and 10th date, we could get them together! Sorry, I'm often guilty of looking WAY further ahead than is really necessary. Bad Tammy. No pressure, honest. I will only talk about actually having a first date whenever it's a possibility — promise!

Moving onto dirty little secrets… ok… skipping dirty little secrets. For now. That's totally 5th to 10th date stuff. You must earn those!

Craziest thing I've ever done on a dare, recreation wise. The most daring thing I've done lately is try an "ollie" on my son's skateboard, and failed miserably. What about you? What have you done, and what do you continue to enjoy doing?

I can't think of anything else at the moment. Really looking forward to a reply. I check my inbox every day, hoping… wishing… ;-)

Tammy

From: Michael Friese
[kaloogan@netscape.net]

Sent: July 27, 2005, 2:44 a.m.
To: Tammy Tyree [tyree@telus.net]
Subject: Trying not to disappoint you!

What an excellent surprise to get an email.
I was a little worried that my ramblings in
my last letter had made me seem like a
raving loon and that you had quietly
slipped away. Now that I know the reason,
or at least perhaps your kind explanation
while pondering the possibility, I can
honestly say that I can relate to the busy
"excuse." I am just getting home from work.
I am surveying during the days this week
and split shifting nights to fill in the
gap left by yet another defector. My staff
is dwindling.

Enough about work for now. Have to save
some boring talk to tell when I am old.

Okay, on to the horse. Two years ago on
Thanksgiving, I went to visit Linda and her
boys. When I got there, she had just
finished reading a newspaper article on a
local group that rescues horses from the
slaughterhouses and sells them to suitable
homes. She had just bought a new farm and
was moving in at the end of the month, so
she was trying to figure out how to find
the money for a horse. Being the easily
intrigued type, (some would say "simply,"
but hey…) off we went for a drive, and next
thing I know I am buying a pregnant mare
and a young stud. Now there is something I
wouldn't normally say! The mare was a gift

to her and the forthcoming foal and the colt were to be investments.

Long story short, newborn horses are adorable and the big dumb lummox of a colt grew on me, so investment ideas dashed like an Enron retirement fund. I am the proud owner of a horse of questionable lineage! The vet figures he is quarter horse/draft horse cross stock, and last time I measured him he was 14 hands high, but I was told last week that he is MUCH taller since I was there last. I guess that is a good thing, as I can't remember the last time anyone referred to me as petite. Linda is training him while I am away. As for the cowboy part, well, I must admit I have had more time riding scooters than horses, but I can get around the block without looking too stupid. I will purchase a cowboy hat and say things like "SHUCKS" and "MA'AM" if you'd like. The whistle on my hat might give me away, though.

All joking aside, he is a beautiful, big fella, and I am looking forward to the day that he can hold my weight. He is just over 2 years old now and may be rideable this fall. I also have an adorable little black dog whom you have already met. I named her "D'fer" as in "D for Dawg," much to the disgust of my many friends who said a girl deserved a prettier name. So when it came time to name the horse, I came up with H'fer. Well, the death threats were coming by courier, so "Morgan" became the prudent choice. Some people's sense of humor leave a wee bit to be desired!

Food. Other than things in a half shell — ie: oyster, clams, etc. — I will eat just about anything. I think I am growing scales from all the fish I have been eating these days and I like chicken just as much as beef, so I think we could agree upon a suitable menu for our first date.

Okay, so let me get this straight. Women, discussing men, at the hairdressers. Sounds a little far-fetched, but I haven't had a good leg pulling in a while, so what the heck, I'll buy it. It is nice to hear that someone had something nice to say about me. It means all that money that I spent on friendship fees wasn't a waste! My landlord and his wife are wonderful people, but I don't really know their daughter, so it is flattering that my name came up!

I have not committed to renting the house from Earl, and he could have changed his mind by now, but in the spring, I had told him I liked what he has done with the place and I need to find a bigger place anyway. He said I could either buy or rent the place from him, so you never know! We may be neighbors soon!

As far as the bike riding comparison that you seem to be fond of, well let's just say that somewhere down the road I will show you some of my riding scars. Perhaps date 5 or 6? My training wheels were my best friends, you know!

While my son has not yet pointed out women I should date, he is not against it. We were actually discussing it last week (no names though, as he is not a registered hair stylist)! He thought it would be good if I started seeing someone, as he thinks I might be a little lonely. Kind of cute, but kind of sad too.

The family date comment does not scare me, as it sounds like fun. I am also guilty of far too much forward thinking and examination, so the honeymoon comment does not throw me off either, though it brings up ideas of vacations to exotic locations (always the daydreamer)! That your kids think you should find "the one," however, is a bit of pressure. I mean it sounds kind of like I should come in wearing a cape and tights! Again, not afraid of a little dress-up fun! Would they settle for thinking that I am just "the two"? How does this rating system work and is there a test? Can I buy the condensed notes and cram beforehand? I mean, come on, I want to make it to that 5th to 10th date so I can hear these dirty little secrets! HELP!

Okay, panic attack over.

I'm okay now, really.

I think that skydiving has to be about the ballsiest thing that I have done to date, because of my severe, irrational fear of not being able to fly and falling to the Earth as I scream and wet myself. I'm still here and have landed several times, dry pants and dignity intact, so I guess I got over it. While I know what a skateboard is, I've never heard of an ollie, so you may already have me beat in the bravery department. As for what I still do, well… um… I guess I need to get out there and start doing some things again, so as not to sound too boring. I would love to get back into scuba diving, as I always found that to be quite relaxing and exciting at the same time. I guess I have always seen myself as more of a fish than a bird. Any desire to slip into some tight, form fitting rubber suit and get wet? Man, if the last letter didn't convince you I am an idiot, I might actually be safe with this one!

Well, my alarm will go off in about 3 hours, so I guess I should get some sleep before I get silly. No questions tonight, but you are not off the hook. I will wrack my sleep deprived brain tomorrow to think of some new, prying pop quiz to throw at you. Perhaps something as deep as "what's your favorite color"? I will not say good-night, as I am sure that you are dreaming pleasantly as I write this. Perhaps of some tall blonde figure in a cowboy hat and cape? Rather, I will say good morning, as I hope this puts a smile on your face to start the day.

Just so you know, if you found this amusing, no, I am not a professional come-dian. If you did not get a chuckle, well, as I already stated, I don't do this for a living (luckily).

Oh yes, one more thing. I have HIGH SPEED now, so I will try out the whole messenger thing. I am new so be gentle because even though my internet is now fast, my fingers are still in the same gear and my wit is sometimes in reverse.

Have a great day!
Michael

From: Tammy Tyree [tyree@telus.net]
Sent: July 27, 2005, 1:29 p.m.
To: Michael Friese [kaloogan@netscape.net]
Subject: On the floor, laughing!

To say that your email "put a smile on my face" is a total understatement. Laughing my ass off until tears were falling is more like it. I knew you had a delightful sense of humor, but a GREAT sense of humor? You've been holding out on me…

Morgan is a wonderful name for a horse and the perfect horse for you! I too need one that's at least 16 HH, or it looks like my feet are dragging on the ground. I am so touched that you did that for Linda. How gooey sweet are YOU!! I haven't spoken to Linda since before she moved and didn't even know she did! I'm happy for her. You'll have to bring me up to speed on how she's doing now. And how is it you and she never hooked up!? Or perhaps that's one of the biking scars you have to show me? You made the right decision to keep Morgan, and I gotta tell you that the mental pic of you with a cowboy hat was GREAT, until I pictured the whistle to go with it. THAT had me holding my sides, laughing until it hurt.

Dinner will be an adventure and I'm really looking forward to it, although I'll probably have too many butterflies running around in my gut to get much food down…

You didn't get around to answering my questions about your son, but I'm sure we'll get to that. My oldest has a wicked sense of humor, I'm warning you now, as she told me to tell you she can't wait to meet and dissect you — nice, eh? She is looking forward to the cape and tights, by the way. Please try not to disappoint the girl.

Let's see. The rating system for "the one." This is in its initial development stage. I could tell you how you're doing so far though, based on very rough, untested evidence. We'll use the "scale of 1-to-10" scenario.

One the subject of having the ability to make me laugh — 12

One the subject of being a great dad — 10 (from what I know so far).

About being able to cook romantic, candlelit dinners — 8 (have yet to try them).

About being a cowboy — 10 (regardless of

how well you ride, that you own a horse stands on its own).

About having much in common — 10.

About being a sappy romantic — 8+ (has yet to prove it, but the general impression is good).

About being interested in my kids — 8 (again, has yet to prove it, but the general impression is good).

About willing to try new things — 10 (this applies to Dress Up, ollies and so forth).

About being taller than me — 12!!

About being able to pick up after himself and keep his house clean — ? (not enough information available to rate).

About being good looking — 10+!!

About non-smoker, social drinker — 10 (evidence accumulated from dating profile).

About being compatible in a "private" area — ? (not enough information available to rate, but we're hopeful!)

I think that sums it up so far.

Disclaimer: the preceding ratings are solely based on untested, written evidence, and the final rating is subject to a series of personal experiences, which could take months to years to complete. The testing is concluded upon the acceptance of a marriage proposal, so don't let it go to your head JUST yet…

That was fun.

I noticed Earl is back in town, for now anyway, and I had to stop myself from

charging his door today and insisting that
he draft up a rental agreement with your
name on it.

Now for the question period of our
program:

Previous questions about your son still
apply.

What movies do you like to rent/go to,
and are you strongly opposed to the occasional chick flick?

Do you have any hobbies, and if so, what
are they?

How many brothers and sisters do you
have, and where are they?

That's probably enough to keep you down
to about 2 hours sleep tonight. Just think,
if things work out, this won't be the ONLY
time you lose sleep because of me!

Tammy

From: Michael Friese
[kaloogan@netscape.net]
Sent: July 28, 2005, 6:41 a.m.
To: Tammy Tyree [tyree@telus.net]
Subject: Good morning

Hope you had a good sleep. It has been a
long night here and I now have to go to my
"day job," so this will have to be a quick
letter. I couldn't imagine a look of disappointment on your face today from finding
an empty inbox.

It was neat chatting with you last night

on MSN Messenger. I still prefer face-to-face conversation and would rather be there to see yours. However, it was a little closer to having a chat than writing an email. Last night I spent most of my spare time trying to figure out if there were enough hours in the day for me to drive home for the long weekend and slip in a dinner. All things considered I think the best course is to wait until Labour Day. My mission for the weekend is going to be to catch up on my sleep and send some pictures to you.

Quick question; how tall are you? Guessing from memory, I am thinking 6-feet, but not sure if the difference is 2 or 3 inches between us?

No, Linda is not one of my biking scars. Our friendship is a bit of an enigma to many, but she is closer to me than my own siblings and I will often introduce her as my sister. I will bring you up to speed later, and perhaps we could even go to her farm for a weekend visit a few dates down the road! Sneaky way to invite you to a weekend in a hotel, huh?

My son is turning 12 in a week and this is the first birthday he has spent away from me, which feels a little strange. Moving my 12-year-old hormonal son next door to a 15-year-old girl might be like having a cat in heat! You might find him on your doorstep spraying the porch! It is actually quite funny to see him going through this awkward period of life. The teens are coming with an onset of acne as well. Makes me kind of happy to be an old fart sometimes, and well past that stage.

Well, my crew is here to pick me up (late again, but I'm not complaining today), so I will have to wrap this up for now, but I will write after work!

Have a great day!
Michael

From: Michael Friese
[kaloogan@netscape.net]
Sent: July 29, 2005, 5:57 a.m.
To: Tammy Tyree [tyree@telus.net]
Subject: Ideas for date #?

I was sitting at my desk trying not to drift off when I noticed an old copy of a Beautiful BC magazine with an article on hot springs in the Kootenays. As I was reading it, an idea occurred to me. Have you ever been to the Nakusp Hot Springs? It is really beautiful there in the winter, and they have nice little A-frame chalets for rent. I couldn't help but think that it's a great place for 2 people to disappear for a weekend. No phones, no TV, a cooler of food and a good bottle of wine. Spending the whole time soaking, hiking, having a romantic dinner (with candles, of course), breakfast in bed and whatever else 2 consenting adults do when there are no children around to hear. Do you know anyone who might be interested?

Okay, next less serious question; movies. Well, I am pretty diverse on this and have a reputation as the worst person to send to the video store without specific directions, as I gravitate to the "worst movies ever made" section. Our local movie store keeps a special stash of crap no one would rent, just to put out when I walk through the door. I am good at taking directions, though, and will come home with whatever I am sent to get, even if it comes with its own box of Kleenex. I will even sit through the movie without making faces or gagging noises, but if the person I am cuddled up to makes a comment on the moisture on my cheek, I will feign a cold or a random bug in the eye to maintain my macho image. How is it I keep telling you all these things? I have a weakness for a good horror movie, not that they've made many good ones lately. I am not talking about the slasher type movies, but more so a good thriller that makes you jump if you're lucky. Okay, I am feeling manly again now!

I have a hobby collecting antiques. Usually when a man says that, it is just a way of saying "pack rat," but I have a genuine love for my job and history, hence I own a rather large collection of antique survey equipment. I have bought old equipment and fixed it up, either to be usable again or for display, with the delusion that I will resell it for a profit. So far, none has left my collection. My friend up here says it is because I am a hillbilly and naturally gravitate to shiny objects, but he is from Northern Alberta, so really it is like the pot calling the kettle black.

I used to go cross-country skiing, but it has been a long time. I can no longer downhill ski, as I damaged my knees badly in an accident when I was 17, and it is coming around to haunt me. They cannot take the side pressure from slaloming, and so waterskiing is out as well. But I have hiked up the odd mountain just to see what the world looks like from the top!

Siblings; I have two brothers, one is 40, the other 43. Yes, I am the baby, but one would never know it by looking at us. They are pretty good people overall. We have never been very close, but I still look forward to the annual progress calls and the occasional mid-year call for counsel and advice. My middle brother is dating a girl younger than me and has no children, but has 3 cats. The oldest brother is single, but has adopted his stepson from a previous marriage and lives with him. They are both living on the coast.

I think that catches me up on my assigned homework. If not, I throw myself on the mercy of my taskmaster and beg that her punishment not be too lenient. ;-)

Okay, my turn.

What was it you always wanted to be when you grew up?

What is something that you have always wanted to try, but in reality do not see yourself doing?

Do you like fish?

What's your favourite flower?

Okay, random thoughts and comments time from last evenings MSN Messenger chat:

How is it you know how long your legs are from crotch to toe? Never mind this one. I would prefer to live with the mental image of you measuring yourself!

Yes, we have flush toilets here, but one has to pack the water in from the well down the block, so it is advisable not to drink before bedtime!

I can't say that I have ever had one "strapped" to my ear before, but I have heard of these call phone things you spoke of. I hear they work much better than the string and cup method that we use up here.

Well, it is time for me to head back to work, so I will wrap up. I need to come up with a little pet name for you, I guess.

I know you have a busy weekend planned, so I will not be hurt if you don't respond until next week.

Michael

From: Tammy Tyree [tyree@telus.net]
Sent: July 29, 2005, 10:33 a.m.

To: Michael Friese [kaloogan@netscape.net]
Subject: *sigh*

Okay, you had me at hello. The date idea sounds beyond wonderful, and I can't wait to plan it! (I'M the someone who might be interested, by the way.)

I've never been to Nakusp Hot Springs, just Halcyon, so the whole idea is a treat for me. Funny you should read a Beautiful BC magazine last night, as I was at my mom's for dinner, and guess what I picked up off her coffee table? Gives me goosebumps.

I'm sure your son is having a great time with his mom. At least, I hope so! I have a feeling there is a little more to your story with your Ex, but I am happy to wait until we are together to hear it. My situation with my Ex is quite different than what I imagine yours to be, but still quite sad. No bitterness there either, though, and I'm so happy he's with a lovely gal now.

Sending you to get a movie; noted. If I want you to come back with something worth watching, I'll make you write the title on your hand first. You may have a macho image in front of the guys to maintain, but being a softie in private scores WAY bigger points with me! I'm not in the sappy romance category ALL the time, as I really enjoy thrillers or intrigues and will probably pick one of these off the shelf first!

Me and my girls went to see "War of the Worlds" on the weekend; alien thriller. We were on the edge of our seats the entire time.

I had another one of those stunned "dear-god-we-have-so-much-in-common" moments yet again, after reading that you collect antiques. I owned an antique store a few years back with a group of ladies (a Cooperative). I love garage sales and antiquing and that led me to having a space in the store. Except for a few small pieces, my house doesn't reflect my interest. I've mostly sold my finds, but my dream is to have a house full of really amazing antique furniture pieces. Finding antique survey equipment must be quite a hunt! I think we found another date idea…

As far as the hillbilly comment, so long as you aren't missing any teeth and get along with all other races, I think I could live with that. Gravitating to shiny objects isn't just for hillbillys though. Girls like them too!

I have two brothers and two sisters. My youngest brother and sister are twins and 11 years older than me. My oldest brother is 12 years older than me, and my oldest sister is 15 years older than me. I am indeed their baby. My parents planned to have me, the rest, not so much. Especially the twins! Mom did not know until she was about to deliver that there were two! My dad, who dropped her off at the hospital and went to work, as was the fashion in those days, came back later and refused to believe the nurse when she told him. They had a 3-year-old, an 11-month-old and now, twins. Mom had them all by the time she was 23. It was a whirlwind for her, so when the dust settled, she realized she wanted another girl and got her wish! We were all born in Alberta and made the move west when I was 4. Dad was building houseboats for Three Buoys Marina in Sicamous at the time of our move. My family history is vast and interesting. In fact, there have been books written about my Dutch heritage…

Ok, now for your questions. Holy cow man, I hope you realize how deep you're making me dig here and appreciate my efforts. Ok, here goes…

When I was a kid, I would play with a turned-over egg carton as a typewriter, and dreamed of being a writer or a secretary. I worked for a lawyer in Kelowna through high school and college, then another lawyer for a few years before moving here, so the part about being a secretary came true — but so did the part about being a writer. This wasn't my only dream, however. I was a romantic as a child too, always imagining I would never really have to "work" for a living, as my husband would be wealthy and take good care of me. *sigh* That dream has yet to materialize. I miss youth, but discovered that I really enjoy writing (spawned from the egg carton I assume), and

until I had to step out and work full-time,
I completed a novel and had written several
short stories (mostly erotica), and have
the privilege of calling myself a published
writer (both as a contributor in tasteful
anthologies and not-so-tasteful magazines).
I would like to "pick up the pen" once my
life settles into a part-time routine.

Perhaps you'll have the macho joy of
showing your crew my latest installment in
Penthouse sometime… (I don't actually BUY
those, not magazines, anyway. I have a few
excellent books with short story erotica
though, much more tasteful, but hey, a
girl's gotta make a buck or two now and
then and the mags pay well!)

Something I've always wanted to try but
in reality do not see myself doing… hm…
damn that's a toughie. Thinking… thinking…
nope, nothing! I guess because everything
that I've always had a craving to try, I've
tried! If there is something that I want to
experience, then I try to make it happen. I
don't actually have a list of 100 things to
do before I die…

Oh, I'll tell you the exciting adventures of leg measurement around date 5
or 6!

Do I like fish? Gee, I sure hate to
disappoint a guy, but no, I'm not a genuine
fan of the slimy suckers. I don't
completely turn my nose up at them either,
however, and if one were to cook up a
feast, then I would gladly partake. I enjoy

lobster and crab far more. I have discovered a food allergy to scallops and squid — found that one when my throat started closing up after trying them… if you want to get on my mom's good side (easy, by the way), then bring her a fish. She'll love you forever.

My favorite flower… I'm partial to tulips, daffodils and gladiolas (being half Dutch), but they're harder to find year round. I really like carnations because they're pretty and cheap! I'm not a huge fan of roses, not because they aren't beautiful, but because they just don't last very long! I certainly wouldn't turn my nose up (half-pun intended) at receiving a bouquet of ANY flower, however!

Ok, my turn:

First two questions; right back at ya. I already know you like fish, and I don't assume you're "into" flowers, and I really can't imagine why you'd need to measure the length of your legs, so those other two will have to do for now. I have a day at the beach with my kids planned. It's summer, and our little town is crazy busy with tourists already — yikes!

Have a great weekend. Don't forget my pictures, or the taskmaster WILL have to come up with a cruel and unusual punishment! (Taken from page 82 of "Miss Lacey's Fun Guide to Exploration of Whips and Chains," which I may — or may not — have contributed to!)

Tammy

As I copied our email romance onto these pages, I found it amazing how much of myself I lost through time, divorce and raising children. Writing every day was normal, and I was, thankfully, published several times in anthologies and magazines. It feels like home for me, where I am safe. Being creative fills the void of solitude in the most constructive, moving way. I also recalled the feeling I had as a child about being "taken care of." This has never left me, and now that Michael is gone, I realize – with amazement and a certain amount of disbelief – that I have been, and still am, "taken care of" by him.

As a species, we need to learn to trust our instincts and intuition over everything else, as it is seldom wrong. We all have stories of an "awareness" at some point in our lives, whether it be knowing you'll receive a phone call from your child's school just before the phone rings, or a greater understanding that there is something better "out there." When I read my journals, I find several points of fact, which I will share... later.

From: Michael Friese
[kaloogan@netscape.net]
Sent: July 30, 2005, 12:37 a.m.
To: Tammy Tyree [tyree@telus.net]
Subject: Synchronicity perhaps?

Sorry I did not get to write last night. I gave one of my Native workers a ride home and spent the evening learning to mend fishing nets, and then stayed for dinner. I think I qualify in the "getting along with other races" category. After dinner we sat and had beers around the fire in the back with a bunch of his neighbors, and I was the only white face in the circle, and the only one to not notice. They said they would adopt me into the tribe if I stayed much longer. It will be really sad to leave here, as I feel very much at home.

The fish comment was just a random thought, and it does not disappoint me that you are not a fan. I rarely eat fish, but here, I seem to eat a lot of it, as it is quite delicious when fresh caught. Your comment about allergies took me aback. Anything in a half shell or with over 4 legs, oyster, clams, octopus, are out for me. The effect on me is very much the same; my first discovery included a trip to emergency. Kind of scary, isn't it!

If I was no more sure of my sanity, I would say that I'm imagining these conversations, as the similarities between us are almost incredible.

The idea of a cute little blonde girl playing typewriter with an egg carton makes me smile. It is nice that you have fulfilled your dreams being a published writer. I would love to look at the novel one day. I think that as a little boy I had nothing more serious than the age-old dilemma faced by all males; whether to become an astronaut or a garbageman. Space was cool, but so was being the guy that got to crush people's refuse. Truly lucky would be the man that could do both.

As for more serious career path ideas that come into adolescence, I was already working when I was 11, and knew that I would work in the same field as my father. Logging was my profession for many years, and I was lucky enough to escape into something that I enjoy and isn't so dangerous. I looked into a career as a chef and went to Vancouver to check out the school, but decided that my love of cooking was something that I wanted to keep a private matter, sure that if I had to do it for a living rather than by choice, it would lose its luster for me. I still get a kick out of watching the garbage trucks now and then, though.

The next question is simple. I have always wanted to go to South Africa and dive with the great white sharks. I know it would truly be the event of a lifetime and an adrenaline rush that would last for months, but in all reality, I cannot see myself doing it. To have the dream is enough for me.

I am wandering around the house all alone today, as I have given everyone the day off, and I am supposed to be doing paperwork. I worked on it for a few hours already, and will get back to it for a while this afternoon. There is a concert in the park this evening, followed by fireworks, so I might make the drive and hang out with the family I was with last night. Their kids call me uncle now, so I guess I should show up. Tomorrow I am off to Alaska, hopefully to get some wonderful pictures of the Grizzlies and glaciers for my son, returning late to chain myself to the computer all day Monday.

No homework for you today, as I know that you have a busy weekend and don't need to be digging deep into answering my questions. Next round of the "get to know each other" quiz is up to you, continuing the deep search for knowledge.

Have a great weekend!

Michael

From: Michael Friese
[kaloogan@netscape.net]
Sent: August 1, 2005, 11:37 p.m.
To: Tammy Tyree [tyree@telus.net]
Subject: how's your weekend?

Must have been a busy weekend. I hope you slept well. I did not make it to Alaska, as they asked me to work all weekend. Hope you had fun at the beach with the kids.

Oh yeah! Not to fear. I have shaved my beard and mustache as of yesterday. Will send you some new pictures of a nice smooth face next weekend.

Michael

From: Tammy Tyree [tyree@telus.net]
Sent: August 2, 2005, 7:19 a.m.
To: Michael Friese [kaloogan@netscape.net]
Subject: RE: poor tired girl!

Hi Michael. I will write tonight, promise. Thank you for the pictures! I can see why it's going to be hard to leave that place. So much beauty and culture — but at least you've made friends for life, and you will always be welcome to visit.

The beard's gone, eh? Darn! Kidding… I don't mind facial hair, but nothing quite like a smooth, aftershave-scented guy. I look forward to pictures, though. I think last time I saw you here, you were sporting a beard then as well.

I've had a great weekend with the kids, I will write more tomorrow!

Tammy

From: Tammy Tyree [tyree@telus.net]
Sent: August 2, 2005, 11:08 p.m.
To: Michael Friese [kaloogan@netscape.net]
Subject: Okay — back to the grind…

Long weekend over and it's back to real life!

That's pretty crazy about the shellfish allergies. I don't suppose you have any aversion toward creepy crawly things, do you? Nah, me neither. Hey! One more thing in common. I meant a dislike of creepy, crawly things — not eating them.

So, a space-loving-garbage-man-cowboy-shark-diving-tribal-surveyor, eh? Your mom must be so proud. :-) I have to disagree with you about shark diving though. I think that is totally do-able. You ain't dragging me in there with you, however — that's just downright crazy! Sharks are one thing I have an eerie aversion to (unlike creepy crawlies). Besides, I'd look like a stick of black licorice in a wetsuit. Not really the look I long for.

I'm sure it has something to do with watching far too many reruns of "Jaws" when I was a kid, then going to Universal Studios and having the thing jump out of the water at me — EEEK! Do they not know the permanent damage they're doing to children with that particular attraction? Even now I have to suck it up to step into dark water, lake and ocean — how sad is that?

I was thinking of one thing that I'd like to accomplish — in theory — but don't really see myself following through with it. Getting my class 8 license and buying a Crotch Rocket. I may save that for my mid-life crisis. Hey, it's better than buying an expensive convertible or having an affair, don't you think?

Okay, deep, probing inquisition time…

Red or white?

Cowboy boots or runners?

Clay Aiken or Tim McGraw?

Potatoes or rice?

Bicycles or rollerblades?

Paris or Rome?

Black licorice or chocolate-covered grasshoppers?

And the deepest probing one — ready?

Lingerie: pointless or pretty?

I anxiously await your reply,

Tammy

From: Michael Friese
[kaloogan@netscape.net]
Sent: August 3, 2005, 5:29 a.m.
To: Tammy Tyree [tyree@telus.net]
Subject: deep soul searching in the a.m.!

Glad to hear you had an enjoyable weekend.

I regret having worked through it, as I am sitting here with my coffee trying to fully open my eyes. I am usually a morning person, but today I can't remember why!

Okay, the first cup is down, and I am coherent. Re-read your letter during the break to get the synapses firing. On to the questions first.

Red or white? Wine? Red on most occasions, but I do have both on my wine rack. For a nice, easy bottle over an evening of conversation, merlot perhaps?

Cowboy boots or runners? Don't think that I own either anymore. I will have to do some footwear shopping. Work/hiking boots or sandals is what I have. I think sandals would be my answer, or barefoot in the warm sand!

Clay Aiken or Tim McGraw? Well, let's see… who is Clay Aiken? Actually, my music collection varies. I own some country, but not a pair of cowboy boots, remember? I think I am going to go outside the options again and say Leonard Cohen.

Potatoes or rice? Potatoes with red meat and rice with chicken or fish.

Bicycles or rollerblades? Okay, let's start out with the fact that I have been told that I have no ass. Now, I disagree with this statement because I know I am sitting on something, so I assume that what is being referred to is that I have a small, bony ass. This I can accept because when I cover it in a pair of Levi's, it looks not bad (just my opinion, but it will do for me). Add to this knowledge that I have never been an avid skater, and one can only imagine my first and only experience with rollerblades. They seem like a good idea and look cool when everyone else is using them, but the sight of me careening down the street, swinging my arms like two windmills followed by the whining every time I sit down for the next two weeks is not pretty. Seeing as you don't give me a motorized option, I will take a bicycle. Can I at least twist the hands grips and make "vroom" noises, or would that be too embarrassing?

Paris or Rome? Belize. Sorry, I am a

sort of option "C" kind of guy. Europe, been there, done that, bought the T-shirt. Of course, as a romantic getaway, I suppose I could try again.

Lingerie. Lace… is… sort… of… distracting… what was the question again? I will have to say a little of both. I would not turn down the fashion show if you were offering! But it does not seem like the most practical sleep wear. Of course, a nice pair of flannel pajamas can be sexy too. It's all in how you wear them.

How am I supposed to stay focused on work today? BAD MONKEY!

Okay, less distracting thoughts.

Yeah, I like black liquorice, but I think you are alone on trying grasshoppers. Not a huge fan of creepy crawlies here, though I can manage not to shriek like a little girl when I see them. Slithering and slimy is okay, but over 4 legs and flying or crawling find the bottom of my boot.

So, I am going to take a wild guess and say that scuba diving is not one of your retirement goals, what with it involving deep water and all. Are you really that uncomfortable around a lake? Man, scratch the naked snorkeling off of the honeymoon agenda! :-(

Crotch rockets as a midlife compensator, huh? Convertibles and younger boyfriends are so much easier, no? You just want to break all the old cliches, don't you! Actually, this one I can agree on, I always smile when I see old couples riding across the country. Have you ever spent 8 hours on a crotch rocket, though? 6-feet tall does not lend itself well to being bent over all day like that.

Not that I am complaining about the thought of you in some form-fitting, leather riding gear… (sorry, drifted away again there), but I am more of the custom cruiser kind of guy myself. Biker without the attitude. I can see the need for some long back rubs for you after a ride. Again, not complaining! Did I mention I give a mean massage?

I may have to return to the north in October to wrap up this project, but I will be home in September. Hopefully to pack and move. I tried to get a hold of your neighbor this weekend, but he was too busy to answer his phone, so I will try him at work this week. I can just imagine the 20 questions that I will get out of him. I need to find a bigger place, and I kind of like the layout there. A little close to the neighbors, but I think I can manage. ;-)

I had better get to my paperwork before it is time to leave for work. I sent the crew to do another minor job, so it is nice and peaceful here today.

I will think of some deep insightful questions to send you tonight, if I'm able to stop thinking of the lingerie question. Hope that you had a good day.

Michael

From: Tammy Tyree [tyree@telus.net]
Sent: August 5, 2005, 8:09 p.m.
To: Michael Friese [kaloogan@netscape.net]
Subject: Poor, busy Pooh Bear…

You must be pretty busy lately not to be rushing to your computer to reply to me and ask me all kinds of lingerie questions. It's ok, I understand. I will stay logged into my MSN Messenger if you care to chat with me later. Doesn't matter how late; my sound is on, so the message alert should wake me up if I'm dozing…

I thought of a question! Any tattoos, piercings or weird body things you should warn me about? (Like enormous amounts of back hair, for example.)

Don't forget to send me some pics this weekend! Great day today, hot and sunny. Closed the office at noon and took the kids to the lake! Teehee.

Tammy

From: Michael Friese
[kaloogan@netscape.net]
Sent: August 8, 2005, 5:24 a.m.
To: Tammy Tyree [tyree@telus.net]
Subject: RE: Poor, busy Pooh Bear…

So sorry to have left you hanging out there with no response. I had to leave last week to do some estimates on a potential project and could not get my dial-up to work. I got home at midnight, 5000km later, only to find that the strange bite marks that have been appearing on my arms for the last month are from bed bugs that are living in the bedroom and apparently feasting on me.

Guess who has spent a sleepless night washing all of his linens and clothes in boiling water and scratching at imaginary bugs? Did I mention a touch of O.C.D. in my profile? I have done a web search and learned a lot. After an extreme search of the rest of the house, I quarantined my room and moved to the couch for the rest of the month. The only good part of the week is that my son has returned and will be here until we leave for home at the end of the month.

Lingerie questions? Well, let's just say that I will let my imagination run wild for a little longer in hopes of one day seeing for myself.

Tattoos? Yes, I have two. I have a dragon on my right shoulder and a tribal piece on my right calf. They are both black and gray pieces and nothing too big. Sorry, no Harley Davidson emblems or naked women astride mountains of skulls if you are looking for the bad boy thing!

Piercings? Yes, my right nipple. And before you have the chance to ask, yes it hurt like hell, hence why I only pierced one nipple!

Weird, enormous body thing? Well, I don't want to brag but………… ;-)

Did I mention I wear a size-12 boot? In case we ever go shopping for cowboy boots. You know, just mentioning in passing…

Anyway…

No hair on my back. Actually, very little body hair at all. There goes that hairy chested bad boy thing again.

How nice for you it is sunny there. Here it is rainy, and I am getting quite used to standing in mud puddles.

I promise to write tonight. Have to get ready for work now.

Michael

P.S. Somehow, I can't see you resembling a stick of black licorice in a wetsuit, but I do like black licorice!

From: Tammy Tyree [tyree@telus.net]
Sent: August 8, 2005, 8:16 a.m.
To: Michael Friese [kaloogan@netscape.net]
Subject: Got me blushing… hope you're happy!!!

A size-12 boot??? There *is* a God.

Err, what I mean is… it's nice to know someone with larger feet than me!

Happy to hear you don't have the Harley tattoos and body hair. Happy to hear a lot of things actually… ;-) What you have is plenty of bad boy enough for me, thank-you-very-much. I don't have any tattoos, and I restrict my piercings to 2 holes in each ear. Really exciting, huh? I've contemplated piercing my navel, but know too many people whose piercings got infected. Not a really delightful picture there, sexy belly piercing oozing with green goop. Nice. The tattoo, I would like, but can't decide what or where. That's probably one of those "likely will never happen" things. Or maybe it's a "got really drunk and woke up with a pierced tongue and snake tattoo" event few of us can attest to in our lives.

Sorry that you had to spend the night debugging your place. Sounds horrible. Not so great that you have to spend the rest of your month on a couch either. I've had a similar experience with head lice. Not a lot of fun to have three girls with long hair.

I'm awaiting pictures, not that you don't have enough on your plate already. Too bad — get your priorities straight! Haha. Oh, and a couple smiley ones would be nice. You have a gorgeous smile, so why not show it?

Question to ponder: what would you consider your biggest regret and your biggest accomplishment?

I'll think of more and write later. Got to dash to the office!

Tammy

From: Michael Friese
[kaloogan@netscape.net]
Sent: August 9, 2005, 11:34 p.m.
To: Tammy Tyree [tyree@telus.net]
Subject: RE: Got me blushing, hope you're happy!

I would be happier if I was there to see you blushing.

Sorry about last night. I had some sleep to catch up on, apparently. The weather here has turned, and it is cooking hot. Sitting here in my PJ's sweating. Yes, I do wear pajamas, but only outside of the bedroom.

I guess my experience the other night answers your question as to my feelings about creepy, crawly things. Still can't help scratching and looking over my shoulders. If they had been spiders, I would probably still be in the fetal position.

As for you with a pierced tongue and snake tattoo, well, it would surprise me!

I must admit not being the best at this electronic age in some ways. I still can not link up my camera with this dying laptop, so I will have to wait until I'm in a town with stoplights, so I can have my memory card saved to a CD. What I am trying to say is that there will not be any pictures until after Friday. Of course, I will also need to take some! Smiling in my pictures, huh? Well, I guess I could think of those lingerie questions while having my picture taken.

What do I consider my biggest regret and my biggest accomplishment? What happened to easy ones like "what's your favorite color?"

Biggest regret? I've been giving this a lot of thought today. Still haven't come up with one thing that I would have changed that would not have cost me more in the long run. I have always been an analyzer of the events of my life and cause and effect, and I know I would not be the man I am today without the experiences that made me this way. I guess I could pick one of many minor mistakes in business and personal life, but in true retrospect it has been a good life. Hope that is not too sappy of an answer! Oh yeah, I wish I was taller! Does that count?

Biggest accomplishment? I guess that would be the little person in the other room who thinks that I am the greatest dad and the biggest pain in the ass, all at the same time. Not an easy accomplishment. Apparently, it requires about 13 years to do so. They should surgically remove boys' hormones until they are 18 and moved out. I have never had someone constantly ask me a question and then look at me like I am an idiot when I answer. I am not looking forward to high school. When I asked him how he would feel about Dad dating, I am sure that his thoughts were, "anything that gets him out of my hair."

I know that these are not terribly exciting answers, but I am a kind of simple guy. Not looking for the "American Dream," just my little piece of happiness and hopefully someone to share it with. After all, what is the point of having 20 acres to roam around on if you have to do it all by yourself?

Now I will have to throw these same two questions right back at you so I can better understand your hopes and ambitions.

So, I am bad boy enough for your tastes, huh? Well, I am not that bad or boyish these days, so I guess our tastes are, once again, along the same lines. I guess I had a bit of a "bad boy" stage in my life, as do most men I know, but I was always too damn responsible to get too out of line.

Of course, if you really want to try out page 82 of "Miss Lacey's Fun Guide to Exploration of Whips and Chains," I could pretend to be bad!! (You know, of course, that the first time you leave me alone in your bedroom I will look in your night table to see if you actually own said book!) Assuming that I see said room… alone… not that I am snoopy…

Could you perhaps help me remove this size-12 foot from my mouth?

Okay, let's just mentally delete the ramblings of an idiot that does not know when to stop talking, and move on, shall we?

I have not forgotten the fact that you are a published writer of erotica! I would like to read some of your work someday. :-)

Question period!

Favorite author? Last book read; fiction and nonfiction? Last movie that made you cry; this should be an easy one for you! Favorite meal to cook? To eat? Popcorn; buttered or unbuttered?

I am off to bed (sofa), but I will write tomorrow with more "thoughts and incoherent ramblings from the North."

Michael

P.S. Sorry, I just can't bring myself to sign it "Pooh Bear"!

Our conversations slowly migrated to MSN Messenger, so there appear to be gaps in the emails. Although this chapter is quite lengthy, you can certainly see how our budding romance began and quickly escalated, blossoming into a full-fledged romantic partnership. As we spent two months emailing back and forth, we truly developed feelings for each other that later turned into love and, not so much later, commitment.

Although the only parts of the emails that were changed were blatant spelling and grammatical errors, I feel it's important to continue the rest of our email stream for you, so you can fully comprehend the depth of our cyber romance. Also, a large remainder of this story relates to our meeting, and the universal simmering of intention and coincidence. Besides (although you may disagree), I think a lot of the notes we passed back and forth were damn funny!

From: Michael Friese
[kaloogan@netscape.net]
Sent: August 10, 2005, 9:11 p.m.
To: Tammy Tyree [tyree@telus.net]
Subject: RE: Ramblings from the North

All right, now who's blushing!

First off, an admission. I am a wee bit shy. Those that know me have a hard time believing this, but in all honesty, I am not one for making the first move. This emailing and messaging back and forth is a unique experience for me. I can honestly say things via cyberspace that would take me longer to "spit out" if we were actually sitting face-to-face. I will admit that I am a little nervous about meeting you when I get home, but we seem to be so compatible that I am sure it will be comfortable.

That said, I know that if you had not written to me first, I probably would not have asked you out for fear of rejection. I only say this so that you know I am not a player.

Okay, let's call this MORE RAMBLINGS FROM THE LONELY NORTHMAN!!

In regards to our MSN conversation questions last night: PJ's; sexy, more to strip off. Like it would require any effort on your part! They would be in the corner and out of sight at the first signs of interest! May I say though, it sounds like your choice of a long negligee for bed-wear is just a tad too long? Hiding legs as long as yours is truly a shame!

And, on that note, yet another reference to your legs! Trying to distract me from a previous comment, perhaps? Regarding my wanting to be taller than I am; I always thought that 2 more inches would be great, but I guess that is a guy thing! Before your mind goes "there," I'm talking about height here, remember?!

Kids/hormones; well, already stated! Were we this bad?

Canadian dream; I like your idea of a large piece of property with a rambling house on it! May I add the guest house as well so that when kids and grandkids visit there is a place for grandma and grandpa to go wander naked, out of sight?

Your reference to interesting items on your nightstand. Okay, that is just teasing and you know it! Bad monkey!!! Got me daydreaming though!

My favorite author — okay now… must… think… about… things… other… than… sex… now! Trying… ah hell, I'll just fake it! I used to like Stephen King, but the last few left me feeling cheated in the end. Jack L. Chalker, Zelazny and Harlan Ellison are a few of my favorites. Last book, well, time has been short, but I am reading the latest "Harry Potter," if that doesn't sound too childish. Spend more time trying to read training manuals without falling asleep than I do actually engrossed in an excellent book.

Last movie… well, you know… this is an admission that is told to you at extreme threat of displeasure if you disclose it to other male-type people! "Terms of Endearment" is a guaranteed "turn your head and sniffle" movie, but lately I am becoming more and more sentimental, and if I am sitting at home alone watching a sappy one, I get this strange feeling in my throat. Enough said!

Popcorn; whatever way we serve it. I like butter, but don't put it on by myself. I do not have that 18-year-old metabolism anymore.

T.V.; I haven't had cable for over 3 years now. There are only a few shows I like and I have my mother record them for me in the fall/winter season, but during the summer the television is only there for watching movies via DVD. I know you are going to ask, so the T.V. shows are; "CSI," "Law and Order," and (shameful admission) "Survivor."

I'm really not a fan of hockey, but happy for you to watch the game while I cook dinner, or if it is a late game, heat massage oils and light candles! I do like a riveting game of curling, however! Perhaps you could coach me on things to say about hockey so I don't embarrass myself in front of the guys.

Things I like to cook; various pasta

dishes or perhaps something out of my German secret recipes to eat — I would have to be honest and say Eggs Benedict is my favorite. Hard to get a good one made from scratch, though. I too enjoy wonderful food and being as I stand still all day, it is a fight not to be 300 lbs. We could always be two fat, naked, old people wandering around our 20 acres. Might work better than a fence for keeping out the neighbors, you know?

Yeah, I don't think Pooh Bear will stick (fingers crossed). I could always suggest a few nicknames — i.e.; Sexy, Good Looking, Honey, Awesome-Lover-with-a-Great-Set-of-Hands-and-a-Tongue-that… Sorry. Kind of ran wild there for a minute! My apologies for any nasty thoughts that I may have put in your head!

Potential rental; the neighbor is not answering his phone, so perhaps he has rethought the lease terms we had discussed this spring. If so, his loss, as he is losing a good tenant and I can always drive over from anywhere in town in, like, what… 2.5 minutes? Might be for the best, as you would have been sick of me before I got to that date where you tell me all those dirty little secrets. Would have made for some easy access to late night visits though, if one were so inclined?

This is not fair, by the way. You just answer my questions and then return them to me, so now I have to come up with more.

Here is my latest attempt to find a crack in the "perfect" image that you are creating:

In your honest opinion, what is your worst characteristic?

When you stand in front of the mirror and look at yourself, what is the first thing that you criticize?

Now, do it again, but this time naked. Does your opinion change?

We all have our regrets — relationship wise — for poor decisions, but do you have a "one that got away?" If so… if he called you tomorrow and wanted to catch up on old times, would you be excited?

What is the thing that you wonder about most, when you think about me?

Refuse to answer any of these questions that you want, knowing that I will also answer any you do.

Have a great sleep!

Michael

From: Tammy Tyree [tyree@telus.net]
Sent: August 10, 2005, 11:32 p.m.
To: Michael Friese [kaloogan@netscape.net]
Subject: Hockey's too violent anyway…

Warm up the massage oils, baby! I enjoy hockey, but what you're offering is hands down worth missing the entire season… Bertuzzi who?

Now, I find it a LITTLE hard to believe

you're a shy guy. Although there is something to be said about being free to
express oneself in this manner rather than
face-to-face, true. However, I really don't
think that will be much of a problem. If I
had never actually met you face-to-face
before, then maybe. As far as making the
first move, don't be shy! Nothing is sexier
than a guy who takes some initiative and
"goes for it" and isn't afraid to throw a
gal up against a wall now and then… ;-)

As for the player part; please. I knew
that about you the entire time. I am not a
player but am guilty (as charged) at being
a wee bit of a tease. Just shut up and
enjoy it. ;-) Definitely not big on dating
around, though. Much happier being a "one
guy kind of gal." I would rather "get to
know someone really well and one day maybe
realize you think of them more often than
not." I believe I'm quoting you there, and
I totally agree.

I'll draw up some plans for an awesome
guest house… perhaps just one room with a
four-poster bed in the middle. Great idea.
;-)

Dissing my choice of nightwear? You'll
understand when you see it. I mean, IF… ;-)

Eggs benny? Who did you ask to find out
my favorite breakfast of all time? You and
my daughter talking behind my back? Is this
one of those amazing coincidences we seem
to have? We should make a list of them!

I was a bit stunned when you made that

comment about The King. I had the same feeling the last few books he created. Kind of felt cheated, almost like he had started something, then got too lazy or emptied his idea box to finish with a great ending.

Your favorite authors? Would that be "Quest for the Well of Souls" by Jack Chalker? And Roger Zelazny of "The Complete Amber Chronicles?" And I'm assuming you mean Harlan Ellison of the "Strange Wine" fame? Excellent and very intriguing taste! If you are presently sitting in shocked, excited silence that I would know these authors and their works, relax. I can perform a search on Amazon.com easily. I do, however, look forward to reading them, so I can gain a better understanding of your literary interests.

My oldest daughter had a conniption fit when I told her you're currently reading "Harry Potter." He is a read, respected and loved dude in this household. She is also in the 6th book in the series after having read the first 5 about 10 times each. She was wondering if you'd marry her — haha.

Ok, how is it one or several lucky ladies have not scooped you up in the past few years? I gotta tell you that if you were even the slightest bit romantic, you'd have my vote. That you're MORE than that is making me a little crazy! (Dammit, I should shut up now…) Candles? Massage oils? Cooks? Size-12 boot? Cries (ok "chokes up") at movies? I know you think you're all sappy and not manly and stuff, but dear God, please don't ever change!

Could we just go from a first date straight to a honeymoon in Fiji? (Ok, your turn to pull MY foot from MY mouth!)

Oh, and I love your various ideas for pet names. The last one especially; NOW WHO'S TEASING! Argh!!

Funny about the "perfect image" I'm creating — haha. I promise I've done nothing more than tell God's honest truth about myself. The only time I'd have to fib is if you asked me how much I weigh.

MY questions are hard? You win! "Refuse to answer any you want…?" Please. You honestly think I could refuse you anything? I mean that in a completely "Jeopardy," 20-questions kind of way. I'm up for the challenge.

My worst characteristic? Well, gosh, that's a toughie. First, let's check the definition. "A feature that helps to iden-tify, tell apart or describe recognizably; a distinguishing mark or trait." Oh, ok thanks. Then the answer would have to be my freakishly long toes. I also have rather long, knobby fingers too, but my toes are quite epic, and all thanks to my Dutch ancestors.

I criticize the jiggly, fleshy part under my arm and the slightly roundish "mummy tummy" that I believe I'm stuck with for all eternity. Those parts I curse when naked. Fully dressed, I have no complaints.

I actually feel pretty lucky to have the body that I do after 4 kids! I never got one stretch mark on my stomach, just a couple on both hips. So, if a slight layer of extra padding is what I'm stuck with, I can live with that.

Never had a "one that got away." Have a few minor regrets, learned from every relationship I've had (which I can count on less than one hand), and am so ready for the "real deal."

The thing that I wonder most about when I think about you? What makes you think I think about you? Kidding! Haha. Do I have to pick ONE thing? Geez, okay. I wonder if you're a good cuddler and a good kisser (or both at the same time). I realize you may not be the best judge to answer this one. Perhaps your hillbilly Albertan friend can help you out?

You are the King of questions. I bow, humbled by your mastery. I answered all of them, so right back at ya, babe! PLUS:

If you knew I was busy or needed a "night off," and my kids were sitting around bored, what initiative would you take with them (or would you) and what would you do with them?

And… socks or pants. What do you put on first?

Enjoy your day!

Tammy

P.S. The neighbor packed up a U-Haul and left for the week, back this weekend to collect more. "Easy access" and "late-night visits" sound like something that we should take advantage of at every moment! I like the way you think! Secretly hoping the rental thing works out!

From: Michael Friese
[kaloogan@netscape.net]
Sent: August 11, 2005, 6:14 a.m.
To: Tammy Tyree [tyree@telus.net]

Subject: You are great to come home to, but even better to wake up to!

What a treat! Another email so quickly. You'll have me trained to respond faster if you keep this up!

Not to worry about the shy part. It is true, but only in the initial stages. Once I get to know people, I am much more outgoing. I hang back in social situations and listen until I am comfortable, but once I am, I can be the life of the conversation. As for taking the lead and throwing you up against the wall, well… I think I could arrange that!

Your knowledge of my favorite writers had my heart skipping a beat there, until you admitted your search. Was almost another one of those spooky moments!

Nicole sounds sweet, and I am flattered, but I kind of have my eye on this other really wonderful and sexy lady right now. Break it to her gently, will you please?

Fiji for a honeymoon, huh? Okay, I'll pull on the ankle and you say ah!

Pet names were just helpful suggestions, but will wait for one of my own. As for your weight, I would never dream of asking a question that I would not be willing to answer myself. I am not concerned about that as I am pretty sure that I could lift you, but finding a door large enough for carrying you across the threshold at night would be tough for 2 people our size. I love the idea of you not being able to refuse me anything. (In a completely "Jeopardy" 20 questions kind of way.) Could make for interesting pillow talk.

Sounds like we could have stupid toe trick contests. I can pick up a penny laying flat on the floor with mine. Can you tell how exciting my evenings are? How is it that your toes grab people's attention? Do you deal cards with them at parties? Usually not the first thing people see, you know? Your fingers, however, are something that I had noticed before and caught myself wondering how they would feel running down my back.(Not appropriate for having in the bank, I know, but you were the highlight of my paydays that year.)

Well, I guess it is my turn to self critique, so here goes.

My worst characteristic dressed; my nose. I have always thought it looked a little out of place and too large for my face. Didn't get any better every time it

144

got broken. It is like a magnet for anything that flies at my face, perhaps because it is too large to miss.

Worst characteristic naked; well, let's just say that I miss that 19-year-old metabolism. My weight seems to fluctuate more and more each year. Slim down in the winter, put it back on in the summer. Backwards to everyone else. Hey, my nose doesn't look so big now!

I used to think that I had a "one that got away," until we met up again for the first time in 2 years and had a coffee together. It was actually quite funny, because she also thought the same thing, until we sat and talked for about 4 hours and realized that we were two completely different people than the ones that we were mentally picturing all these years. It was kind of funny and sad at the same time. I guess some memories are better left just that. Other than that, I have always believed the past belongs in the past and is better left there. Never been one for trying things one last time.

If my distant memory serves me well, I think I used to be able to wrap my arms around someone and work my lips at the same time, but it has been a while so it may be like that bicycle thing we were talking about. (And the hillbilly life has never been my thing, sorry. Besides, I would never come between a man and his cousin!)

Okay, I would need more info on the last

one, about what to do with your kids. I mean, are you busy, burned out or just wanting some peace? If you wanted to get some work done, I would take the kids out and leave you at home alone. Taking a break from being a single mom, I would come hang with the kids and send you out. Wanting some alone time with me; well, I am not above shamefully buying the kids off with cash and sending them out so we can be alone! As for what to do with them; well, I would have to get to know them and what they like, but I am flexible and actually can be fun. Anything from an afternoon at the pool to a pleasant hike or even a stim- ulating board game. Does anyone in your house play chess?

Have a good day.

Michael

P.S. Pants first, always! There is nothing sexy about a man in his boxers and a pair of knee-high sweat-socks. Nothing! And just so that you know, I do not see socks as an option when wearing sandals. Just in case you were afraid of that!

After this email, my reply appears to be missing, likely answered through MSN Messenger. Again, I am amazed that I had printed these emails and kept them at all! As I rewrote them, so many memories came flooding back to me. Those little details of life that are not usually on record and not memorable enough to stand out, but relevant just the same, as it paints the sweet picture of our budding romance and the solid build of our relationship's foundation.

We are nearly at the end of the romantic, dorky comedy, my friends, and I will spare you any further minutia. Just a few emails later, in which we discussed work, life and the misadventures of my 5-month fight with a local roofing company that took forever to complete the new roof on my house, we finally found ourselves at a point of Michael wrapping up his work to come back to our small Canadian mountain town for the September long weekend.

Finally, we were going to meet in person! Not for the first time, but for the first time since our digital courtship began! The anticipation of our first date was unreal. Butterflies weren't flitting around in my belly; they had been devoured by a flock of sparrows that continually dipped and dove around my insides. We had both built up our expectations of each other, and it was finally time to face the truth. Would we truly be compatible? Would he be everything my overly-romantic heart desired?

Reading back through these emails, I see that the part of myself that I had kept closeted, my beliefs and spirituality, didn't deserve a space in cyber-land. As I write and ponder the reasons, I believe it was because I wasn't ready to expose that part of myself to Michael yet. I know I was always reading, researching and studying other religions, beliefs and miracles, but I kept them safely to myself, lest I "burn at the stake." Closeted spirituality would be the theme of my life, until a comfortable number of years into our married life had passed, as well as the final catalyst of Michael's untimely death, propelling me into the magical life I am living now, which I promise, dear reader, you will see... later.

CHAPTER 6

Shower

March 2-4, 2019, Mexico

The day after Katrina and Casey arrived was the best I felt in what seemed like an eternity. Finally, I would receive answers to a lot of the questions that passed through my mind during my endless days and nights. Questions that Michael, in spirit, or the hospital staff did not answer. Or, perhaps they had. I hadn't yet realized that I was experiencing the aftermath of a major concussion, and all the information I received could only pause in my brain for a few seconds of contemplation before sinking into the black abyss.

Michael had awoken me during the night, again in what I could only guess were the proverbial "wee hours." The still silence that preceded his "chats" was louder than the hospital noise, as I was transported to a vacuum of nothingness, fully relaxed, my body encapsulated in warmth and limitless love. Then his voice, so deep and resonant, began: "*It happened this*

*way for a reason. I had to leave you, but you know I will always
be with you. We have and will always be together."*

I took so much comfort in his words, in the sound of his
voice. All of this was meant to be. Something within me felt
the truth behind that statement. Laying on that horribly
uncomfortable clinic bed, with its thin sheets and no pillow, I
felt the truth in his words, and they made me feel like I was
floating on clouds, weightless, painless and free. I remembered
when I was a child how I always knew that, as an adult, I
would be looked after. I didn't truly understand what that
meant, other than what my mother wished for me; find a good
man, marry young, have children and be "looked after." That
was all she truly wanted for me. To be secure and have a
simple, peaceful life. But the knowing that I would be looked
after came even before my mother expressed her deepest
wishes. My innocent, naive, young mind just *knew* that I
would always be ok.

Michael gently whispered again, his words fluttering
through my head, *"I made sure everything was in place. I
didn't want to leave you, but it had to be this way."*

Everything was in place...

The realization flooded through me, my eyes widening.
Michael had life insurance *in place,* didn't he? I felt like this
was something I should know, just *know,* but the details
eluded me. I could recall recent conversations in the previous
months leading up to the accident. Brief snippets of our
conversations whispered past me, visions of sitting together at
our table on the deck of our Belizean home, deep in
discussion.

"If anything happens to me, you'd be ok," Michael had
told me. "We have the life insurance, the property in Belize,
and the houses in Canada would take care of themselves with
their renters, or you could sell them." In our almost 12 years
together, we had accumulated a decent portfolio of RRSPs,

savings and property, something Michael was extremely proud of. Before we had met, he didn't own an RRSP, paid for everything in cash and didn't own any property. I owned the home I lived in and had a tidy amount of RRSPs and some savings, but not a lot. What we built and saved and bought, we did so together and with a shared end goal in mind: retire at age 50 and enjoy the rest of our lives doing whatever the hell we wanted.

But the Universe had other plans for us, as Michael was trying to tell me now. Snippets of the past few months crept into memory. He had turned 50 in 2018, less than a year before the accident that took his life. In December that same year, about two mere months before the accident, we were in Belize for our annual 6-month Snowbird trip between stints of summer work. Michael noticed a substantial increase to his life insurance payment on his credit card – twice.

"What the hell is this?" He demanded, immediately irritated, assuming the insurance providers were dummies and had overcharged him. Doing the simple math, the first large payment was taken six months after his 50th birthday. As per the insurance company's policy – the dues had increased.

"Cancel the policy, or reduce it to reduce the monthly payment!" I insisted. Michael merely grunted and stomped out to his tractor, lighting his "thinking stick" en route. I insisted numerous times after that day, letting him know that, unlike most things, this wasn't something that I could deal with for him, and it definitely wasn't going to go away on its own.

"I'll deal with it when I'm back in Canada," was his final response. That would be two or three months away! I thought it rather asinine to bear the extra financial burden for a few more months, when a simple phone call could solve the issue, but that was Michael. Stubborn. And when it came to his tractor and playing on the property over dealing with anything on Canadian soil, he would always choose the former.

As I realized what this meant for me now in being looked after for the rest of *my* life, I could forgive every stubborn tic he ever had. Lying in that hospital bed, recalling the conversations, even the frustration with him for not making that phone call, I bawled. His reluctance to reduce or eliminate the life insurance policy was part of the Universal plan, and therefore, no coincidence. I could hear Michael's voice as the tears streamed down my face.

"*There is no reason to be upset or to mourn me,*" he continued, his voice filling my head, softening my heart and drying my tears. "*This plan has been in place since before your birth, as it is for all people. It was my great honor to be involved in its development and execution and to have the opportunity, once again, to be in your presence on Earth.*"

The tears flowed from a bottomless, unseen pool. Waves of comfort washed over me by his words; I was so in awe of my experience and what lay before me. What would come next in my life? What was the rest of *my plan* that Michael spoke about? It was too much to think about now. Trusting that things would unfold as they did, I let go and drifted off in mild physical discomfort, but vast emotional ease. I didn't feel so alone, knowing Michael was there with me, and my family was only a few blocks away and would visit soon. I felt the weight of his body curl up beside me, the scent of his luxurious cologne wafting in the air around me. I dozed until Casey and Katrina came to visit, as promised.

When they arrived, a flutter of commotion, emotion and excitement ensued. Hugs, touches and kisses abounded, Casey looking fresh from finally getting some rest after the last 48 hours of having none, the previous night's tell-a-tale red eyes now settled, sparkling blue and bright, but I could still see the pain hidden behind those soulful blue beauties. Her long legs, elegant arms and hands already looked tanned and healthy. She had her long dirty-blonde hair tied into a ponytail to beat the Mexican heat and out of the way, so she could easily attend to her priority: take care of Momma.

Katrina offered hugs and kisses, finally semi-rested and comfortable in simple summer clothes and flip-flops, her long dark hair knotted at the top of her head, highlights of silvery grey sparkling under the hospital's fluorescent lights, and her long, wildly-polished nails clicking away at the phone in her hand. She wore cat eye glasses, the shape and style of a vintage pinup with sparkles at the high corners. With her large breasts and thin waist, she was the epitome of Strawberry Skulls meets Betty Boop. She was ready to take command and get to work figuring out what needed to be done to bring me home.

Adam and Vera thankfully came for their daily visit. They introduced themselves to the girls and explained the next steps of my release. I listened but couldn't absorb the conversation. It all seemed like a foreign language and so very monumental. I felt like there was no point to even listening to things that were out of my control.

"Can I go now?" It was all I could think about. I didn't want to be here, I wanted to be back in Canada, holding my grand-baby and my other children. I wanted my pillow and the comfort of my friends and family.

"No, not yet, honey," Katrina told me. "You have a few more days in the hospital until you are well enough to leave." Damn.

Katrina is a short, sassy, no nonsense kind of girl. A tiny tornado, an absolute force to be reckoned with. We worked together in the financial field for a few years before I left to work on the road with Michael. She was top salesperson, and later, top Branch Manager. If there was a job to do, she got it done. Did she have the occasional meltdown during the process? Absolutely, but she pushed on and, more often than not, overshot her targets. I was utterly amazed that she jumped to my rescue, but I could honestly think of no one better for the job. I may be almost a foot taller than her, but in this moment, she was the giant, in control and taking charge, and I couldn't have been more relieved.

Casey tended to her Momma during their entire visit, half-listening and half-partaking in conversation with Katrina, Adam and Vera, but mainly, she focused her attention on my comfort and care, and I loved having her beside me. She would curl up on the narrow mattress and snuggle me the best she could, the awkward neck brace and IV in my hand making it tricky. I could feel her beautiful energy flowing through me, and wished I could adjust my position to get a proper snuggle with my 24-year-old girl.

"Momma, you still have blood on your face, hair and eyes," she told me softly, her long, thin fingers gently pushing my crusty hair away from my face to view the source. Unsure where the source of the blood was coming from, she lifted the hair on the left side of my head and found a rather substantial bump. Later, I would vaguely remember knocking heads with Michael as the Canary rolled endlessly. This was the most likely reason for the swelling and blood. Michael's head was tougher than iron, rock and steel combined, but none of it could protect him from the fatal injuries he sustained in the accident.

"Can we give her a shower?" Katrina asked the nurses, once Adam and Vera had exchanged contact information with her and left. She was in full command, using the translation app on her phone for all non-English conversations that she couldn't otherwise communicate through hand gestures.

"Si, si," the nurse replied. She explained that they had neither the time nor staffing to give me a shower and that we would have to be very careful with moving me over to the bathroom, going slowly. It would be the first time sitting, standing or walking since the accident, and, presumably, I would be dizzy from the concussion, or even collapse from not using my legs or feet for the past couple of days.

The nurse placed a plastic stool in the bathroom, a room that served as both a toilet and full shower. They didn't have any shampoo, just a small bar of hand soap and a washcloth, but it would do. Katrina and Casey assisted me, as I slowly swung my legs around until I was sitting up on the edge of the bed, then waited for my signal that I was ready to continue. My head spun hard, a swirling vortex of mushy brain matter recently scattered and jarred, once again trying to find its place within its protective cavern. It wasn't a fun ride. I waited until my stomach caught up with my head, hesitating briefly to ensure I wouldn't spew my morning broth all over Casey. *Wait,* I thought. *Did I even have broth today? Did I even see my social worker yet?*

Satisfied that the broth I may or may not have had earlier would remain in my stomach, I slid off the side of the bed, my arms and hands held by my rescue team as my feet connected with the cold tile floor. Kat and Casey on either side of me, one arm over each of them for support, I took my first, trepidatious steps. The walk from the bed to the bathroom took forever on newborn fawn legs. We took our time. It was only a dozen steps to the bathroom, but it felt like a mile. One foot sliding in front of the other, I was grateful for the cool, smooth tile beneath me. Upon arrival to the cold, green-tiled, multi-purpose hospital bathroom, they seated me on the small stool, constantly supporting me by holding my arms, and closed the large bathroom door. I desperately wanted to take the useless neck brace off, but that was a definite "no" from the nursing staff. It was "too soon and too risky," according to the expert nurses. I wondered if they even realized how useless the too-large brace really was.

Katrina ran the water until it was warm, while Casey,

maneuvering to support me with her arms or legs to lean on, removed my thin hospital gown. Exposed and shivering, the warm water was a welcome relief. Very slowly, they washed my hair, face and the rest of what was reachable or exposed. They also cared for the bedsores that were already developing on my back and behind from the numerous bed pan uses trickling urine over my buttocks and lower back but never being cleaned up afterwards, just left to sit in my own juices.

As they bathed me, I could see the red water swirling down the central floor drain. My blood and Michael's blood, a horrific mix of the two. I closed my eyes and wept. Casey lifted my hair away from my face and washed it the best she could without touching the swollen purple egg. They noticed that my left ear was also bloody – and sparkling with fragments of glass! We tried to piece together whether or not the left side of my head broke the front window of the Canary, or if it rubbed through the glass during the rollover. Not that it mattered; either way, there was glass, and a lot of it.

The girls did all they could to rinse out my ear, muttering their disgust at the staff for not having got around to this task themselves. It did seem a little odd that nothing had been done to remove the blood trail from my hair, face, hands or ears in the time I became a guest at the ever-popular, 2-star resort, "Hospital Comunitario de Bacalar," but my guess was that my injuries didn't seem severe enough to require stitching up. Plus, allowing boo-boos to air dry and scab over saved the cost of bandages.

After showering and drying me off, they dressed me in a fresh hospital gown and had me sit on the stool while they went to change the sheets on the small clinic bed. The bed sores made sense now – not only was my urine allowed to trickle down my rear without being wiped up, there was no bottom sheet provided for the bed, just the mattress, which was more like a plastic-covered, 12-inch piece of foam. The girls quickly swapped it out with the thicker plastic-covered foamy on the now empty bed beside mine (when did *that* clubhouse member leave?) and requested a second sheet to use as a mattress cover. I could see for the first time that it was more like a gurney than a bed. The only way to elevate it was the hand crank at the foot of the bed, which my social worker had done for me previously. Even with the switch of the mattresses (which did offer a small reprieve to my aching body), it was impossible to get completely comfortable.

"Can I have a pillow?" I asked, as they tucked me back onto my gurney, completely forgetting that I had asked Vera to search for one the day before and the nurses before that. Katrina inquired and found out that such a luxury was to be denied. "It's just so uncomfortable without one. It's hard on my neck." In times of tragedy, the small things mattered.

"We'll see what we can do, sweetie," Katrina promised.

"Also, this neck brace doesn't fit right at all. Do they have a smaller one?" Katrina inquired on that as well, but also returned with a "no." She promised to find a pharmacy that would sell a more fitted one and bring it back with their next visit.

The only other request I had was for some decent food. "My social worker brings me broth, but when she is gone, they bring me cereal for dinner. With milk *and* a whole apple!" I told them, reverting to a rather childlike behavior. I don't drink milk or eat much dairy, so I had refused the previous evening's meal. "It's that or some soup with big chunks of food in it, or an entire piece of fruit, and it's impossible to open my jaw wide enough or chew." Or grasp a spoon or fork with my crumpled hands, or even speak properly. Although, I wasn't having much trouble with that last one at the moment, knowing the Complaint Department was open for business. I loved having my personal delegates with me. They could surely set things straight, especially if I was forced to stay here for another few days.

Tucked into the somewhat softer bed, the upper part of my body elevated, Casey did her best to cuddle me. It brought such comfort to have her there, although the look in her large blue eyes was so sad. It was difficult to look at. Her loss was my loss, and mine hers. I knew she was in a tremendous amount of pain from losing her step-dad. She and Nicole had lovingly nicknamed him "Papa Bear," and I watched in awe how their relationships with Michael blossomed over the years. He was their go-to for advice about life, as he'd had what seemed like lifetimes of experience on the subject. Michael would beam with pride if any of the kids came to him for advice, and he provided it thoughtfully, always with encouragement and love.

Casey and I, freshly showered.

QUESTIONS

I ran the gamut of questions now that my team was there. Where were my things? The suitcases? My passport and wallet and

Michael's things? Again, Katrina drilled the nursing staff, finding out what she could in translation. The nurses brought what the ambulance attendants had given them, which wasn't much. They delivered a large tan-colored beach bag with a tiny white pattern of dogs and cats on the outside and a creamsicle-colored interior, replete with blood splatters inside and out. Michael had bought me the bag when we were doing a short work stint in Winnipeg, Manitoba. It was a purchase to benefit the local SPCA. I really loved that bag, a small reminder of Michael's generosity to the cause, as he paid far more for it than what they were asking.

Seeing the blood splatters sent ripples of horror through me. Was this my blood, Michael's, or both? I remembered the bag being in the back seat of the Canary and imagined there must have been blood smattering throughout the whole interior as well. Shivering, I asked Casey to remove the contents. There was the bloody shirt and skirt they cut from my body, the Mexican ring I had been wearing on my right hand, the pair of earrings I had also been wearing and Mike's good cologne, my favorite on him, but nothing more. This was what I had come in with, what I had been wearing on the way to Cancun.

"My husband's things, where are they?" We asked the nursing staff, who merely shrugged in answer. Vera and Adam were eventually able to fill in some gaps. Anything that would have survived the crash would be in police custody and would also be part of the release paperwork we would have to complete in the next few days. We could then claim our belongings and, most importantly, Michael's body. One of the biggest issues Adam was having was convincing the Federales to release Michael's body into Adam's custody. He couldn't get clearance without a police report being signed and filed by me, the widow. Adam and Vera explained as much to Katrina, but all was kept silent from me. They would process as much paperwork as possible before my leaving the hospital, but the statement from me was something they could not complete without me being present. Adam had me sign a certain amount of paperwork before Kat arrived, but what it was for, I couldn't recall. I just felt that I could trust them, and thankfully, my instincts were still firing well on that point.

Another thing Adam, Vera and Katrina graciously kept from me was a discussion around viewing Michael's body. They asked if this was something that I would want to do, but recommended – *highly* recommended – that I did not. They told Katrina that the body was damaged so badly that viewing it would surely make me highly upset, or worse. I do recall them asking me if this was something that I had wished to do, but I gave them a firm "no." I didn't need or want to see my husband in that way. I had seen enough in the millisecond my eye opened immediately after the accident to know that he no longer looked like Michael. Knowing what damage he had sustained assured me that I didn't need to look further. I also knew that Michael was no longer *there*. He was with me, and he was *perfection*.

The only other piece of jewelry that I had was my wedding ring. That large orange citrine with its rows of diamonds he had proposed to me with. It was cruddy with dirt and blood, even after the shower, and still firmly on my finger amidst the swelling. I contemplated the ring and the swollen purple finger and heard Michael chuckling, his deep guffaw rumbling through my head. Then, I knew.

"He did this on purpose!" I said to the girls, holding up my ring finger, showing off my mini-eggplant.

"Who did, honey?" Katrina asked.

"Michael did. He made sure that I hurt my finger, so whoever stole most of our belongings at the scene couldn't take my ring off. He never wanted me to take it off."

Katrina and Casey both smiled and cooed at the notion. I relayed some messages that I had received from Michael, being honest and open about what I had heard and felt in the past two days. I watched Katrina's face with curiosity. How would she take that truth? Would she believe me? I shared about hearing him say that I could "be a Vegan now," and we all laughed together. Appeased that she seemed to accept my new reality, I felt comfortable in relaying more of the messages that I could remember.

Casey lit up with awe and understanding of what had taken place, which didn't surprise me in the slightest. She was already on her own path of spiritual development and growth; this would simply add to her own "knowing." The ability to channel from the other side was comforting and exciting. "Does he have any messages for me?" She asked.

"I'll need paper and pens," I replied, "and as soon as I can grip a pen to write, I will ask."

Until sometime later, I could only imagine writing the messages out as they came to me, not speaking them, so pens and paper would be a requirement. I would also need a host of other things. As there were no suitcases to be found among my belongings, that meant I had no clothes to leave the hospital in, and I surely would not wear the blood-soaked, cut-up clothes I came in with. Casey disposed of the bloody items after asking if I wanted to keep them, but I declined.

The girls made a list of things to purchase. They stayed until lunch hour and requested food alternatives for me, as I had a "special diet," which was truly only certain food preferences (no dairy) and the obvious inability to chew anything that wasn't as soft as baby food. The hospital staff did their best to accommodate, at least I chose to believe so, but the foods were just too difficult to eat, and it would appear that the residents of Bacalar who frequented the hospital didn't have food allergies or sensitivities, so the staff couldn't understand mine. Katrina and Casey would also find foods that would be easier, healthier and more palatable than what the small hospital *could* offer.

COINCIDENCES

At some point after the girls returned with my requested items, Casey began scrolling through the many thoughtful messages from friends on her social media. Suddenly, she sprang forward in surprise, saying, "Oh, my God! Tanya was there! By accident!" Apparently, Casey's friend Tanya and her boyfriend Jim, both residents of our small hometown back in Canada, were vacationing in the area during the time of the accident. Learning the story of how Tanya and Jim, had come across our accident scene absolutely floored me and solidified my belief in non-coincidence. I could feel the vibrational energy alive in the Universe, and in that moment, I knew without a doubt that our life path lay before us long before we come into our 3rd-dimensional realm.

This particular chain of coincidence started an entire year before the accident actually happened, when Tanya had been at a retreat on Isla Mujeres, just off the coast of Mexico, and she was told by an acquaintance that Bacalar was truly a wonderful place to visit. One year later, Tanya and Jim made their plans and were on their way to Bacalar in February 2019, about the same time Michael and I had left our Belizean estate to begin our trek to Cancun. During their stay, Jim contracted strep throat, and in his foggy, fevered state, he decided he wanted to visit some healing mud baths he had read about on Tripadvisor. In his groggy state, he was mistakenly convinced the mud baths were at the Chancchoven Mayan Ruins. Tanya knew they were not, but she couldn't convince Jim of it, so off to the ruins they went. Once they had arrived and discovered there was, after all, no mud to be found, they visited the ruins before heading toward the *actual* lake of mud. On their way, they happened upon our accident scene, which had taken place only a few minutes earlier.

As it turned out, Jim had medical training and had assisted where needed when they arrived on the scene. It was actually he who had determined Michael's state and covered his face with a towel they had in their vehicle. Apparently, I was incoherent, on my knees outside of the Canary, repeatedly mumbling, "I don't know what happened." Tanya wasn't completely sure of who I was, but she just "knew" that I was from her own small hometown. Locals surrounding the accident asked Tanya, in Spanish, what I was saying. And here's where the "coincidence" gets even freakier: Tanya, not fluent in the language, was – *much* to her surprise – able to understand what they were asking, **and** could answer in Spanish – just as I had been able to in those moments after waking in hospital!

When the local authorities and ambulance arrived on scene and placed me on a backboard – with the dreaded neck brace in place – and took me to the Bacalar hospital, Tanya's instincts were to follow the ambulance, but Jim's ill health and exhaustive state meant they should get back to the bed-and-breakfast they were staying at in Bacalar. The lady who owned the bed-and-breakfast, Jenny, was an American expat who'd retired from her previous career of emergency response planning. This was also an amazing coincidence. Jenny helped Katrina and Casey with details relating to where they needed to go, who to talk to and what to do to take me home.

Tanya had heard from a mutual friend that Casey was on her way to Bacalar, and that it was her mom and step-dad who were in the accident. Tanya and Jenny set out to find the hospital I would be at, and an "emergency response plan" was created. They would bring Casey and Katrina sustenance upon their arrival to their own hotel and assist with the language barriers and so on. They did, indeed, bring the girls food and things they may need the night they arrived in Bacalar, but Tanya said nothing of being on the scene the day before. She felt it was more important that Casey rest, knowing there would be time to tell her story in the days ahead. Hearing it all, it absolutely blew me away at the "small world" we live in, and I am so very grateful for Tanya's and Jim's care and concern.

The "coincidences" continued to pile up long after leaving the hospital and returning home. Michael and I writing our wills and preparing the estate documents for Nicole *just prior* to heading to Belize in October 2018. My conversations with Michael about me being okay if anything happened to him. The life insurance payment jumping up to over $500 a month and Michael not doing anything about it. The accident being so close to Bacalar, between the Canadian Consulate and the funeral home that brought Adam and Vera to me. Katrina obtaining a new Mastercard only two days before the accident happened, which enabled us to take care of so many expenses during the whole ordeal. Thinking about it, it was no coincidence that Katrina came into our lives in 1999, approximately 20 years before the accident happened. She needed to be here and have this experience with us, to support us and love us, her fierce strength desperately needed during this time of crisis. As I took stock of all these "coincidences" and so many more I'm not able to include here, I realized how everything, *my entire life* leading up to this... it was all so non-coincidental, and it was enough to make my head spin right off my shoulders.

TROY

After chatting about this amazing new detail and all of the coincidences in general, the girls started making shopping lists and planning their afternoon. All conversation stopped when we heard heightened voices coming from the hallway, one distinctly male and accented. To my absolute delight and complete surprise, my friend Troy burst into my room! Troy and his wife Anne lived on their farm in Belize, about 4km from our property. Troy, an ex-military, average height, tough-as-nails bloke from Ireland, still held a lofty Irish accent. He packed a 9mm sidearm on one hip and a sheathed buck knife on the other. His demeanor and weaponry commanded respect from fellow villagers, and that is what he received. His lovely wife Anne, born and raised in Germany, serves as a doctor in the Belize City Hospital. They had been in Belize for 4 years prior to Troy's and Michael's first meeting over our property fence one sunny November day. Troy, driving his shiny new tractor, was on his way to cut the grass on their secondary piece of property close to ours. Michael, on our much older, not-so-shiny Kubota clunker, noisily roamed near the fence, moving dirt from one pile to another. Troy stopped and got Michael's attention. They chatted for quite some time and became fast friends.

"Troy?" My eyes widened, stunned at seeing him right there in front of me. Wasting no time, Troy started in on his reason for being there.

"I just wanted y' to know how incredibly sorry Anne and I are at hearing of Mike's passin'," his thick Irish accent heavy with grief and concern. "I also wanted y' to know not to worry about a thing on the property. I've gone and changed all the locks on the sea cans and 'ave the house secured. Everythin' is safe."

"Oh, Troy, thank you so much!" Once again, I was flooded with relief and gratitude. Until this point, I hadn't once thought about what might happen to our property. I had even forgotten that my niece, husband and their daughter, who visited for a week before we left for Mexico, were staying on the property an extra day before they headed back to Canada.

Sadly, the reality is – and Troy was all too aware of this –

knowing there was a death of the property owner, the house, sea cans and all of their contents were at risk of being "picked clean" by the locals. Belize is a beautiful country, and we could never bring ourselves to call it "third world," but it was definitely poor by North American standards, and, as with any country, it has its own issues of theft and violence.

Anne was also there, but the clinic staff wouldn't permit her to come into the room with Troy, as Katrina and Casey were there also, and the clinic had visitor limits. I was flabbergasted that they made the 4-hour trip for a 5-minute visit, just to let me know everything was ok and to put my mind at ease. They were, and still are, the most amazing friends I will treasure forever, and they continued to maintain, secure and care for the property in the months that followed.

Troy and the girls exchanged contact information, so each could keep the other up to date on my progress and the plans for me to leave for home. Troy promised he would continue to take care of things on the property, even if that meant staying in the cabana (which he did several times), and to keep in touch. We said goodbye and wished Anne well, thanking Troy for taking the time to come. Then the girls left and let me rest after the eventful morning and set about finding the items on the list. Kat had brought two cell phones, knowing mine was missing; she left me with one of hers and helped me log into my Facebook Messenger so I could communicate with friends and family. Because I now had a phone and access to the outside world, I was able to read the posts the girls made on Facebook and the messages people left for me. I replied to a few, but my cranky, crooked hands made holding the phone or typing on the tiny keypad a tiring challenge. That night, I slept well, Michael's snoring ringing a soft, gentle hum in my ears.

March 2, 2019

Nicole's Facebook and Go-Fund-Me Post: *"Mom is about the same today. Groggy and really sore, especially in her ear, jaw and neck. She still has healing to do there before we can bring her home, but she is very happy to have people there with her now. It's difficult for her to speak for long periods because of a sore jaw, but she wanted to make sure everyone knew she loves them and is so thankful for everything that everyone has done. The family members who are with her are working hard to make sure her needs are met and helping with all of the arrangements that need to be made. She is able to rest much easier now. Thank you so much again to everyone. The amount of support and well wishes we have all received is absolutely incredible. We will never be able to properly express our gratitude towards you all."*

March 2, 2019

Casey's Facebook Post: *"Mom is recovering well and hoping to return home soon, and she wants to thank each and every one of you for your messages, your kind words of love and the incredible support during this time. She will reply to everyone when she is able. If you want to send her a message specifically you can do so to myself or Katrina, as we will be answering messages when we can."*

UNSCATHED

When Casey and Katrina returned the next morning, they had a good supply of food in hand, the scent making my stomach growl. They fed me delicious soups they purchased at a restaurant near their hotel and as much soft fruit as I could handle. The biggest prize was a fluffy pillow they had "borrowed" from the hotel they were staying at. What a luxury! Instantly, the discomfort in my neck and head eased when my head hit the pillow. The nurses were a little stunned at the receipt of my prize, yet happy for me and my newfound comfort. My intermittent naps and the night's sleep were now so much deeper and more comfortable.

They also brought me journals and pens! Several! I held up my still-crumpled hands and asked how much writing they thought I'd be able to do? We laughed at this. The girls just didn't know what this newfound ability entailed and how much needed to be written, so they grabbed everything they could find. I looked forward to being able to dive into those journals as soon as I was able. We visited for as long as we could, reviewing some events as I remembered them, trying to piece it all together the best that I could. Mostly, they just sat with me, held my hand, stroked my hair and kept me company, which was more than I could ever ask for.

By now, I fully believed in the Universe and my angels, and that the plan for my life was unfolding before me. I was swimming in the large pool of coincidence, and I felt like I was ready to face the inevitable in some sense. Because of the communication I'd had with Michael, I felt relieved and assured that he was safe in the best place possible, and that was something. What I really wanted to know next was the extent of the accident itself.

"Can you show me a picture?" I asked Casey.

"Are you sure, Momma? It's horrible," she replied.

"Yes, it's ok. I'd like to know." Casey brought the news report up on her phone. The girls had maintained cell service since leaving Canada, even purchasing service on the plane so that they could stay connected with family back home on their arrival and so on.

I couldn't believe what I saw.

Our beautiful yellow and black Canary, the Jeep Michael was so very proud of, lay on its side in a twisted, scattered mess on the shoulder of the highway. The hardtop, roll bars and front window were ripped off, tossed in a shamble of twisted metal, glass and plastic along the highway. Michael's thick, limp body lay beside the vehicle, his legs still resting inside. My body lay on a backboard further away, but my legs were near Michael's head. It almost looked as though they had rested his head on my shins. His face and torso were covered with a red towel, compliments of Jim and Tanya. My elbows were bent, holding my hands upright, the neck brace already on me. I couldn't recall any of it, not one second other than opening my eye to register the truth of our situation.

How did I survive this?

The Canary, mangled post-accident.

Conversations with Nicole came back to me. I could understand her devastation and astonishment at my survival, and not just that, but virtually walking away "unscathed." I gave a silent prayer of thanks and gratitude and wondered what it all meant. To me, this was absolute confirmation that I survived to fulfill my life's purpose, just as Michael had told me. There was a bigger plan in play, and since the accident pictures didn't add up to the injuries I currently had, I fully believed that was the truth. I shed no tears when viewing that photo, only sat in total awe of my reality. "*I will always care for you.*" Michael's words rolled through my mind. This knowing that I had even as a child had proven true in so many ways.

"I need to call Oma," I told Casey, "Oma" being Michael's mother, the step-grandma to my children. I couldn't imagine the pain she must be in, having lost her second son of three. We dialed her number in Canada, and when I said, "Hello, Mum," she gently breathed an, "Oh Tammy..." in return. We chatted only briefly, but during that time she let me know she was making calls to all of Michael's family members, and I made her promise not to search out the news or pictures of the accident. I wanted so desperately to spare her the pain those images would surely cause. I hung up the phone and turned back to Katrina and Casey. They held me once again, soothing me. Then it was back to the business at hand: get me home.

Next, I called my son and spoke with him, listening to the hitch in his voice as he did his best to push back the tears. "Come home, Mom. Just come home. I need you here with me," he sobbed.

My heart ached to hold my boy. It was a pain worse than what I felt losing my husband. My boy has a way of tugging on all of our hearts, his sisters included. His being the only boy in the family made him extra special, like the sprinkles on top of the banana split – the best part of us all. I promised him we were doing everything we could to get me home as quickly as possible and told him I couldn't wait to see him. I believe that was the only conversation I had with him during this time, other than group chats with him and his sisters, something we still do daily, no matter where we all are in the world. The journey home was just beginning. Being the patient, I had no clue, but the process to release me, Michael's body and the paperwork that ensued was going to be arduous. Without the help of our Consulate, Adam and Katrina to oversee the requirements, it would have been a nightmare worse than the accident itself.

After hearing about and reading the messages people had been sending to Casey, Katrina and Nicole, I thought that doing a Facebook Live would be a good idea. I probably shouldn't have insisted, as I was in really rough shape and looked awful, but I was following my heart and my intuition. Knowing there were so many concerned people, I hoped that by doing the live, they could find some peace and hold space for my healing. I had great intentions of being brave and strong, letting people know that I was ok, but when the broadcast started, I couldn't find my words. I got quiet, but with help from the girls, we thanked everyone for their support and told them I was ok and hoped to be home soon.

DISCHARGED

The day of my release from the clinic couldn't come soon enough. I enjoyed visiting hours with the girls; they were true rebels who overstayed the posted hours and broke clinic policies – bringing in outside food and being too loud – but we didn't care. There was a lot of planning and paperwork to complete if I was going to be on a plane to Canada any time soon. Katrina was constantly on her phone, adding WhatsApp and messaging via text or voice to Adam, the Canadian Consulate and, of course, family. She was a fury of fingers over the next few days, texting, voice messaging, calling and organizing whatever needed to be done to bring me home. To this day, we don't know what we would have done without her there. I couldn't imagine any of my family having the will or ability to get things done like Katrina did during those tumultuous days in Mexico. Adam and Vera also made the hour-long trip from Chetumal to Bacalar every day to provide updates, find out the status of my injuries and prepare for the next steps. It wasn't a simple task, releasing Michael's body and getting me home, but Adam was eager to complete what needed to be done. He was also a little frustrated by the process, as we would learn a little later.

The girls went shopping for some clothes for me to leave the clinic in, but, as is typical for a small Mexican village or town, the pickings were slim and rather tacky. They brought me a few choices of underwear (all brightly colored, lacy and barely my size) shirts, shorts and so on. Most of what they found was straight out of a bad 80s MTV video, a copy of anything Madonna had worn during her "Papa Don't Preach" phase. Most had brazen gold sparkles and were smattered with rivets and lace. It was clear that every Mexican clothing factory was well-equipped with a Bedazzler. Thankfully, they could find a couple of simple T-shirts and a pair of nice lace shorts, but it wasn't without digging through piles of bargain base-ment throw-backs like K-Mart shoppers at a Blue Light Sale. The funniest piece of clothing they found was an 3XL T-shirt, emblazoned with a cartoon female body (no head). The front of the shirt was a print of the full-busted cartoon body wearing a Mexican flag bikini. The back was the full-bottomed cartoon in the same flag bikini. This was a typical tourist T-shirt that made the wearer look as if the skinny bikini body was hers (or his). The girls thought this would make excellent pajamas and a seriously funny joke. It was definitely hilarious and made me laugh for the first time in what felt like weeks.

The girls also scoured the town of Bacalar until they found a pharmacy that sold medical supplies and purchased a proper neck brace. Katrina then had to convince the clinic nurses that the brace would do a lot more for me than the current one would. They made the exchange, and I felt enormous relief, allowing my neck to relax into the new, fully-supportive wrap. I promised the charge nurse – who rather scowled at the idea that the simple yet firm and form-fitting soft neck brace would do a better job than the large, too-big, rigid one – that I would keep it on 24/7, until my doctor deemed it able to come off.

I was really willing to do anything if it meant leaving sooner than later. I'd eat the cereal for dinner, force my jaw around the firm apples or choke down the weird broths and sandwiches that held no nutritional value whatsoever and were impossible for me to eat. The pain in my head and jaw made chewing and even breathing uncomfortable, but I had started walking to the bathroom on my own with support from Casey when she was there, and very slowly on my own when she wasn't. It took forever to walk from the bed to the bathroom without feeling dizzy and woozy, but I made it, rejoicing in small victories. It was a far better feeling than doing my dookie in a bed pan while impatient nurses waited to *not* wipe me up and take it away.

Our actual anniversary date, March 3, passed without the usual aplomb. The day escaped me at the time of its passing, as most things did in my foggy, concussed state, but it was realized in the days to come. I don't think it even came up in conversation, and if it had, I would have avoided reminiscing. My anniversary gift was brought to me by one of the nurses. I was presented with a large yellow manila envelope containing my X-rays. Until that moment, I had no clue that they had taken X-rays after the accident, but here they were! The large, plastic grey and white transparencies of my spine showcased the crook of my scoliosis and the zipper of the shirt I was still wearing for the picture. They punctuated the end of my life with my husband, an eerie memento of our last honeymoon vacation.

The day of my release, March 4, was an exciting one! Adam and Vera were there to escort us to our hotel in Bacalar. Transferred to a wheelchair, I said a cheery goodbye to my plastic-covered hospital bed. I was then wheeled out to their vehicle, a large, comfortable Escalade. I settled into the back seat, Casey and Kat beside me, and we made our way through the narrow streets to the hotel entrance, not far from the hospital. The streets were lined with colorful stores, restaurants, flowers and trees. It was truly quaint, and I felt so liberated being out of the clinic! I noticed Katrina softly crying by my side. We'd done it. One major event, busting me out of the hospital, was complete. Katrina and Casey posted to their Facebook walls:

"WE BROKE HER OUT!!!! Now the big hard work begins. Our Consulate guy

will be here in a couple of hours so that we can begin working through all of the

individual details. Insurance information has finally come through, and we can

also get started on that. Most everything was pending Tammy's release, so this is

a huge relief. We still don't have a timeline for when we will be home. We are

feeling the love in massive abundance. Thank you all so much."

Sometime after we had arrived home and I was fully healed, the girls told me that the hospital staff and care was, in fact, incredibly frustrating to deal with. They were not permitted to bring outside food into the hospital, but I was not able to eat anything that was provided for me, so they had no choice. Unfortunately, that meant bribing the security guards and nurses to allow them to sneak in soft fruit, soups and over-cooked pasta noodles. Shortly after the girls started sneaking in food, the hospital stopped bringing me meals altogether, but they still had to pay someone off to sneak the food in.

At times, they would even have to bribe them to come and see me at all. Because I had very little sense of the time of day and acted solely on impulse or direction from Michael and the messages he provided, I would sometimes text or call Casey with the phone Katrina left for me and ask her to come to the hospital to bring either food or pen and paper so that I could dictate messages to her. This was always outside of hospital visiting hours, sometimes as late as 11:00 p.m., but Casey never refused or questioned my requests, just did as she was asked, bribing her way in to see me again.

This explained why they referred to checking me out of the hospital as "breaking me out." They went through three doctors to do so, however, the first two refusing to allow my release, and the third finally agreeing, partly based on the improvement of my condition and partly because of Adam's insistence. We still needed to get the required documentation completed in order for him to obtain Michael's body and bring it to the funeral home to be handled properly. The girls felt like they were visiting a prisoner, one that had been sentenced to life with no chance of parole. If they could, they would have brought the proverbial cake with a file in it. As hard as Adam, Katrina and Casey tried, begged and pleaded with authorities to release his body before my discharge from the clinic, the authorities would not budge. In the meantime, Michael's body lay in a state of decomposition that should never have been allowed to occur.

FREEDOM

Once released and now free as a bird, I savored the sights of the quaint little town. The hotel was as colorful as Bacalar itself, and the hosts were warm and welcoming. Everyone was aware of the circumstances that brought me there, as it had been plastered all over the news for days. I was the mystery woman who lost her mystery husband in a horrific car accident five days previous. In Mexico, there was no censoring of graphic pictures, so they could all see just how horrific it actually was.

Thus, anything that we required to make our stay more comfortable, they would oblige. I felt like a princess, which would have been to Michael's liking and standards anytime we traveled. This time, however, there was a disturbing hole from his absence.

Our room was on an upper floor of the open, airy hotel, which meant climbing a flight or two of circular stairs. I was moving extremely slow, only recently having found my feet during my nightly visits to the clinic bathroom. Casey and Katrina offered their arms always and wouldn't allow me to move even an inch without one of them there to support me. I was dizzy, woozy and concussed, as I slowly took each step up the brightly-colored stairwell. The feeling of "being hit by a Mack Truck" was an understatement. When the girls had me settled into the large, comfortable queen-sized bed I would share with Casey, they bustled about, getting food, magazines and anything else I would need to be at ease.

I appreciated the comfort of a normal bed like nothing else on Earth. I had developed a bad case of bed sores on the thin, plastic-covered mattress at the hospital, and my festering wounds had not been attended to at all by the hospital staff. Casey and Katrina purchased the necessary first aid to administer before tucking me in. There was no TV in the room, and we kept the radio off. No sense in having anything on; it was all in Spanish anyway. Preferring not to see any further images of the accident itself, we kept the one-eyed monster off.

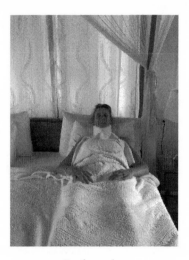

Comfort, at last.

The room, hexagonal in shape, was resplendent in mahogany trim with a large, four-poster mahogany bed in the middle, hosting a walk-through closet and large bathroom and shower. The soaker tub was actually in the main room near the bed, hidden behind what looked like a large mahogany bar. Katrina had a hot bath nearly every night that we were there, even though she had difficulty navigating the in and out of the deep-seated bath. She got high-centered one evening, when she had to reach outside the tub to retrieve a slippery soap. Casey was quick to the rescue, assisting one sudsy Katrina back into the tub in a fit of giggles and splashing. The large shelf unit behind the tub was mirrored, giving the room a much larger feel. It was the "honeymoon suite," but the trip we were on was the furthest thing from a honeymoon.

Paying for the hospital bill, the hotel and anything related to my care and return was in the hands of the very capable Katrina and Nicole. By this time, the Go-Fund-Me had risen to an astonishing $34,000, thanks to the kindness of the very large staff of the company that Michael was contracted to. One close friend, an administrator on a Calgary, Alberta job, had sent the news of Michael's passing and the Go-Fund-Me link to the entire staff via email. My sister Kate had also sent out a mass email to the school district she worked for, boosting the number even higher. Overnight, the fund rose from $10,000, to $34,000 and change. I was in awe of the messages that people had left on the Go-Fund-Me page. The continued kindness of so many strangers kept the tears of gratitude flowing.

At last, the first step of "Operation: Bring Tammy Home" was complete. I was out of the clinic, in a comfortable bed and once again connected to the outside world and my family back home. In the days that followed, what I had hoped would be a simple matter of signing documents, releasing Michael's body and venturing home would end up being a long, arduous and painful time. As it turned out, the next few days were full of frustrations, criminal activity and insidious blackmail. It felt like "home" was never going to arrive, as you'll find out... later.

CHAPTER 7

Love

2005-2012, Canada

A little over two months after our "You've Got Mail" romance began, Michael was bringing his son home on the Saturday of the September long weekend, as he would start high school in a few days. Michael expected to do some sightseeing and stay overnight halfway through their return trip, so we set our first official date for Sunday evening. However, Michael's son really wasn't that interested in visiting yet another tourist attraction, as he'd had his fill on the summer weekends when his dad pried himself away from his work to take him on an adventure. He just wanted to get home, so they pushed through and arrived late Saturday evening. Michael called me upon his arrival, just before 10 p.m.

"I'm back earlier than expected! I have to shower and shave, but then I was hoping to come over for a hug and a chat on the porch, perhaps?"

I was ecstatic! And also freaking out! He was back early, and my home was a disaster! I dashed through the house like a fireman searching for bodies in a 5-alarm fire, waking Nicole and Casey up in the process. All hands on deck, we cleaned, tossed, tucked and washed up as best we could in about 20 minutes flat. It was rather hilarious, fun and exciting. At least, I thought so, but I think the girls agreed. They were just as excited to meet Michael in the flesh after listening to their mother's "Michael this and Michael that" chatter for the last few months. The girls slid into Nicole's main floor bedroom when we heard a soft knock on the front door.

I silently prayed my armpits didn't stink from the sudden house cleaning frenzy, wished that I had time to apply makeup, or, at the very least, a bra. I decided that any nipple protrusion would make up for the lack of mascara and lipstick as I reached for the door and opened it. There he stood; tall, blonde, clean-shaven with beautiful, deep denim blue eyes and an incredible smile, which I remembered fondly from our very first meeting. He was wearing jeans, a denim work shirt and leather jacket. As he leaned against the door frame, I realized how well he filled it. He was a large man, both in stature and weight. Although only a few inches taller than me, his build made him seem much taller. He was barrel-chested with a slight "beer belly," something he must have diligently culti-vated while he was up north eating all the wonderful food he'd told me about, but his appearance wasn't unattractive. Quite the opposite. He was a little Zeus and Poseidon rolled into one.

"Hi!" He grinned, hands in his coat pockets. He was wearing a 90s-style leather jacket, black with different colored raglan sleeves and a racing stripe here and there. I half expected to see a leather "8-Ball" on the back, as per the style, but thankfully, there was not, as that may have been a deal breaker.

"Come in!" I said, trying to hide my nervousness, appear

relaxed and beautiful with nipples in check, all at the same time. He stepped inside, and I closed the door behind him. I moved in for the hug first and brushed his lips with a quick, solid kiss. His lips were soft, as he barely had time to form a pucker in return. The scent of his aftershave was a heady, deep, woodsy scent with a hint of ocean breeze. Heavenly.

"Oh! Nice!" He seemed surprised by the kiss. Was I being too outgoing? After all the emails in the months beforehand, it seemed right! I took his coat and asked him to come in. He removed his boots and followed me down the hall past Nicole's bedroom door, and then left into the small but cozy living room. He didn't notice the four eyeballs peering through the crack in Nicole's door, or the hushed giggles that followed us down the hall.

We sat on my blue sectional couch, he on one part of the L-section and me on the other. We chatted for at least an hour before I heard Nicole's door open and the girls popped out. I had totally forgotten about them! They peered through the open decorative wall spaces between the hallway and living room. Casey asked if she could go back to bed now, and after introducing the girls to Michael, they both went back to their own rooms, giggling. Michael questioned why I had locked the girls in the room to begin with, possibly a little concerned about my parenting methods. I had to admit to the last-minute Clean Fest, in which the girls took part.

I poured two glasses of wine, and we chatted late into the night. Still on separate parts of the couch, I rested my bare feet beside him, and he immediately started to massage them. Eventually, I moved beside him, and we started making out. Feeling rather like teenagers in the backseat of dad's station wagon and heady with the wine, we slipped upstairs and continued our evening. My children may choose to skip this part – or they may not, as I'm sure in their own lives they can attest to similar circumstances – but my wish is that their experiences are 100-times better than mine. I can tell you that the first time with Michael was NOT fantastic. I think if anyone tried to tell you their first time with their significant other was absolutely brilliant, I will happily call that the biggest pile of bullshit.

Let's face it, all romance writers are lying, and the best ones have been setting us all up for failure. We were clumsy, as if two dorky teenagers were figuring out which parts did what for the first time. It was not the passionate, stunning love-making session I had envisioned. I think if I were to survey most of my friends about their first times with their significant others, I would find that a very small percentage would say they were absolutely mind-blowing. This was not one of those times. Later, when Michael and I would try again, and then again, we both relaxed enough to become completely immersed, and the fireworks flew.

Up until that first night, I assumed Michael was absolute perfection. He may have been boasting a bit of a beer belly, but that, I knew, was understandable and completely fixable. He was handsome – roguishly so – with beautiful light blonde hair and gorgeous eyes. He had large, masculine hands and legs with large calves from his years hiking miles over job sites. After months of online chatting and spending hours in person, and even after our first, clumsy love-making session, I knew we were perfect mates for life. It was only when Michael fell asleep beside me that I discovered his fatal flaw – he was a snorer. Not just any old run-of-the-mill snorer, breathing in, then blowing out, like so many do. No, his snoring was EPIC. He sounded very much like the locomotive freight trains that passed through our town, a mere thousand meters from my home. In fact, in my sleepy state, I thought it was a freight train that was passing by my home, louder than usual.

When I discovered that it was neither a locomotive, nor a coffee percolator or some weird combination of the two, but that it was, indeed, Michael's snoring, I was stunned. The perfect image I had of this man was now officially cracked. That wouldn't do, but it also wasn't a deal-breaker. I knew I would just have to be a little imaginative and buy a case of earplugs, should this relationship climb to the levels of our dreams. I woke him up, reminding him that I didn't want my girls finding him in the house when they woke up. He hastily got dressed, gave me a lovely kiss goodbye and tip-toed out of the house. I fell back into a noiseless sleep. Later that morning, I received an email from him.

From: Michael Friese
[kaloogan@netscape.net]
Sent: September 4, 2005, 10:43 a.m.
To: Tammy Tyree [tyree@telus.net]
Subject: Good morning beautiful!

Well, that was a little more than a chat on the porch now, wasn't it?
   I slept in over here and woke up about half an hour ago. I have had this stupid little grin on my face ever since.
   Is this what it feels like to wake up beside an angel?
   I'll call you a little later.
   Michael

I, too, was grinning and excited. What a night! Despite the clumsy lovemaking, there was obvious chemistry between us, and we had so much in common that furthering our relationship just made sense. We had spent weeks communicating via email, really getting the chance to know each other, so actually being together (a.k.a. "going steady") was the next logical step. Although we hadn't mentioned it the night before, we both felt a closeness and connection that neither of us had in previous relationships. We had covered so much ground through our communications but truly only just scratched the surface. That evening, Michael picked me up for our first official date. Nicole was old enough to babysit her little sister, so I was free to go. We went to a restaurant just outside of town, which used to be owned by a lovely German couple, but it had been sold and turned into a place that attracted many of the "sledders" who stayed in the nearby hotels, close to the snowmobiling areas.

A young man wearing jeans, a black-and-white checkered flannel shirt and a ratty baseball cap seated us. He provided menus and a wine list. We ordered a bottle of wine, which was delivered and uncorked prior to anyone taking our food order. We held hands across the table, sipping our wine and enjoying deep, delightful conversation about life, our pasts and our dreams for the future. As we sat, I noticed people come in, sit, eat and leave. Our bottle of wine was poured and re-poured until empty, but the staff still hadn't taken our food order! We had been talking for three hours when we called a server over and mentioned that no one had taken our order. Mortified, the server brought us another bottle of wine, this one on the house, and shortly after, our food.

It was such a delightful, insightful evening. I didn't bring up my beliefs in spirituality and metaphysics, as I was still learning and also had a deeply-rooted fear of persecution, one that had been with me since childhood. It didn't seem to matter this time, as we were still getting to know each other, but later, I regretted not being more forthcoming with opening up that part of me far sooner. Michael delivered me to my door, and we spent a long moment saying goodnight. He had to head back to work in the next day or two, so we were grateful for the time we had. Little did I know, that would be a running theme of our life together. The morning after a good night's sleep, I received another email from him, written the night before.

From: Michael Friese
[kaloogan@netscape.net]
Sent: September 5, 2005, 10:59 p.m.
To: Tammy Tyree [tyree@telus.net]
Subject: To a beautiful lady at bedtime!

Hey you!
   I can't free myself up to come tuck you in, but sure wish that I was there.
   Probably for the best, otherwise people might think that I joined us at the hip or something just as silly that they usually accuse teenage lovers of.
   I have to tell you that this has been a bit of a surreal whirlwind two days, and I am enjoying the ride COMPLETELY! I can't look at you without being dazzled at how pretty you are, can't listen to you talk without being amazed at how sweet you are. You are actually more of a sappy romantic than I am.
   I am sure that it is I who has cast the spell on you. Or perhaps, your mother dropped you on your head as a child and it affected your senses. Either way, whatever the reason that you see a plain, humble person such as myself in such a wonderful light, I hope the effects are long lasting,

as I am proud to be your boyfriend! (OK, I even sound like a teenager).

It will be hard for me to leave again. The only thing that will make it bearable is the months we will have to make all of our silly dreams come true when I return.

Sweet dreams lover,

ME

Although we hadn't yet said it, we both knew we were in love. We had spent enough time together, talking and truly getting to know each other, and everything so far seemed like pure magic. Over the next couple of days, my girls and I spent some time with Michael and his son, and Michael and I had another "adult sleepover," wherein I woke to the sound of his snoring once again and booted him out early, lest my girls wake up to find him there. We tried to spend as much time together as possible, knowing he would soon return to his work in northern British Columbia until November or so.

We reminisced about the months that he came to the bank to gather his pay, and he admitted to letting the guys go before him until I was available, so he could spend a precious few minutes in my company. He also admitted to hearing me in my garden then rolling D'fer's tennis ball into my yard on purpose, just so he could mosey over to see me. His revelations touched me, my heart and head fluttering. Then, on the only visit I made to his basement suite apartment, I was utterly shocked to see my business card – the one I had given him several years prior with my personal extension written on the back – adhered to his fridge. He blushed and admitted his crush went even deeper than keeping this small memento of our brief meetings.

The biggest admission, however, was the real reason he

had a profile on the dating site in the first place. Michael was over at a friend's when they discovered my original dating profile on Lavalife.ca. He hadn't known until that moment that I was single and immediately created a profile for himself so he could connect with me. He wasn't able to finish his profile in time and connect with me then, as he had to head to work. When he revisited the site weeks later, I had already taken my profile down. Frustrated but assuming the laws of fate were fast at work, he left his profile alone, and it was eventually migrated over to Date.ca, a subsidiary of Lavalife. That was where I found him, 3-4 years later.

This *alone* proves to me the truth of non-coincidence that permeates each of our individual lives, and that if things are part of a grand plan, *they will be made manifest*. Although it would have been far easier to connect if Michael had just picked up the phone and called me, his shyness and belief that I would find him unattractive forced the Universe to intervene. We *must* be together. For nearly 15 years, our paths had crossed time and time again, until finally aligning. Having officially met in the flesh and "consummating" our relationship, we continued documenting our love affair via email.

From: Tammy Tyree [tyree@telus.net]
Sent: September 6, 2005, 7:12 p.m.
To: Michael Friese [kaloogan@netscape.net]
Subject: RE: To a beautiful lady at bedtime!

I think that when you get back from work in November that you'll still have to send me amazingly sweet emails that I can read repeatedly, as I really enjoy a good giggle and blush… ;-) In fact, even when (or if —

although I'm leaning toward WHEN) we someday move into that big house together on our vast ranch, I'll STILL make you send me emails. I keep them all, you know, and will probably still be reading them when I'm 90 — I'm just THAT sappy…

I really couldn't think of much else other than you today, which was wreaking havoc on me while working this afternoon. This HAS been a whirlwind few days and a GREAT couple of months. I've enjoyed every minute as well. I can't believe how incredibly sweet and genuine you are and how the butterflies in my stomach are making me dizzy from all their activity. For today I thought maybe I was coming down with some strange stomach ailment, then realized that it wasn't an ailment, it was just YOU!

sigh

Can't wait to see you later so I can gush in your ear…

ME

XOXO

From: Michael Friese
[kaloogan@netscape.net]
Sent: September 7, 2005, 7:12 a.m.
To: Tammy Tyree [tyree@telus.net]
Subject: My favorite Teddy Bear!

You would never know that I am someone who suffers from a sleep disorder. Is this because of a warm, sweet, cuddly woman

187

beside me, or a result of the long, knee-weakening lovemaking sessions? I will bet the latter, but a majority of the former. You are just the cutest little thing when I roll over in the middle of the night and wrap myself around you again. Did you know that you also make little growling noises in your sleep?

You had mentioned walking with pride around town with me yesterday. Well, I am brimming over with it whenever I am with you, as well as the desire to tell everyone what a sweet and wonderful person you are underneath the blinding good looks.

I wish I was there this morning to cover you with kisses to start your day, but I am looking forward to the day when I do not have to sneak off in the morning and can linger a little longer with you before wandering off to make you breakfast in bed.

I will call you a little later to gush more sweet things in your ear and distract you from your day!

Good morning, babe! :-)

Michael ended up extending his trip home by a couple of weeks. We spent as much time together as possible, getting to know each other in a deeper way, as well as getting to know each other's children. We were creative with our intimate endeavors, finding time to just be with each other while the kids were in school, going out for a drive or a walk or just cuddling on the couch. The first time we professed our love to one another, I took the initiative. I was having trouble NOT saying it, not that I was waiting for him to do so first, just sitting with my feelings, making sure they were real, grounded and true.

"I'm totally in love with you," I finally blurted, after a particularly juicy make-out session.

"I'm in love with you too!" He grinned. We both sighed deeply. It was such a relief to jump this particular hurdle, and really, what had we been waiting for? Michael told me that he had confided in a friend that he was finding it so difficult to hold back saying "I love you." He didn't want to put any pressure on me, but as it turned out, we were both biting it back for the same reason. A few days later, Michael had to head back to work. Phone calls slowly replaced the emails, in which my girls talked to Michael too. We still sent the occasional email, however, which delighted me to no end.

From: Michael Friese
[kaloogan@netscape.net]
Sent: September 18, 2005, 6:45 p.m.
To: Tammy Tyree [tyree@telus.net]
Subject: You sexy thing, you!

Hey you, just checking my email and thought that I would drop a quick line to say

I LOVE YOU!!!!

Just in case you were unsure!
Me

From: Tammy Tyree [tyree@telus.net]
Sent: September 21, 2005, 6:11 a.m.

To: Michael Friese [kaloogan@netscape.net]
Subject: Morning baby!

Woke up at 5 this morning for some strange reason. What were you doing at 5 a.m.? Hope you slept ok after that long ride back to work. I've decided that sleeping with you is definitely better than sleeping alone — and I don't even mind the low growls and snorts from your side of the bed. Kind of miss them, actually. Rather comforting. Might have to tape you some night and run it as I'm drifting off…

　　If there is a luckier girl in the world, I'd have to meet her myself to believe it. You're the sweetest, most wonderful man there is, and I love you to pieces. Hoping you will still feel the same way about me after being away for a few weeks!

　　Have a great day, babe.

　　ME

　　XOXO

From: Michael Friese
[kaloogan@netscape.net]
Sent: September 21, 2005, 7:23 p.m.
To: Tammy Tyree [tyree@telus.net]
Subject: RE: Morning baby!

Slept in, long day. Going to nap! Call you soon.

　　Of course I will still feel the same, silly goose.

```
I LOVE YOU!!!!!!!!!!!
Sleepy now...
```

My girls were excited that Mom had Michael in her life, right from the start. They always wanted to know if he had emailed or called and got just as much delight to talk of plans as I did. Michael was a father figure they desperately needed in their life, after their own father and I had divorced years prior. My other two children lived with their dad but remained close with their siblings; however, they didn't get to spend as much time with Michael as they would have liked to. Michael often sent brief emails to my girls, as he did his own son, which delighted them to no end, and in particular Casey. As Casey grew into a young lady, the two of them developed quite a bond. The girls would enjoy Michael's wine collection, sometimes *with* Michael, and other times, sneaking a bottle – or 12 – behind his back, which they'd joke about later. Michael tried to teach Casey how to drive a standard, being as patient as he could be while she ground out the clutch on his vehicle. They teased each other and bantered endlessly when Michael would return home, and he loved every minute of it. We wouldn't know until after Michael's death how important and deep their connection truly was, and it became even deeper after his departure from this Earth.

```
From: Michael Friese
[kaloogan@netscape.net]
Sent: September 22, 2005, 5:36 p.m.
To: Tammy Tyree [tyree@telus.net]
Subject: To my girls!

Nicole and Casey:
```

I wanted to say hello and let you know I made the trip back okay, and I'm thinking of you; I have been doing this for a long time and it has never been easy to leave for work and leave my son behind. It was even harder this trip because I was leaving behind 4 people that I care about and will miss very much. The last few weeks have been wonderful getting to know you and spending so much time together. I have been missing you and think of you both often. I am looking forward to coming home more than ever and doing all the things that we will get to do as a family over the winter.

The house I'm renting here seems so quiet and empty without your voices. I would give you both a big hug if I was there. I miss you.

Please be patient with your mother, as I know she must be whining with me gone. She is sappy, in case you hadn't noticed. Write to me or call if you feel like it.

I am counting the days until I return.

Michael

From: Tammy Tyree [tyree@telus.net]
Sent: September 22, 2005, 8:20 p.m.
To: Michael Friese [kaloogan@netscape.net]
Subject: RE: To my girls!

HI MIKE! It's Casey. I love you, and by the way, mom is being sappy and driving us BANANAS!!!! Only I am writing to you today because Nicole is at dad's. I'll talk to you later, and I miss you lots. From one of your girls.

PS: I am counting the days until you return too, I MISS YOU!

XOXOXOXOXO

Having Michael in our lives was truly wonderful. All the visions I had made for the man of my dreams had come true. I believed in the Law of Attraction and had used it to manifest this wonderful man. Eventually, I shared my list of desires for the perfect partner with Michael, and he was so proud to check off the *entire* list. He would bring that list up time and time again throughout our relationship, as we moved into our future together, and our dreams became bigger and bigger.

MOVING IN

In early October 2005, Michael wrapped up his job sooner than expected and was coming home. I was so excited! On the night before leaving, his friends took him out to celebrate and say goodbye. I received quite a funny email from him that night and am including it here, exactly the way he wrote it to me.

From: Michael Friese
[kaloogan@netscape.net]
Sent: October 5, 2005, 1:06 a.m.
To: Tammy Tyree [tyree@telus.net]
Subject: hello baby

Hi there baby

I am a whee bit drunk. Sorry I did not call again tonight. I told the guys that I was leaving this weekend and they insititede they take me out for drinks and so now it is after midnight and I am reaaaaally late to call yooooou but thinking about you so I thought I woouldsay hello./ It was nice all the "we will miss you's and such but keep thinking how much I want to talk to my "baby".

Probably not making much sense right now,, bAUt really wanted to say HI

. I love you, and I MISS yOU.

Thhhhhhiiinnkinng   nasty   thought about you!

Love yo with all my heart

mICHaell

Hilarious.

Michael came home that weekend. Once he unpacked and settled into his basement suite, located right beside his mother's house, we could take up where we had left off, enjoying our time together, having him and his son over for dinners and so on. On one such occasion, the girls asked Michael when he and his son were moving in. This came as a bit of a surprise, but a delightful surprise just the same. I was planning a work-related trip in November, so I asked Michael if he could stay at the house with the girls and make sure they were ok. He heartily agreed.

I didn't end up taking that trip but moved Michael and his son into our home instead, a mere five months after we had started our "You've Got Mail" romance. Life was a wonderful new normal. There was definitely a period of change, during which Michael was at home for the winter "break up" part of the construction season. We enjoyed family time together, Michael spoiling all of the kids and me. We already knew we were heading to a bigger commitment, however, when three months into our relationship, Michael bought me a horse! Since Michael had a young horse of his own and knew of my love for horses, we made a trip with our friend Linda and found Southern Hayze. Hayze was a retired school horse; a 17 hands-high Hanoverian Warmblood, and he was perfect. He was also 16 years old, calm and patient. Just the boy I needed after having retired from consistent riding when I was a teen.

We boarded both of our horses at Linda's farm until we could secure a facility in our hometown the next year. Michael went on a rampant eBay buying spree of all things horse-related. We had more tack, blankets, saddles and bridles than any one person could use in one horse's lifetime, but that was who Mike was. "May have overdone it a little" was his catch-phrase, and it was also the truth! Sometimes to the state of overwhelm. But being back in the saddle was incredible! We would make weekend trips to Linda's to ride together, the wind in my hair and my horse's mane as we rode through endless trails, "posting" in the Australian saddle Michael bought for me (a combination of western and English – great for trails or jumping) and communicating with my horse on a deeper level. It was all so glorious.

Michael had officially spoiled me and my children. He studies my eclectic collection of jewelry, clothing and lingerie to better understand my tastes. He would also quiz the kids on their likes and dislikes and mentally note the same, then spoil us all on a whim. He enjoyed cooking for the clan and would even do laundry; I remember a particularly cute moment when Casey and I found him folding freshly-cleaned socks and underwear on the living room couch. We looked at each other and whispered in shocked surprise, "He's doing laundry?" An alien had entered our village, and it was delightful.

For our first family Christmas, the kids got lost in a sea of wrapping, tissue paper and boxes on the living room floor. Michael bought me more lingerie than I would ever end up wearing, but I certainly appreciated his efforts and happily gave him private fashion shows. He bought the girls tickets to an up-coming Avril Lavigne concert and spoiled us all with so many things. I truly thought life couldn't get any better. Being spoiled was so much fun! We were slowly integrating and sharing our lives, joys and frustrations. It was a tricky change for me to be raising another son, one that hadn't grown up with my kids at all, and there were definitely going to be difficult times ahead once Michael returned to work in the spring, but I was hopeful everything would remain as rosy as it had been these past few months.

PROPOSAL

When Michael and I first got together and even after the first few years of our relationship, I wasn't yet ready to expose my spiritual beliefs or abilities. I felt a nagging fear of persecution at being, once again, "burned at the stake," as I had been by my Holy Roller brother throughout this lifetime, and I believed I was quite literally burned at the stake in a previous one. I couldn't quite put that infernal finger on it, but the nagging voice in the back of my head told me to keep my beliefs to myself – at least for now. I had quietly been working hard on honing my intuition and reopening my gifts and abilities that I had as a child. Intuition is a naturally occurring "sense" we have all been given, and honing in on that can be an amazing tool for you to have in your toolbox. It can, however, cause disappointment when you "know" certain things that are about to happen in your life. For instance, your mother-in-law is about to call, or the call you're getting is from your kid's school, or you get the nudge to take the right path instead of the left one, when sure enough, there is a big black bear lurking on the path not taken.

In my case, it was that Michael was about to propose. This happened in Fall 2006, about 14 months after we first started our "You've Got Mail" romance. I would have enjoyed a surprise engagement and even thought, "Oh no, no, no!" Because I knew that his proposal would be nothing "super special," and I secretly wanted romance, passion and a big deal made of the event. He was, after all, my Knight in Shining Armour! I never thought that with four kids I would be attractive to anyone else – **ever**. But Michael wanted a big family, and my kids loved him, so to him, I was a dream come true. His Happy Meal Deal with all the toys, bells and whistles included. On the day of his soon-to-be proposal, knowing what he was about to ask me, I scuttled around the kitchen, busily wiping up and looking outside at the beautiful evening and glowing moon.

"We should go for a walk!" I suddenly suggested.

Yes, that would be better. At least under the moon I could claim it was super romantic. I ran upstairs to change and bundle up, and, to my dismay, Michael followed me. Darn. As I sat on the bed pulling on warm socks, Michael kneeled down in front of me and brought the ring box out from his jeans pocket and opened it. Inside was a beautiful 2-carat citrine, with three lines of .25-carat diamonds on either side. It was breath-taking! I gasped. He knew me. He knew I wanted nothing traditional in a ring, a relationship or a wedding, and he gained a lot of points by getting the first one right. I held the ring, mesmerised by its uniqueness and sparkle, the previous thoughts of the perfect proposition vanished. Everything was, once again, rose in perfection.

The actual proposal itself, however, would quickly taint

this: "I was wondering if you would do me a favor and be my wife?"

Seriously? Do him a *favor*? I had to laugh. It was just so sweet and also so terrible. It was probably the worst proposal in proposal history, but adorable and funny as hell. Naturally, I said yes. What other choice was there, really? Refuse him with a "try harder?" No. He was clearly a boatload of nerves, perspiration dripping down his furrowed brow. To the day of his death, Michael often referred to his proposal saying, "I should have done better, could have done better." I would simply smile at him and giggle, neither agreeing nor disagreeing. The outcome remained the same. He would also say that he would marry me over and over, every day, for the rest of our lives. He was so honoured that I'd done him such an enormous "favor." I often wondered who had truly done the favor? It was completely mutual.

Michael wanted to elope to Vegas, rent a limo and have a drive-through wedding at a typical Vegas chapel, but my girls wouldn't hear of it. They wanted a real wedding, a big "to-do." They were celebrating Mom's happiness, and my kids were so in love with Michael; they just wanted the day to be spectacular and special. We appreciated their thoughts and feelings, and, as girls do, they had Momma's man wrapped around their sweet, dainty little fingers. We couldn't possibly disappoint them, and I was happy to be on their side. I had settled for an "ordinary" proposal and agreed to do Michael the "favor" of marrying him. I was ready for a grand gala in return!

WEDDING

We married on March 3, 2007, at Summerhill Pyramid Winery in Kelowna, BC, two hours away from our hometown. My very own brother Rick structurally engineered the winery's pyramid, where they aged their organic wines. It was, and still is, a beautiful Okanagan landmark. The wedding was a small and intimate affair, with only direct family members in attendance. For my side, that meant 34 people, counting siblings, nieces, nephews and my mom, my father having passed away over two years prior. My Holy Roller brother and I were on speaking terms during this period, so he and his wife and sons were in attendance. It wasn't long after our wedding that my brother either snubbed me or other members of my family once again, and we would spend another couple of years in silence. Michael quickly decided he had no patience or love for that particular brother and wanted nothing to do with him, as he had seen firsthand the distress and anxiety my brother caused me and my family. For Michael, the total of his family count took only one hand, including the thumb, so we extended the invitation to Linda, her two boys and the boy's father. Linda had been the sister Michael never had, and it wouldn't have been the same without her and her family present. With the minister and his wife, who were old family friends of my parents, we had 46 people in attendance.

I had found a lovely cream satin halter gown at my favorite clothing store, Le Château, just a couple of weeks before Michael had proposed and thought that it would make a beautiful wedding dress one day. I didn't buy it then, but I knew the day would come that I'd need one. Indeed, it did, and the day after Mike's proposal, I drove to Kelowna to see if the dress was still on the rack – and it was! For the thrice marked down price of $99! This was a double bonus, as they'd marked it down yet again since I was there earlier. I knew Michael would be proud of his thrifty fiancé. I also found two beautiful, matching sage green satin dresses with a beautiful brown and gold floral pattern for my two younger daughters, and a soft, velvety brown halter dress for my oldest daughter, all at "Attention K-Mart Shopper" prices.

For the boys – Michael, his son and my son – we rented simple beige suits and found coordinating ties with white shirts. The bucks we saved on the girls' dresses were more than made up for in the suit rentals, but it still seemed easier and less expensive than purchasing suits that the boys would surely grow out of within a few short months. My son was shorter than both Michael and his own son, but in the next two years he sprouted to a solid 6'3", taking on the Dutch genes of my family with a vengeance.

The wedding was a lot of fun, and we went as "cheap" as possible, despite the gorgeous venue, knowing we would rather spend more on a honeymoon in Vegas, which is exactly what we did. My oldest daughter, Nicole, served as both Maid-of-Honor and photographer. She had to be creative, as she was the last to walk up the aisle before me and had just enough time to grab her camera from my mother seated in the front row and snap a few pictures as I progressed down the aisle. Even though we were standing in front of our combined families, both Michael and I were incredibly nervous. This was reminiscent of the first time we had met in my home after two months of online dating. This time, however, we were making a real commitment to each other in front of our friends and family – one to last a lifetime.

The simple ceremony took place in the dining room of the winery, in front of a massive stained-glass window. A small creek ran through the room; the floor around the creek and the restaurant was made of natural stone. It was earthy, yet decadent. During the ceremony, the minister cleverly and respectfully asked for our blessing from all of our children, and he spoke of joining our two families under God's love and care. It was moving, beautiful and absolutely perfect. After the ceremony, we moved to a second dining room, where they had set up a small head table for me and Michael and several other long tables on either side of the room for our guests. We played a few silly wedding games, had some laughs, a little wine and then cut into the two cakes we had purchased from Costco the day before. We were truly "The Clampetts" with a pretty, shiny gold bow on top. Simple, unadulterated and unapologetic, yet we could pull off polished and classy when we wanted to. Perhaps a better description would be "Brady Bunch" with fewer children, but I don't believe Mr. and Mrs. Brady would get up to nearly the shenanigans we would in our life together, classy or not.

After the ceremony and reception, Michael's family drove home with his son. My children drove back with my mother, who would care for them while we were on our honeymoon. Michael and I stayed for one night at the Manteo Resort Hotel. We booked a suite on the top floor with an incredible view of the lake and a soaker tub in the bedroom next to a shower surrounded by glass walls, opposite the fluffy, comfortable bed. We took advantage of the room's amenities, but I was a little concerned that if we didn't consummate the marriage, then we wouldn't be doing so for another few months. We planned a whirlwind honeymoon in Vegas, then Michael would have to return to work immediately after our return.

Everyone knew Michael for something besides his brilliant mind; his ability to fall asleep within a few seconds of sitting down. Not laying down and closing his eyes, no. Rather, his head would bob and eyes would close within five minutes of him *sitting down*, anytime except for meals. It was partially because of his overtaxing work schedule, and partly because of years of failing to keep his health in check, too busy to concern himself with the importance of such things. Michael was a workaholic. When he was working, it would be 16-hour days and short sleeps, which he then had to make up for on his time off. This evening, I was concerned that Michael would fall asleep the moment his head hit the pillow on that fluffy honeymoon bed, crushing the rose petals and chocolate mints. I had to be creative, keeping him busy with talking and laughing, reminiscing about the ceremony and reception, all the while trying to relax and enjoy the luxurious soaker tub. He actually fell asleep for a few seconds, fully dressed, until I joined him and insisted (with a modicum of convincing) that we top off the day in our own special way. Naturally, I succeeded, and for a few minutes we had wedded bliss, then we each fell into an exhausted, shared sleep.

HONEYMOON

The next morning, we set off for Las Vegas. In the planning stages of the destination for the honeymoon, we narrowed the choices down to Mazatlan, Mexico, at an inexpensive 2-star resort on the Pacific, or Vegas. When I saw that Tom Jones had a regular gig at the MGM Grand Hotel, Vegas it was, as Tom was one of Michael's favorite singers. I bought tickets to his show, which nearly matched the entire cost of the trip, including flights. We stayed at the cheapest place we could find – Circus Circus, and if you have ever stayed there, you would agree it has maintained its circa 1970s charm! It was merely a place to rest our tourist-weary heads at the end of the evening, so looks didn't matter – Tom did.

It was worth every penny to see Michael's face light up in that theater once Tom took the stage. We sat in the second row of a plush red velvet booth with a small table between us. They served us drink after drink while the show went on. I have never been a big fan of Mr. Jones myself, but I truly enjoyed his performance that evening; in particular, when one lady threw her panties onto the stage – something that happened often, from what Michael described to me. Tom threw them back at her, however, when he saw she had not graced him with her own underwear, but a cheap pair bought earlier that day at K-Mart – the tag still attached! I asked Michael if he would consider ripping off his jockey shorts and tossing them to the purple-suited crooner. Since he appeared to be his biggest fan, this made perfect sense to me, but Michael, rather red-faced, declined.

We enjoyed several other shows that trip, including Blue Man Group and a jousting performance at the fancy hotel shaped like a castle. We did very little gambling; I could lose a 5-dollar-bill faster than the aging waitresses served drinks, so I soon gave up. Michael would get up super early, as per his usual, and spend some alone time in front of the slot machines until I joined him for breakfast at a much less vampire-like hour. We would then hit the strip, walk the usual ten miles a day, checking out the sights, sounds, musical fountains and as much free "stuff" we could find, until settling on another show or event to go see.

It was a really wonderful honeymoon and the start of an amazing lifetime of honeymoons we would take together. We agreed to take one every year, as close to our anniversary as we could. That was a pretty sweet deal, to be sure, and we would end up being the envy of all of our friends because we actually did so, every year except the one when Michael had to have his gallbladder removed and couldn't travel. Some years, we took *two* honeymoons, one in the Caribbean and one in Europe or Eastern Canada, depending on the invitation from friends, weddings to attend and so on.

Upon returning home to the Canadian cold, Michael spent less than 48 hours at home before returning to work, which, for him, was on two jobs, one on each side of our hometown, less than two hours in either direction. He left me to create a new normal for myself, my two girls who lived with us and Michael's son. The next five years would be the most trying time of our marriage, one that I don't wish to elaborate on here for its irrelevance to our romance. Suffice it to say, the pressure and strain of raising a teenager that I had not raised from childhood took its toll. I had to adapt to Michael's unique set of rules for his son, most of which I didn't agree with or practice with my own children, so two sets of rules under one roof was hardly fair and impossible to manage. We would butt heads constantly, as I argued against several of Michael's methods that were not effective ways to entice peace and cooperation from a young, stubborn, independent mind.

In our life together, I had only one regret, and that was that I should have said "no" to Michael and his son moving in so soon after we started dating. Perhaps if I had taken more time to become closer to his son, understand and observe the way he was being raised by his Ōma when Michael was away at work and the relationship between all three of them, I would have felt differently. But alas, I was far too eager to start my fairy-tale life with my Knight in Shining Armour. I was in love and wearing a rosy shade of glasses. Because of this, I never gained a proper foothold on my relationship with his son, and we never became close.

Regardless of the valleys and accompanying hills, Michael did more than his best to support us. With my encouragement and support, Michael went out on his own as an independent contractor and became the most sought after heavy civil engineering consultant in Western Canada. When he was hired as survey manager on the Anthony Henday ring road project in Edmonton, Alberta, we purchased a home there so he'd have a nicer place to live than the dive hotels he was used to. We rented the extra bedrooms to the company he contracted with for a few of their workers. I was still living in our hometown, working in finance and living in the home I had purchased after my divorce with two of my girls. We had long since renovated this home to suit our needs, and we were officially building our estate, one piece of property at a time, and celebrated our efforts. Together, we created more wealth, stability and shared dreams of what could be possible for us in the future, creating the ultimate vision for our lives. We took leaps of faith that few have the stomach for, and truly, were living the ultimate dream.

REVELATIONS

A few years and a few honeymoons later, I was finally able to crack open my spiritual beliefs to Michael. This happened after several sessions with a hypnotherapist who helped me dive deeply into my past lives. I always had a *knowing* and a belief that Michael, my children and I were meant to be together, but I ached to know more. For what purpose was I with this man? And, more importantly, why didn't I feel safe to divulge my belief in all things spiritual?

My meeting with the hypnotherapist started out as any therapy session does, with an in-depth interview about who I am, what issues I would like to resolve and so on. Once the initial one-on-one work was complete, we moved into the hypnosis session. By this time, I'd had several years of practicing self-hypnosis and was slowly working on earning my own degree as a hypnotherapist, but I wanted to work with someone who could assist me from the level of knowledge, experience and understanding that this therapist could.

The only questions on my mind were, "Why do I have such an issue with baring my soul to Michael," and, "What is the connection between myself and my three daughters?" As I settled into the comfortable chair in her office and listened to the therapist's induction, I allowed myself to let go, and the veil between my conscious and subconscious mind lifted. Then... *BOOM.* The first image came to me, with the intense clarity of where I was in space and time right at that moment. I was sitting on the dewey, mossy ground beneath me, hiding behind a very large and very old growth tree.

"What do you see?" The therapist asked.

"I'm sitting on the ground," I replied. She asked me to describe the place I was in, the clothes that I wore, the smells, sounds and every detail I could see to determine the time period and place I was in.

"I'm deep in a forest. There's moss, wet moss, and so many trees. There's hardly any light from the sun, maybe it's stormy... yes, I think there's a storm."

"What are you wearing?" She asked.

I looked down at my body. I was sitting on my buttocks in such a way that my legs were both tucked beside me, but not visible. "A dark green or black... dress or cloak..." I replied. "I can't see my feet or hands. They are hidden under the cloak. I'm tucked up against a tree... I'm... hiding..."

"Hiding from what?" She prompted.

I paused for a moment. In my mind, I expanded my view of my surroundings to include the rest of the forest beyond my seated area. There was a path in the distance. My eyes followed the path further, until I saw a man seated on a great black horse. He was wearing a cavalier hat and a doublet over a white linen shirt with a high lacy color. His breeches met with high white knee socks, and a leather riding shoe completed the ensemble. I peered closely at his face, then I gasped. *It was Michael.* This man didn't look like the Michael I knew and was married to now, but it was definitely the essence of him. His soul, in another life, another time, another body.

I sobbed.

"What is happening now?" She asked.

"It's him! It's Michael!" I sobbed again. It was complete and total understanding, a realization of my question being answered in that one brief moment.

"What is Michael doing there?" She prodded.

"He's... hunting... me..." I cried.

"Ok, you're perfectly safe. He can't hurt you," she reassured me. "Rise above that scene and float above it. What year is this? Where are you?"

"It's... 16th century. Somewhere in France in the 16th century. I can't see a year clearly," I replied.

"Good, that's good. Do you have a home you can visit now? If you do, be there *now*," she directed.

"Ok, I'm there." I began to describe what I saw. "The house is more like a cave, dug out of the edge of a small hill. There's grass growing on the roof, one small window and a wooden door. There's only one room. In it, there's a large fireplace with a... a... cauldron." I couldn't think of a better word for it, but saying it just seemed so strange, and yet, realization flowed over me. Was this the life of a witch that, as a child, I *knew* I'd had? Astounded, I continued. "There are herbs hanging from the roof rafters, drying. They're hanging over a wooden table. There's a shelf with some bottles... I can't make out what's in them. I'm a healer!" I paused, taking in my surroundings and a wonderful, peaceful feeling of *home* enveloped me like a warm blanket. "There's only a small bed in one corner and a wooden rocking chair in front of the fire. I like to sit in the chair, rock and watch the flames."

"Good, very good," the therapist replied, encouraging me to stay with the vision. "Enjoy your time there for a while longer. Get a feel for your life there, in that time, in that space. Did you help people? Can you sense what people's opinions of you were?"

I could. I saw various visions of me going from home to home, assisting with births, deaths and illnesses. I could feel a great respect from the fellow villagers, and I could feel their love and told the therapist as much.

"See if you can find a connection with your daughters during this time," she prompted. I sat in silence for a few minutes, enjoying my little home in the woods. Then, I felt the connecting lines between myself and my three daughters as they appeared. First, Nicole.

"I'm with Nicole! She's about my age, and she's a very dear friend and fellow healer. She has beautiful red curly hair, and she's a real spitball of a woman, like she is in this life! She's in childbirth, and I'm assisting!" I was giddy, excited to be with my then-friend, now-daughter, during this incredible time for her. This was years before the birth of my granddaughter in this present lifetime, but that giddy feeling followed me through the centuries and lives we lived.

"That's fantastic! You're doing so great! What about your other daughters? Do you have a sense of them in this lifetime?"

"Yes! They are also healers, but not from my village. We know of each other and are even friends, but we live in separate villages, a fair distance from one another," I replied, elated at this revelation.

"What is the purpose for you four to be together in your current lifetime?" The therapist asked, knowing this was one of the questions I had. I paused, allowing the knowledge to float through me.

"To build... power," I replied.

"Power for what purpose?" She asked.

"To show people, to make them understand that they have the power within themselves to heal," I replied. "That we are all connected, that there is no past, present or future, there just *is*." I felt an enormous peace flow through me.

"Good, very good. Remember all of what you are experiencing here. Now, let's go back to Michael. Remember, you are perfectly safe. He cannot harm you," she reassured me. "Go to where he is in that lifetime, interacting with you. Can you find a moment in time or an understanding of how the past life relates to this one?"

I was immediately drawn to a disturbing and tragic scene. I

saw myself tied to a pole in the center of our small village.
There were dry branches and sticks piled up around my feet –
I was about to be burned at the stake. I looked over the crowd
of people gathering from our village. No one was bitter or
angry toward me; I could still feel their love and respect. Any
bitterness they held was directed toward the men who had tied
me to that stake, one of them being Michael. I focused on the
connection between us, and there was one definitive one. I had
sensed it at the pathway at the beginning of the vision. *He
knew I was hiding behind the tree, and he chose to ignore me*!
He turned his horse around and shouted, "There's no one
here!" He *wasn't* the man that eventually found me and
brought me to the pire. At the pire, he hovered in the background, not assisting but also knowing he wasn't able to put a
stop to what was about to happen. He was only following
orders from... *MY BROTHER.*

I gasped audibly and started to sob again. The therapist
asked me to share what I was witnessing at that moment. It
took a while for me to describe the scene to her and the realization that Michael was an unwilling participant in my demise.
But, *my brother*... his role in that life was short but hauntingly
similar to the life I had with him now. He was the fire and the
brimstone then, and he would be again, in another life and
another time, with me. The one I am living now. Wanting to
relieve me of my emotional upset, the therapist brought me
out of hypnosis without making me watch as they burned me
at the stake. It wasn't necessary for me to live through that
again. I knew what happened, when and how, and the questions I had coming into the session had been answered.

Flood after flood of understanding washed through me. In
this life, Michael was with me to protect and love me, the
opposite role he played in the life where he was partly responsible for my death but could do nothing about it. Past lives and
interactions between people in our soul groups are often the

yin and yang of experience. What I couldn't fathom at that time, and even now, are whatever lessons my brother and I have to learn and how to prevent our history from further repeating itself.

I went home from my session and waited for Michael to arrive. Once we had settled in for the evening, I told him I really needed to share my experience that day. I took a deep breath... then let it spill. I told him about my experiences as a child, as well as the *knowing* that we'd had a previous connection sometime, somehow, and what the hypnosis session revealed. Michael gave me the benefit of his rapt attention. He listened in silence, at times stroking my arm or thigh, encouraging me to go on amidst my tears. He shared neither a belief nor dis-belief in what I had to say, only held space for me and respected my experience. He didn't get up and leave or try to "burn me at the stake," and for that, I was truly grateful.

In the months and years following, I was pleasantly surprised at his encouragement to continue my spiritual growth. He persuaded me to obtain my Reiki Master certification, something I had been hoping to do for some time, and to set up a small office in our home where I could take clients. He was also supportive and encouraging when it came time to finish my degree in hypnotherapy, and I was relieved and grateful for his love and support, which lasted the remainder of our marriage. In fact, we supported each other in the best ways possible. As I wrote this chapter, I looked back in my journals and found this note from Michael, given to me about a year into our marriage. It is one of several that I received from Michael over our life together, and it sums up our success and our feelings for one another beautifully:

I love you, my wife, with all of my heart. You are my foundation. Everything I achieve is because of your support. You calm me when I am tormented, and your faith gives me strength and courage. No other could ever mean as much to me. I base every goal I have on rewarding you with happiness. For the rest of my days, my first and last thought each day will be of you. I would marry you a thousand times over and still have a thousand more "I do's" waiting on my lips. If I achieved no more in my life, I would be a success from your love alone!

Little did we know that only 11 years and 362 days after our lovely, inexpensive family wedding, our dreams would come to a crashing, Earth-shattering, iron-bending halt in a way that was too unreal to fathom.

CHAPTER 8

Belize

March 2009 - February 2019, Belize

The annual honeymoon planning was usually left up to me, as Michael's work schedule left him very little time to plan such things. I would provide him with a few options, ensuring there was always a cheap option, middle ground and over-the-top. Michael's preference would gradually shift from cheap to over-the-top as the years progressed. Our honeymoon trips, precluding our first trip to Belize, were Mazatlan and Newfoundland. Then after our first and subsequently several trips to Belize, the travel was interspersed with trips to Portugal, Cuba, Palm Springs and Cancun. But the majority of our honeymoons were in Belize. Traveling there was a lifelong desire of Michael's, so for our first trip, we booked three weeks to do it right.

It was a long time for me to be away from my girls, and that was incredibly difficult; having their grandmother (my mom) "babysit" them was tasking on the pre-teen and teen. I kept in contact with them as much as possible, using the limited wifi available on Caye Caulker, the small touristy island off the west coast of Belize. The world's second largest barrier reef skims the entire length of the country, only 43-miles off the coast. The humidity, turquoise blue waters and salty air was a wonderful change from the bitter cold of the Canadian winter. After a week, my facial pores opened and purged their contents, as tiny whiteheads formed over my entire face, and the copious amounts of freshly-squeezed fruit juices (watermelon being my favorite) we consumed on a daily basis cleansed me from head to toe, inside and out.

We were on Caye Caulker for a week before we met with a group of our friends there, Linda and her boyfriend being two of them. We rented a 3-bedroom apartment above a building supply store large enough to house three couples for two weeks. It had everything we needed to make our daily dose of pina coladas and guacamole with the only avocados we could find on the island – black market ones smuggled in by a guy from Mexico, risking a visit to Hattieville Prison as he did so, as avocados were out of season in Belize at that time, and importing food goods was illegal! We had a standing order with the local avocado smuggler to buy everything he had at the equivalent to .25 cents US per avocado, so we were never without a good guacamole.

Michael and I decided to take a couple inland trips during our stay, so we had Jan, the lady who owned the apartment we were staying in, arrange transportation for us on the mainland. We were decidedly NOT tour bus folks, having spent some time on one during our trip to Mazatlan the year before. Once was enough, thank-you-very-much! Jan had just the guy – Solano, a registered tour guide who was ready and waiting for us and a couple of our friends as we disembarked the island hopper ferry in Belize City. Solano took us inland on two occasions. The first, to take a river boat tour to Lamanai, an incredible Mayan ruin in the Orange Walk District of Belize. The tour was absolutely epic, and once I had experienced one ruin, I knew I wanted to experience them all. There was just something about the vibration of the place, roaming the acres and acres of ruins, walking on them, around them and into them, imagining what life would have been like for the Mayans centuries ago. On this particular site, survey markers could be found almost everywhere, which pleased Michael greatly, surveying being his career. It became a game of who could find the markers first, and I always won, which drove him nuts. We took picture after picture of the ruins, the markers and each other. It was an incredible visit.

For our next trip to the mainland, we went for a river tube ride and a visit to a zoo. The river ride was slow, lazy and relaxed, sitting in large black inner tubes, floating through a couple of cave systems along the way, always directed by Solano. The zoo was and still is not a zoo at all, but a rescue for animals illegally held in captivity or injured by vehicles or hunters. The cages really weren't cages at all, but rather, loose fencing around large chunks of natural jungle, ones that the animals could actually crawl out of if they felt so inclined. The only completely secure fencing was for the birds that needed to remain in captivity and the jaguars, for obvious reasons. After this trip inland, we nurtured a desire to see the entire country. Possibly, this would be an amazing place to retire, so we made a plan to come back next year.

The next year was the only honeymoon-free year in our life together. Instead, Michael went in for surgery to have his gallbladder removed and spent the remainder of the year in a blur of work projects. So we made the trip back to Belize in 2011, again for three weeks. And again, it was difficult to leave my girls at home with my mom, and I know they weren't too happy about it either. They were both in their teens now and very likely capable of handling themselves for three weeks, but

I worried, so my mom agreed to stay. On this trip, we toured the entire little postage-stamp-size of a country from top to bottom, ending our trip in Caye Caulker. From there, we embarked on a 3-day sailing trip with Raggamuffin Tours to a handful of the tiny islands scattering the coast of Belize. We did a ton of snorkeling, fishing, drinking Rum Punch and sun-bathing until Michael was a lovely shade of lobster.

Most people we meet assume Belize IS an island; however, there are actually 300 small islands dotting the coast of Belize, and most visitors stay on Ambergris Caye, never making a trip to the mainland. For our trip inland this time, we rented a small car, which turned out to be a rather large mistake, as some (okay, almost all) of the off-highway roads were tragically in disrepair and potholed. The car – an Indian-made equivalent to a Ford Fiesta – was like packing two large circus clowns into a flimsy tin can. We had to call the rental company to replace the vehicle when we made it to Punta Gorda, the furthest south we had planned to travel. They did so, and within a few short hours, we had another small vehicle to use and abuse. We never rented anything larger on that trip, being mindful of our budget and still playing the mad savers game.

The landscape further into Belize is so lush and inviting, nothing like the Savannah you see as you get closer to the coastline. We went almost as far as the Guatemalan border and stayed one night in a newer "expat" development off a very beaten track. As we traveled the Hummingbird Highway towards Hopkins, we knew it was here that we wanted to retire and started making plans. The landscape along the summit of the Hummingbird Highway reminded us of our hometown in Canada. Lush, tropical mountains surrounded us like a humid hug. It was a scene right out of Jurassic Park, and if a giant T-Rex had stepped out from the trees onto the road, I wouldn't have been surprised. This area was so much like home, but whenever I looked closely at the trees and realized that they were all palms and *not* fir, pine or cedar, I felt an incredible rush. The beauty of the landscape in that area was absolutely breathtaking.

The next year, we traveled back to Belize to start property shopping. There, we met with a Canadian ReMax Realtor named Wanda who had moved to Belize a few years previously. She showed us several properties in the Southern District, one we were particularly fond of, as it boasted its own natural hot pools. The criteria was running water through the property and at least 20-30 acres. On this same trip, we decided to venture out on our own, sans Wanda, and take a look at some properties we had seen posted on other realty sites and private listings. One 30-acre piece boasted a full 500-feet of riverfront, so we decided to locate that property and hike around a bit. When we arrived, we parked the rental car and entered the property through a gated, overgrown driveway. We were immediately met by a small, machete-wielding Belizean who came out of the bushes from the right side of the property.

Startled and unsure of our next steps, Michael introduced us as people who were interested in purchasing the land. This revelation altered the demeanor of our new friend, and he introduced himself as "Manuel," a born-and-bred-Mayan-Belizean, and offered to give us a tour. He lived with his family on the property next door, which was owned by a Texan doctor with the same name as my husband. The doctor and his wife only came to the property two months out of the year, their cabana on the highest hill with no electricity, but it pumped water straight from the cool, clean river.

This particular piece of property was called "Three Hills," as the landscape flowed up one hill, down the other, up another hill, down and up and down to the river on the far side. It was lush, full of "jungle" and, according to our tour guide, hadn't been "chopped" for at least two years. Once we made our way through the property, machete-wielding

Manuel chopping a path for us ahead, we found the river and followed it to the adjacent property. There was a vast difference between the un-chopped land and the very well-kept 30-acres of which Manuel was the proud caretaker. There was no "jungle," just large, beautiful trees and tightly-trimmed grasses throughout.

We met Manuel's lovely wife Petrona and their three children at our tour's end. Manuel, seeing that we "gringos" were quite thirsty on this incredibly humid day, clamored up the nearest coconut tree and chopped a couple of ripe coconuts for us. He then slid down the tree and – using the same machete he used for all of his grass cutting, jungle chopping and coconut gathering – chopped a hole at the top of each coconut large enough for us to drink from and carved a spoon for us to scoop the coconut meat once the drink was done. We were in absolute awe of his time-honored skills with a knife that was, frankly, half his size.

Michael and Manuel

New friendship forged, Manuel and Michael exchanged cell phone numbers and promised to keep in touch. Manuel, in his broken English, expressed great excitement for us to purchase the parcel next door and become their neighbor. This family, who lived very simply in a slat board, slapped-together home with a thin thatch roof and dirt floor, were the epitome of the Belizean people. They were very happy living simply and very welcoming. Petrona proudly showed me the interior of their home. The walls were sheets, ropes tied at two corners and hung from the rafters. Each person had a hammock for a bed, with the exception of their youngest – the 3-year-old slept with Mama on hers. There were simple shelves for their clothing, cleaned in the very river we had walked along, beaten on the large river rocks and hung on rope lines to dry in the sun beside the house.

Petrona excitedly showed me her prized possession, a natural gas cookstove, dirty from overflowing pots of rice and beans, but it was a step up from the usual clay and fire cook-stoves most of their fellow villagers still utilized. A propane truck made its regular weekly runs through the village, stopping to fill the 25-pound tank her stove ran on. The children had no toys, other than the ones their father made out of wood. I made a note to purchase backpacks for the children when I got back to Canada and to fill them with school supplies, toys and games for our next visit. We left Belize with hopeful hearts. Wanda kept us abreast of any new listings, and we added them to a growing file of "potentials" to see on our next trips.

In 2014, we made our way back to Belize for more property shopping. Michael had been in touch with Wanda and other realtors in the area and had a rather large list of properties he wanted to narrow down before my arrival, so he left five days before me. He met up with our friend Linda, and they celebrated their birthdays (only days apart) together. I arrived on Michael's actual birthday, and that very day we hired a guide and, with Linda, took the Monkey River tour from Monkey River Town to a howler monkey sanctuary. Along the beautiful, winding Monkey River, the tour guide pointed out birds, turtles and the occasional small crocodile sunning themselves along the shore or on a fallen tree. He stopped the boat and allowed Linda and I a few minutes to cool off with a swim, minding the location of the crocodiles looming just off shore. When the crocs slid off the muddy river bank and dove underwater, it was time for us to get the hell out and leave the area.

We parked and hiked into the sanctuary, where many howler monkey troupes lived. It was spectacular, seeing the small black monkeys in their natural habitat, loving on their babies and jumping from tree to tree. They were quite used to seeing humans below, so they didn't pay us much mind. Our guide made grunting and howling noises, which riled up the males and got them all howling, a practice the tour guide community is no longer permitted to do. We then spent the next few days being tourists, cave tubing, hiking and so on. Along the way, Michael showed us one particular piece of property that he had seen the week prior. He thought it was the most appealing and was sure I would agree. I definitely did. It had 13 acres on one side of a rather wide river and eight on the other; plenty of land to build on and grow tropical fruit. We made plans to meet with the selling realtor and set about purchasing our Belizean Dream.

We would go on a total of 13 "honeymoons" and were heading to our 14th when the Universe skewed our plans. We usually went in March, but for a couple of years, we managed to fit in an extra trip and call it another honeymoon. It was really all Michael's idea. The theme of his life seemed to be spoiling me, and, like I said, who was I to argue? He felt so honored that I did him a "favor" and married him, and he continually celebrated the fact that I said yes. Our marriage was what a really good marriage should look like. Even though we spent a majority of our time apart, Michael worked away from home (maybe that is truly the secret sauce to a good marriage). We made our time together a priority and celebrated throughout the year. Michael didn't get the drive-through-chapel Vegas wedding he was hoping for, but we did make a pact to renew our vows in the drive-through on one of the anniversary trips we would surely make to Las Vegas in the years to come.

BUILDING

In January 2016, the honeymoons changed from traveling *away* from our home in Canada, to traveling *to* our property in Belize, which was exciting in itself, but not as much as being on a "real" honeymoon would have been. The bloom was falling, petal by lustrous petal off the rose, only to be replaced with a new, lovely tropical flower, full of promise and fulfillment (at least for Michael) for a well-earned retirement in the years to come. I began to feel more and more like Michael's assistant, helping him build his dream while trying to figure out where my own life fit into it, unsure of anything but taking one step after another, blindly following his lead and waiting for a universal sign. We made plans to build a "healing hut," which he jokingly referred to as my "witch's house" – a nod to the past life I had shared with him and was now free to talk or laugh about. I absolutely loved that he accepted me for both who I was then, and who I'd become in this current lifetime. I welcomed his ideas about my witch's house, wanting to build it as close to my past life vision as possible, but with river stone walls and more windows!

We planned on building several other cabanas on the property, one for each of our children that I could rent out when the kids weren't visiting, and an area on the property for yoga, meditation, swimming and so on – perfect for hosting retreats. We were trying to plan ways for my life and work to integrate in Belize, despite the tug on my heart to stay rooted in Canada. I could see the potential with staying on the property, but not clearly. There was just something "amiss," like I was waiting for the proverbial shoe to drop. I tried to find a balance between life in Belize and life in Canada, but the pull toward my life path on Canadian soil was far greater. Universal knowledge had given me clues as to what my future held; I just had to be patient enough to let things unfold.

VISIONS

Having "come out of the spiritual closet" with Michael several years prior to all this, I worked hard to complete my Reiki Master training and was mentored by two particularly gifted healers in my hometown. Their sessions were much like mine are now, being both a channel and conduit of healing for my clients. My mentors, however, were able to channel messages for their clients from the other side. This was something I had not yet accomplished, my connection with Source not yet as deep as I knew it could be. I attended my first private session with one of these women, Michelle, which was particularly illuminating – a complete foreshadowing of my life without Michael in it. Michelle and I were merely acquaintances, me having attended her meditation class series, and our discussions were always around the work, not our personal lives. She had never met Michael and wasn't privy to any aspect of our life together. This made it even more fascinating. My late father came into the session and explained how powerful I truly was, that I had a mission in my own life to complete and no walls could be placed in my path. He said I had one foot in Canada, and one in Belize, but I would be back in Canada in due time.

Michelle wrote over nine pages of messages from my father and the other side, and they are safely tucked in my journals, which I re-read from time to time. My journals are shockingly full of tidbits of the visions I had for my future during meditations and spiritual journeys. I saw a future on my own without

Michael. I saw travel and teaching others. I also had a great sense of being financially secure, independent, happy and free. I also started dreaming of life without Michael in it. I didn't know then if that meant that we would separate or if he would pass on, but I shared my visions with him and my yearning for doing the healing work that I felt drawn to do, work that couldn't necessarily be done while living in Belize.

Michael understood and honored my feelings. We discussed renting an apartment for me in Canada when I felt the time was right, living in Canada full-time and visiting him every few months. He was determined to stay in Belize, and I was determined not to. We were also determined *not* to divorce. This just wasn't an option for either of us, despite potentially facing a long-distance relationship. The most difficult part for me was the separation from my children. I felt so compelled to keep them close that the thought of living full-time in another country and away from them truly devastated me. In many ways, the echoes of my past life regression session haunted me. It was important to maintain the connection with my children and "to build power," as I had revealed, but I felt less so when thinking about living separate from Michael. My heart held its priorities in place.

JOE

As we continued to build our estate, Michael hired a local contractor to clear the copious amounts of scrub bush from the property, which he did prior to our arrival, sending updated pictures throughout the process. He had his dozer-operator push the brush into four long rows to be burned in the dry season. The land turned from a sage green hue to one of earthy, rich red. The soil in Belize is full of clay – the good kind – the kind I knew I could wear on my face or even soak in a tub full of the stuff. Not that I was planning on doing either.

More likely, I would attempt to make pottery from the red mud one day in the future, just as the Mayans did in the past. Our property was located on lush, fertile soil, the kind where even a whisper of a seed lodged in a crack of clay would flourish. One such seed from a Ceiba tree had done just that, and Michael was delighted that the contractor avoided dozing over the 20-foot fella. The Ceiba tree is also known as the "Tree of Life," and this became Michael's pride and joy on the property because it was something the land had *given us*, not something that was later planted by our own hands.

Our contractor had done an incredible job but advised us against leaving the property unattended. It was time to hire someone to stay on full-time. He couldn't suggest anyone that he knew to be trustworthy and available, but he warned us not to hire a "Caribbean" or anyone other than a Mayan, as they proved to be the most loyal and hardest workers. We immediately thought of Manuel, the Mayan-Belizean that we had met four years earlier and kept in contact with, so we went south to chat with him and his wife. Manuel's caretaking abilities were exceptional, and the property he lived on was still tidy and trimmed. It would have been marvelous if Manuel and his wife could be persuaded to leave their current residence and job to work for us! This, however, would not be the case, as Manuel was very devoted to his current employer, and, as we found out, was raised in the village on that very same property where they lived, so he wouldn't dream of leaving it.

He did, however, know of someone who would be available, and that was his own brother, Jose. Jose and his family lived in Ontario Village, toward the east side of Belize, closer to San Ignacio. Manuel wouldn't attest to his brother's character or work habits – he said that would be for us to decide – but he connected us with Jose and off we went to meet up with him, get to know him and show him the property. We were hesitant to hire Jose, as Manuel refused to provide a positive reference, but we needed someone on the property and we needed him *now,* so we were willing to take a few risks.

As it turned out, our meeting with Jose – "Joe" – went well. His job working as caretaker for the Ontario Village school was coming to the end of its contract, and he was anxious to find more work. He did a fine job of convincing us that he was the right person to caretake our property and seemed to get along well with Michael right from the start. There was no time to obtain references for our potential employee, and this wasn't a usual practice in Belize anyways, so Michael said he would give him a 3-month trial period. Joe wasn't exactly sure what that meant, but he was determined to make us proud and protect the property with his very life, should it come to that. We conceded and made arrangements for lumber and supplies to be delivered to the property so Joe could build a home for himself, his wife Amanda and their three boys. The materials would arrive in a shipping container we had also purchased as a storage space. This 40-foot sea can would also be Joe's home for the duration of his building their new family home, the rest of the family to join him after the home was built.

Michael and Joe walking the property.

There was an unlimited fresh water supply in the river running through the property, and we bought him enough supplies to "camp" in the sea can for what would likely be three months before his home was complete. He was provided a saw, nails, hammer and any other tool that didn't require electricity to run it. This was, however, what Joe was used to, so there was no complaining, only gratitude in spades. Joe was all set to move onto the property the next day and excited to start his new adventure. The next morning, we were scheduled to leave Belize and travel to Cancun for our "real" honeymoon. Michael left the cabana we were staying at in Sleeping Giant Rainforest Lodge at 5:30 a.m. to go to Ontario Village, pick up Joe and take him out to our property to await the arrival of the sea can full of materials to build his home. Michael came back to the lodge a couple hours later to pick me up at our prearranged time and explained that he had NOT picked up Joe, but he had to deal with the delivery of the sea can himself.

"What happened?" I asked. "Where's Joe?"

"He's in jail," Michael answered, clearly upset.

"*WHAT*? What happened?" I was astonished. This was a freaking nightmare! We were due at the airport in a few hours, and our caretaker had done God-knows-what to land himself in the clink. Were we wrong about him all along?

"He and his brother-in-law got into some sort of fight last night, and Joe chopped him." I was horrified. "Chopping" someone meant that he had taken a machete and cut his foe, causing injury... or worse.

Oh my God. "How bad is it?" I asked.

"The brother-in-law is in the hospital, and Joe was taken away by police. He's been in jail all night. We have to go pick up Amanda and the boys and take them to the station to sort this out." Michael could be a patient man, but he had a defined set of limits, which had now been reached.

We made the half-hour trip to gather Joe's family and find out what had happened. We got a little more of the story from Amanda on the drive from Ontario Village into Belmopan, where Joe was being held at the local police station. Amanda's sister was also in tow, as she was a witness to the altercation between their brother and Joe the evening before. Amanda was very hesitant to give the whole story to "Mr. Mike" for the simple fact that he was, first, a man, and second, Joe's new boss. She was afraid of what Mr. Mike might do to Joe, and Joe desperately needed his new job.

We parked and walked a short distance to the station. I took Amanda and her sister aside, away from "Mr. Mike," and got better details of the story. Their brother was known to cause the family a lot of issues, starting with Joe and Amanda getting together in the first place. Joe was Mayan, and Amanda a "Caribe" or "Creole." The blending of two heritages in Belize could produce just as much animosity and prejudice there as anywhere else in the world by closed-minded, non-loving adults. They also explained their brother was an alcoholic and worked as little as possible, living up to the "lazy" reputation handed to many of the Creole nation in that small country. Their own mother wouldn't condone the relationship, and our construction contractor had warned us against hiring "that kind" just a few weeks earlier. The prejudice was rampant; whether it was deserved or not was debatable.

Amanda's brother had threatened to "chop" their baby boy if Joe didn't produce his half of the money Joe had gotten from Mr. Mike for half of a shared lawnmower. The lawnmower was utilized by both Joe and Amanda's brother for earning additional money cutting people's lawns. Joe intended on taking the lawnmower to the new property in order to keep some of the weeds at bay while he was building their home, so he asked Mr. Mike to purchase half. Joe hadn't yet had the opportunity to pay Amanda's brother his half before he showed up at their home in a drunken stupor, wielding a machete and demanding his money. Joe jumped to the defense of Amanda, the baby and his boys and "chopped" his brother-in-law, cutting into his shoulder. The brother went to the local clinic to get stitches and called the police on Joe.

Joe was taken to the Belmopan police station for questioning, but I feared with the judiciary system not exactly organized or trustworthy that he could potentially spend weeks in jail before ever going in front of a judge. I relayed the ladies' story to Michael, and we stepped inside the station. Being white and female, I was given immediate attention, while Michael stepped back, crossed his arms and observed. The policeman I spoke to was cordial and accommodating. He told us that Joe was not being charged, just questioned, but couldn't say when. I explained that he was our employee and was required to be on our property within the next hour, as we still had a flight booked and scheduled to leave Belize City soon, and we still had to drive the hour to the airport, return our rental truck and get through security.

For a moment, I thought we would have to "sweeten" the

deal in order for us to have him released, but instead the officer in charge escalated our case and assured us Joe would be set free within the hour. Satisfied with his response, I checked in with Amanda and her sister to let them know what was happening. I asked if they would like to bring their brother up on charges. Both ladies were taken aback by this, not even realizing that this was an option for them. They just assumed that because he was their brother and because he was a man, they would have no choice but to continue to live with his abuse. Amanda admitted that she wanted nothing more than to leave their village and start a new life, far away from her brother. Even though our property was only an hour from their village, they would be well enough out of sight and out of her brother's grasp. I walked back into the police station and spoke to the officer in charge once more. I described the victimization that Joe's wife and sister-in-law had endured from their own brother and said they had decided to press charges. He explained that in order to do so, I would have to take them to the police station nearest their district, which, as it turned out, was just outside of Belmopan – thankfully, not quite as far as their village.

Time was running short, but since we had to wait for Joe's release, we thought we should help the ladies out. We all piled back into our rental truck and set off for another police station, not even ten minutes away. Once we arrived, Michael stepped even further back, lit his "thinking stick" and waited for his advocate wife to state the ladies' case. Once I had explained the circumstances to the female chief of that particular station, she led Amanda into her office and her sister to another officer's desk to take their statements. In rapid-fire Creole, Amanda and her sister explained the events of the night before, while Michael and I waited outside.

Michael wasn't saying much, just lighting cigarette after cigarette, as he did when he was under pressure. We would potentially have to cancel our flight and our stay at our luxurious 5-star resort, and we most definitely did NOT want to do that. Due to the short cancellation notice, we would be charged in-full for the trip. With silent prayers, we waited for the girls to finish their statements and clamor back into the truck. Michael noticed a familiar lawnmower just inside the police station and asked who the owner was. When he found out that it was Joe's and had been confiscated after his arrest, he explained that he was now half owner of the lawnmower and should be able to take it. The police chief refused, stating that Joe would have to claim it himself. We decided to leave it and let Joe deal with it once he was out of jail.

Amanda asked if we could drive them back to Ontario Village, but I had a better idea. I just couldn't let them stay there, knowing their brother could be out of the hospital and, potentially, now posing a larger threat. They would have to pack up and move their things to our property three months earlier than anticipated, and with her sister and sister's child as well. I explained my fears to the police chief and asked her to assign an escort to the ladies, watch them as they packed their belongings and then put them on a bus heading to our property. Incredibly, she agreed. I knew without a doubt that had Amanda requested the same treatment from the chief, she would not have been granted the courtesy. Being a "gringo" in this foreign land garnered much in the way of respect that the locals could not.

We said goodbye to Amanda, the kids and her sister, then back to Belmopan police station we went. Joe had not yet been released, but they assured us he would be within the next hour or two; we had no choice but to head to the airport. Michael was very silent on that hour-long drive. His potentially damaging decision to hire someone he didn't yet know that he could trust was eating away at him. Once we arrived at the airport and were awaiting our turn at the security line, my cell phone rang. It was Joe! He had been released and was on his way to pick up his lawnmower and travel by bus to the property. Hurrah! He spoke to Mr. Mike about the events of the previous evening, his honesty, admission and apologetic nature easing Michael's angst. He promised to keep in touch daily while we were in Cancun. The sea can was set to arrive in a few days, and Joe would have to be present to receive it. Joe and Michael kept in touch with daily phone calls while we took a much needed break on the beach in Cancun.

In June of that same year, Michael traveled back to Belize for a week in order to purchase and plant our orchard of trees on the property, just before the rainy season arrived – the optimal time for planting. He had gotten to know a local Mennonite tree farmer and purchased the bulk of our citrus, coconut, mango and nut trees there. He also planted a copious amount of starter seeds for Joe to maintain, and they built a make-shift greenhouse near Joe's newly-completed home. Joe's home was very plain; no electricity, no stove, fridge or toilet, and the interior walls and ceiling of the home were unfinished. The 20x30-foot home was divided into three rooms: one bedroom for Joe, Amanda and the baby, one bedroom for the two older boys and a main area of the house with a hand-built picnic table for the boys to do school work in the evenings.

Joe built doors and windows (no glass) that could be padlocked from the inside or out – security being a number one priority for all homeowners. When the house was closed up, you could barely tell where the walls ended and the doors or windows began. He built everything out of the siding Michael had provided. The only gaps were between the outside walls and the roof; easy access for bats, lizards and bugs, but not human intruders. Joe dug a hole a short distance behind the house and built an outhouse around it. They cooked over a handmade clay fire ring, also outside the home.

Like most Belizeans, they never had the luxury of a fridge or a stove, and they didn't miss what they never knew. Michael was rather impressed at Joe's carpentry skills and felt even more assured that he had hired the right fella, despite the one-off visit to the local jail.

In October, we both went back to Belize to plant even more trees before the rainy season ended. As we only had a week, Joe was left with the job of planting, using a map Michael drew for him. In January 2017, Michael and I got to see Belize through fresh eyes with friends who were visiting the country for the first time. We took them to so many places in ten days our heads spun. It was lovely to show them "our" Belize, and we enjoyed many adventures and explorations together. After our friends flew back to Canada, we went to visit Plett's Builders to discuss cabana plans. We thought it made the most sense for our first cabana to be built offsite and delivered, ready for our imminent arrival the next year.

CABANA

Plett's are the largest "done-for-you" Mennonite home builder in Belize, and they also have the best reputation. We looked at several plans and buildings that were already under construction before settling on a 2-bedroom, 1-bathroom cabana that was 20x30-feet, with wood siding from local trees and a door to a large deck off the master bedroom side. Interior finishes were limited to electrical placement and thin wood paneling (inexpensive) or drywall (very expensive). We opted for an unfinished interior with dividing walls and electrical in place. Since I had experience building and renovating homes with my father, I would handle the installation of the drywall over R-11 insulation; something to keep the cool in and the heat out. Once we had agreed on the plans and put down a deposit, we met with our local contractor to go over plans for an external wash house.

Because the cabana would be delivered with the interior unfinished and would take us some time to complete ourselves, we needed a place to shower, wash dishes, do laundry and – of course – a toilet. Plett's would deliver the cabana to a predetermined location and place it on several large wooden posts, so the cabana would sit 9-feet off the ground, and we would set up a make-shift camping kitchen underneath, as well as a small nursery for the young plants we were growing. Having an open-air, shaded space under the cabana served several purposes and is common building practice in the Caribbean, providing shade from the heat, a place for hanging clothes to dry in the rainy season and so forth. Most homes were only 4 to 5-feet off the ground, but ours would be an impressive 9-feet, giving us a bird's-eye view of the valley we were settling in.

Our previous trips to Belize meant staying in various hotels, but by the next year, we would no longer need to stay anywhere but our own cabana. We were absolutely giddy about this as we headed back to Canada. Two months later, we returned to Belize to inspect the new, long driveway, turn-around, and the start of the wash house construction. Michael hired a drone photographer to take several shots and video of the property in this early stage, and he planned on doing so every year afterward. Seeing the progress was incredible; something to show friends and family back in Canada. During that trip, we celebrated our 10th wedding anniversary at the Sleeping Giant Rainforest Lodge. The manager of the resort had become a good friend of ours, as we had stayed there several times, and he created a truly magical evening for us that included dining on the palapa in the center of the pool, as well as rose petals, champagne and chocolate-covered strawberries in our room.

In May 2017, we first went to Cancun for our honeymoon break, but Michael, apologetically, left me at the resort and flew to Belize to take care of the delivery of the cabana. He just couldn't enjoy his vacation in Cancun knowing the cabana was on its way. It took Plett's about three hours to move the cabana from their location in Spanish Lookout to our location in St. Margaret's Village, with a very special truck equipped with a scissor lift so they could lift the "double-wide" load over the single lane bridges that scattered the Hummingbird Highway leading to our property. Once there, they set to work digging holes for the large support posts, driving the truck between the posts, scissors and cabana held high, and placed the cabana precisely on the 17 posts that supported it. Michael took some video of the process. Upon watching the footage, I was happy I wasn't there to attend; the entire thing looked so incredibly sketchy and difficult, and I wouldn't have been able to watch for fear of the entire house falling! The process of digging and cementing the supports and securing the building to them took only two more hours, an incredible feat!

NEW HOME

By Fall, we were officially semi-retired from our careers and ready to leave the cold north for the sunny warmth of Belize during the winter months. In November, we said goodbye to the kids and headed south for six months, preparing to complete the cabana interior and set up our new winter home. By this time, all of our children were living on their own, with the exception of my youngest daughter Carrie, who was still living with her father and finishing high school. During this winter, I managed to finish the entire interior, insulating, drywalling, taping and mudding each room and tiling the bathroom floor to ceiling. I called on Michael to help only when I had a particularly large piece of drywall to hang high.

Having him help quickly proved to be more of a hindrance, so I was happy to attempt it all on my own. He had never hung drywall before, and it would take longer to explain how than it was worth. He would get frustrated so quickly, partly because he didn't know what he was doing, and partly because outside tasks were calling to him.

I tackled it all on my own, opting to have him help me out later when it was time to sand the drywall tape. I was alone with my own frustrations. The drywalling and bathroom tiling task was incredibly difficult, and I would get so mad at the sweat pouring down my face, arms and hands, losing grip on the sheets of drywall, my eyes stinging with the saltiness. Drinking copious amounts of water and carrying a towel around my neck wasn't entirely helpful. I normally enjoyed the hot weather, but this was beyond ridiculous. How I was planning to cope with being there full-time was impossible to think about.

On top of this, several small things and a few rather large things about our relationship had started to eat away at me. The more time we spent together working on the property, the more distant we became. I craved nature and I missed physical activity. Cycling along the Hummingbird Highway was far too dangerous, and the nearest gym was 30 minutes away; hardly practical. Hiking was a wonderful outing for me, but again, a bit too dangerous to attempt on my own. Michael's idea of hiking or exercise was completely opposite to mine, and if he ever stepped foot in a gym, that would have been a day for the record books. I wanted to remain strong, fit and healthy, but my partner wasn't on the same page.

Truthfully, and in retrospect, Michael's health had been slowly failing the past few years of our life together. As hard as I tried to get him to turn it around, he wouldn't listen to me. He wouldn't drink water, would smoke and eat too much, and it was all contributing to the slow decline of his health and our intimacy. Our sex life had become non-existent. That part had ended over a year before his Earthly departure, due to his physical limitations and toxic cocktails of pain medications he took on a daily basis, his lifelong workaholic tendencies having taken a toll on his body. That certainly applied more pressure on my decision whether to stay in Belize or move myself back to Canada.

Non-existent sex life aside, Mike was an incredibly supportive person, but when I would want to talk about a particularly exciting spiritual experience I'd had or distance healing or hypnotherapy session with a cient, I would only receive a simple nod or "uh-huh" in response. Other than that, he showed no real interest. For him, life was about the end result – retiring on the property. He was happy to let me delve into my own interests, as long as he could have his, which was planning and executing his property plans. We had reached the point of companionship in our relationship. The honeymoons were finally over.

THE CANARY

In Spring 2018, we welcomed the delivery of our 40-foot sea can, shipped from Canada weeks before and containing Michael's mini-excavator, copious mechanical building tools and the majority of our personal belongings. This marked the switch from Canada to Belize being "home." We stored the rest of our belongings in Canada in a single storage unit and rented out both of our houses. The day our shipping container arrived from Canada was monumental for Michael, as he was working on the property and house with limited tools and supplies. The ship was ten days late, being held up in shipping traffic in the Panama Canal, which was more than mildly frustrating. The container had everything Michael would need to complete many small and large projects he had started, as well as my art supplies and various household goods I knew I wouldn't be able to find in Belize.

The sea can also contained Michael's beloved "Canary" – the Jeep we were driving on the day of our accident. Michael opened the container with the giddiness of a school boy. The first item to come out was his orange Kubota mini-excavator, something he had desperately been needing to start running the electrical lines from the pole at the side of the property to the main cabana. Now, his workload would double! After removing the tie-down straps and attaching the battery, Michael drove the mini-excavator out of the container and parked it off to one side. Next, and most importantly, was the Canary. Michael excitedly re-attached the battery to its terminals and fired up the engine. He let it idle while he unhooked the tie-downs and squeezed his way into the driver's seat. There was very little room on either side to comfortably walk around, so Michael had parked it in such a way that getting into the driver's side would be difficult, but not impossible.

I took a video of him driving the Jeep out of the container, his smile so big and excitement clearly visible. When all four tires were on solid Belizean soil he yelled, "The Canary has landed!" We now had two Jeeps in Belize. A silver one we had purchased months before, and our Canary. That, coupled with being white expats and owning a large chunk of property, categorized us as "rich white folk" to the locals, many of whom would stop by looking for any type of work, and sometimes a handout. This was a reality anywhere we'd go. We would always give whatever change we had, but occasionally, it was all too much. We couldn't be in town or walk place-to-place without being approached, the sad truth of the state of the country and its residents.

GRAND-BABY

The next day, Nicole and Shawn came to visit for ten days prior to us heading back to Canada to work for the summer. I got to play tourist, taking them to several sights and on exciting excursions to our local hardware store, so they truly got a sense of what life was like for us there. The interior of the cabana wasn't quite finished when they arrived, but we had beds set up in each bedroom anyways and an outdoor kitchen under the cabana. Despite the building mess, we had a wonderful time. A few weeks after we returned to Canada for summer work, Nicole and Shawn announced they were having a baby, due in December 2018, just two-and-a-half months before the accident took place. I was ecstatic, but also torn. The birth of my first grand-baby was coming on the cusp of our returning to Belize to live for six months of the year. I wasn't sure I had the strength to pull myself away, knowing this new life was coming into our family, nor did I want the opportunity to even try to live apart from the impending bundle of joy.

Michael was definitely at home when he was in Belize. He wanted to stay long enough to obtain his permanent residency and then his citizenship, while I kept one foot in Canada, where it would remain firmly planted. He really only agreed to go back to Canada to work in his industry for another couple of summers, then he'd fully retire at the age of 50. I, on the other hand, was having a little more difficulty fully stepping into life in the jungle. I loved the heat and humidity, except when the sweat ran freely, but the constant summer weather and the misty nights were lovely, even though it was hard to get used to the pitch black by 6:00 p.m. every evening. In Canada, summers are long and winters are short, but in the Caribbean, sunrise and sunset is the same every day, year-round. I was proud of what we were building together, but I couldn't "see" the future unfolding there. It silently unnerved me, and I felt like I was biding my time until some grand decision would be made.

I never shared my feelings with Michael; he was so involved in his new life on our property, and I fully supported him in building his dream. I tried very hard to fit my life into it, to find my own purpose on the land and with its people. We discussed hosting yoga and meditation retreats and renting out the cabanas to foreigners when the kids weren't there to visit, but it was just something else we talked about and nothing I could comfortably say would happen. My spirituality had taught me to trust my intuition, my higher self, but try as I might, the communication lines weren't open. I didn't feel right in my heart and soul but had no idea why. It was merely a whisper in time and a tragedy later that I would receive the answers my soul kept secret from me.

When it was time for my oldest daughter to give birth to my first grand-baby in December, I flew back to Canada to be with her and her partner for the event. The monumental and joyous occasion had finally arrived, and I wouldn't miss that for the world! It was so surreal, holding this tiny infant in my arms just hours after she was born. I could hardly grasp that my oldest daughter was even old enough to have a child, let alone that I was now a "Nana." I was floating, ungrounded, and as I gazed into my granddaughter's beautiful blue eyes, I was already struggling with the thought of leaving for Belize again in early January. I didn't want to let go of this tiny bundle of perfection.

I stayed in Canada for three weeks to help my daughter out after the birth of my first grand-baby and loved every minute of it. Then, in early January 2019, I loaded up Michael's mother to bring her to Belize to visit for the very first time. She stayed with us for the entire month. During that time, she got to experience the property, the planting, the fruit and the food. She was and still is an avid gardener, so we took her to as many landscape places as we could and planted even more trees, shrubs and flowers with Mother's assistance. The heat can take some getting used to, especially for someone in their 80s, and Mother – as Michael always called her, which always seemed a bit "Norman Bates" to me, and I said as much, but Michael would just roll his eyes and say nothing – was no exception. She stayed in the shady coolness of the cabana during the afternoons, reading and resting, taking long naps and early to bed after supper. Because it's dark by 6:00 p.m., we often felt like it must be bedtime right after dinner, and Michael and I were also known to be asleep by 7:30 p.m., partly from total exhaustion, and sometimes simply from boredom.

There wasn't much to do in the evenings. Staying out on the deck meant you would need lights on, which also meant a wide variety of flying insects, including moths the size of my hand (and my hands are not what you'd call "petite") and other annoying flying bugs that would get into your face and just piss you off. We welcomed the bats that would frequently fly through the front porch to grab a snack while we would sit, chat or read, me in the porch hammock and Michael on a rocking chair by the table. There he would sit, plan and smoke, watching YouTube videos on construction, planting, or just reading how-to books. I would normally last about five minutes on the porch until the bugs drove me inside, where I would rest in bed with a good book or in deep meditation. We didn't have cable or satellite TV, and only a data card for the internet, so we didn't have a lot of things to entertain us. We had several gigabyte drives full of pirated movies that Michael had downloaded before every trip, and occasionally, I would make popcorn and we'd watch one together on Michael's laptop.

Mainly, Michael studied, planned, wrote copious notes in

his daily journals and smoked. We talked endlessly about his plans for the property, and I "kept house," making sure he was well fed and didn't work too hard. His workaholic tendencies extended to Belize from Canada, so 16-hour days were his standard. Up at 4:30 or 5:00 a.m., he would watch the sunrise then set to work, doing whatever tasks he felt he had to tinker with each day, until I called him in for a good breakfast and coffee. He needed constant reminders to drink water throughout the day, but he didn't argue. It was always quite hot and humid, so ice-cold water was welcome.

I kept in touch with my children daily through our group chats and FaceTime. My granddaughter was a good sleeper and too young to remember Nana's visit, but Nicole texted me pictures of her growth and adorable faces daily. I was so happy for her and Shawn for their little blessing. My heart longed to be back in Canada, and I couldn't wait until my return at the beginning of March, after our annual honeymoon vacation in Cancun. I was planning to stay with my daughter and the baby until it was time for Michael to go to work again for the summer.

By this time, I was struggling to start my virtual hypnotherapy practice, which was a little difficult, given the half-year of being in a low internet access zone, so working from Canada would give me the boost I needed. I was also starting to feel like I was missing out on the growth and development of my grand-baby, but Michael clearly didn't feel the same. Any adorable pictures or videos Nicole sent me would only get a vacant "uh huh" or "cute" from Grandpa, his nose usually buried in a video or book. The tables were turning for me, and I tried to envision being in Belize full-time, only going back to Canada once or twice a year to visit my children and grandchild, and it wasn't sitting well. I was starting to feel very detached from this life we had chosen. If it truly was for me, only time would tell.

OVERGROWN

Michael had been working especially hard in the months prior to my departure for Canada and the birth of our granddaughter. This was partly due to a series of unfortunate events, which meant we had to fire Joe. When we arrived at the property in Fall 2018, it looked as though the jungle had taken everything back. Nothing was mowed, trimmed, whacked or cared for. There were vines growing all over the outside of our cabana and wash house, and the flowering plants we had so carefully planted were either competing with each other or dying. Joe had had an accident with the little Ford farm truck, and it sat under a tarp near Joe's house, completely wrecked and crumpled. The little Ford had sustained worse damage to it than Joe had admitted to when he called Michael a few months prior to tell him about the accident.

When Michael questioned Joe about the shape of the property, he merely said he had not been well lately and wasn't able to keep up. He hadn't previously mentioned not feeling well, and Michael reprimanded him for not making his illness known so we could have hired additional help for him, rather than let the property be taken back by the jungle. None of Joe's stories were straight. He was clearly lying about the truck, about money Michael had wired him to buy additional trees that were never purchased and more. Upon closer inspection of Joe's part of the property, Michael found piles of empty alcohol bottles, and the truth came out – Joe had a severe drinking problem. He spent the money we had wired him but had not taken care of the property and continually lied to cover his tracks. We had no choice but to let him go.

We met with a representative from the Belize labor counsel in Belmopan to discuss our issues and ensure that we were within our rights to fire him. The representative also met with Joe, then all of us together to sort out an amicable ending to our relationship that had started bumpy and was now ending with far more twists than it had begun. Joe borrowed a friend's truck to load their belongings and move to their new home, a place in the same village where he would be caretaker of another property, and we wished him and his new employer the best of luck. Licking our wounds, we hired several new employees for the next few weeks to get our property back into the shape it had been when we left it earlier that year. We kept the workers on for additional projects, which Michael oversaw, and things settled back to normal by the time I arrived back in Belize with Mother the following January.

When Michael brought Mother back to Canada a month later, I stayed behind to supervise the new workers and the tasks Michael had laid out for them for the week he planned to be away. In Canada, he had his first and only visit with our grand-baby. He got to visit all of the kids that trip, as well as some very dear friends before returning to Belize for the remainder of the winter. His visits were especially heart-felt and enjoyable. To Michael, they were probably the best visits he'd had with everyone in quite some time. The events of that month were a true blessing – that Mother got to visit the property he loved so dearly, and that he was finally able to meet his granddaughter, born in December and not quite 2-months-old. During his visit, he felt the pride and awe of having a granddaughter, and for the first time in his life, he took a "selfie" with her – several, in fact. These would turn out to be truly treasured imprints of the precious few hours they had together, none of which the baby would ever remember, but, unbeknownst to her, were some of the most significant hours in her life.

Michael's only visit with our granddaughter.

When Michael arrived home to Belize, he was anxious to get back on his tractor and continue to level and plant the property. By this time, we had fully mature starfruit trees that produced copious amounts of the sweet fruit. I would pick the ripened gems, slice them and dehydrate them, so Michael could satisfy his sweet tooth with something better than gummy bears or sour candies. We had over fifteen varieties of mango, ten varieties of avocado, five varieties of coconut and every kind of nut tree you can name, all maturing nicely for the years to come. We had plans for a vast garden and shade screen, so the sun's rays wouldn't beat down on the cucumbers and tomatoes, but we weren't quite ready for that project yet. Michael had rented the caretaker's cabana to a friend, now that Joe and Amanda and the kids had moved on, and he was digging trenches with his mini excavator in order to lay the electrical wire through the property to the cabana. He went right back to working his usual 16-hour days, feeling the pressure of getting everything done at once before leaving for Canada for the summer work.

Our 12th anniversary (and 14th honeymoon) was approaching, and we made plans to head back to Cancun. Michael grudgingly agreed to the plans, even though he felt the pull to stay on the property and complete the many jobs he'd started. I insisted that he needed the break and wouldn't put up with an argument from him. He would often get clumsy and careless because he was tired and just wanted to get everything done at once. We made plans to drive our Canary to Cancun for the first time ever, instead of flying.

DRIVE

Sometimes, getting Michael to peel himself away from his tractor was akin to removing a fly from fly-paper. He was stuck either there or on his mini-excavator, adhered to the seat from dawn until dusk, moving dirt around a mostly-perfect property. I would have to trek around, waving at him to come in for breakfast, lunch or dinner, or if it was time to leave, as it was on this particular day. We were all set to head to Cancun, but I sensed Michael was hesitant to leave. I knew I was, in a way, forcing him to take a vacation from the property, and he, being the workaholic that he was, was resistant to leave for the five days we had planned, fearing that nothing would be accomplished in his absence. We had a staff of two or three workers on the property at any given time, and the workers were overseen by a good friend and particularly hard worker. The men had been assisting Michael with pouring concrete, planting, mowing and weeding, basically keeping the jungle at bay while moving forward with plans to build the next cabana, then the next and so on.

I had packed our suitcases the day before, mine separate from Michael's, as I would be heading to Canada from Cancun directly after our honeymoon. Michael would drive the Canary back to Belize, stopping in Chetumal's "duty-free" zone to scope out the shops and pick up any supplies needed on the property. That day, however, we would travel as far as Corozal Town, adjacent to the Belize/Mexico border, and stay the night with friends who were also Canadian expats living full-time in Belize. Their home was a 10-minute drive to the border, and we thought taking the opportunity for a visit and having a nice dinner in Corozal, a place we had only been to once before on our meandering country trip several years prior, was a great addition to our vacation.

"We better get moving if we want to get to Corozal before dark," I reminded Michael, pulling him away from his tractor.

He grudgingly agreed and went up the fifteen cabana steps to retrieve our luggage and haul it to the Canary. My niece, her husband and young daughter had been staying with us for about a week and would remain at the cabana for one more day before heading to the Belize Zoo and Tropical Education Center for an overnight stay. Michael didn't bother to change out of his ratty shirt and shorts, nor his ridiculous yellow clog "Crocs" he had actually purchased for me a few years prior. He found the clogs, a nod to my Dutch ancestry, in a Dutch cheese shop back in Canada and thought I would get a total "kick" out of them. They were handy for slipping on and running outside quickly, but they were much too big for me, so once we packed up and moved to Belize, Michael adopted them as his work boots and wore them all-day-every-day, even into town or out to dinner. He picked up the suitcases and headed to the Jeep, still in his ratty work clothes and rubber clogs. I followed behind, wondering why he was loading everything now and *not* after his shower and change of clothes. As he loaded the luggage and attempted to get into the driver's side of the Canary, I stopped him.

"Um, *NO*. You are *NOT* wearing those shoes on our honeymoon, and you're filthy! Go shower and change!" I insisted.

Grumpily, he trudged off to the wash house to have a quick shower, adorned with fresh shorts, a clean shirt and a pair of grey slip-on shoes. It was an improvement, though not perfection, but I knew what battles I could win and picked them wisely. He was distracted as always, thinking he had far too much to do to slow down and smell the heliconia. Besides, the property didn't care what he looked like any more than he did, so why did it matter? I could only shake my head and smile. Sometimes, dealing with a toddler was easier than getting Michael to agree to anything in those days.

"Better?" He asked, as we climbed into the Canary.

I could tell he was annoyed with having to "get fancy," which he hardly ever did anymore. I had previously bought him new shorts and shirts, ones I would consider nice enough for trips to town or dinners out, but he managed to wear every one of them onto the property at one time or another, and they were now all red and muddied with the clay that was our land. I finally got smart and started hanging his "dress-up" clothes in *my* closet, out of his reach, and would bring them out when we planned to go to dinner or to see friends.

"Yes. Thank you!" I replied, biting back a that-wasn't-too-much-to-ask-was-it remark.

Off we went, silently enjoying the 3-hour drive to Corozal from our property. The area we lived in was lush and mountainous, and we were heading into arid, dry savannah parts of Belize. To this day, it is the only country I know of that can go from ocean fresh to savannah dry to lush, tropical wet in a matter of an hour. That said, the landscape on the way to Corozal is not very exciting; boring, in fact. We would talk about how lucky we were to find the property we had, and how flat, uninticing and difficult it would be to grow anything in the other areas, being so dry.

We arrived in Corozal just before dark and met our friends at a lovely restaurant next to the ocean. We had a spectacular meal and conversation, thoroughly enjoying being among other Canadians. We followed them back to their home, talked over night caps and said goodnight. Their home was clean and cool, with the typical tiled floor and colorfully-painted concrete walls. If you planned to live in an ocean town, you'd better build a home with concrete. The salty ocean air wreaks havoc on wooden homes and anything metal, rusting belongings within a year. We always were grateful to be in an area close enough to visit the ocean, but far enough away that we didn't have to surrender our belongings to salty decomposition.

I had a restless sleep in a bed that wasn't terribly comfortable, in a home that was not my own. I was anxious to get to Cancun, to the resort with lush, comfortable beds, sandy beaches and clear blue pools. I was also anxious to see if this trip would be the catalyst to either rekindle our intimacy, or delve deeper into the discussion around my moving back to Canada. The thought of either occurrence and the subsequent outcome rolled around my brain, making sleep an impossibility. Michael snored his usual percolator beside me, oblivious to my restlessness. Even my earplugs could never completely drown out the noise, and if he fell asleep before me, I would usually have a restless night, as I was now, listening to the uneven breathing. At times, he would stop breathing altogether, until I gave him a little shove to make sure he was ok. He would roll over, but the snoring continued. He was such a talent in the snore division that he could even snore while laying on his stomach.

The next morning, Michael was up bright and early. Letting me rest a little longer, he made his way out to the kitchen to have early morning coffee with our friends. I joined them a short time later, having a lovely visit before making our way out to the Canary, saying our goodbyes for now. They often shopped in Chetumal at the duty-free stores, so they were able to give Michael some advice on what to look for and where, which he planned to do on his way back to Belize in five days' time. Away we went, our friends leading us through town in their own vehicle, as they had errands to run and wanted to make sure we got to the border junction ok. Once we neared the roundabout and turned north, they both pointed out the vehicle windows, indicating the direction for us to turn. We honked and waved and headed north.

Just before the border, we stopped at a rather large "mall," a superstore of sorts, to pick up last-minute supplies, hot sauces and alcohol for me to take back to friends in Canada and snacks for the road trip to Cancun. While we were there, Michael pulled the Jeep up to the outdoor car wash to be cleaned while we shopped. Car washes in Belize consist of a person with a bucket of soapy water, a hose and a shammy wipe, and for the price of about $2 Canadian, you can have your vehicle completely detailed, inside and out. While the Canary enjoyed its "spa day," I found a couple of nice skirts, rather casual in a stretchy T-shirt knit fabric, but skirts were a daily piece of apparel for me, as they were much cooler than shorts or leggings in the humid Belizean climate and less "sticky." We added them to the pile, along with a fresh carton of cigarettes for Michael and his favorite lemon cookies.

Michael would usually buy a carton of cigarettes every time we went to town, and he always brought a few cartons home to Canada when we traveled back. They were much cheaper in Belize, and I guess for the discerning smoker, a decent brand in comparison to the North American model of cancer-causing poison sticks. Michael always tried his best to be sly about his cigarette purchases, the carton costing $65 Belize Dollars ($32.50 US), and he'd try to "hide" his habit from me every chance he could. He also knew he was being silly because I knew he smoked, and he knew that I knew. But he also knew that being with a non-smoker was a point on my list that he, at one time, was happy to check off. He had quit for a while, prior to our getting together, but ever since he had picked up the stress-relieving habit again – which was especially frequent when working – he felt bad about continuing.

Although I was not ecstatic about having a smoker for a husband, I wouldn't judge him for his decision or his deeply-rooted desire to smoke. I offered to do hypnotherapy sessions with him in regards to smoking – which really meant digging deeper into his childhood trauma, the abuse he witnessed at the hands of his father and so on, but he politely declined. Many addicts do. Addictions, whether they are substance or food, can be a tough habit to break, but it becomes easier utilizing hypnosis as a tool for change. When he did smoke in the evenings or below the cabana when he had time to think or relax, I didn't hang around him. I didn't enjoy the secondhand smoke, and thankfully, he never lit up if I was in the immediate area or in the vehicle with him. A couple of times, when he was alone on the deck off of our bedroom, where we had our large dining table, he would light up. This meant the smoke would travel through the open window, directly into the bedroom where I was trying to enjoy a book or a meditation. This got me riled, and the deck quickly became a no-smoking zone.

He was disgruntled yet respectful of my dislike of the stinky stick just as much as he liked them. Joe would refer to them as his "thinking sticks," quite an accurate statement, as he always lit up when he was taking a moment to relax and think. When he was active, digging or playing Tractor Speedway around the property, he rarely lit up. Only in the still moments, or if he got into the vehicle to shuttle off to town for supplies without me would he spark up, marking his thinking activity time. Today, however, was a carton for Michael for the week in Cancun, and a carton for friends back home, which went into my suitcase along with a large bottle of

Old Master Coconut Rum (the best in the world, in my opinion) and bag full of Marie Sharp's hot sauces, both Belizean made. I slipped the new skirts into my tan-colored beach bag in the backseat, and we set off in our sparkly, fresh Canary, tipping the cleaning crew generously. We arrived at the border crossing a short ten minutes later.

The Belize to Mexico border crossing looked a little like something out of a movie studio for a prison scene. There were high chain-link and barbed-wire fences, drug dogs leashed to their assigned officer and several buildings scattered through the area. There was a definite path to follow, depending upon your size of vehicle. Tour buses and regular buses went through one area, trucks another and cars yet another. We went through the wrong line-up to begin with and were forced to back out to move to the car line. Nothing was terribly clear, other than the bus line, as there were no markings delineating the proper path and no signs pointing in the right direction. Strike one for Borderland, but we made a note to remember for next time.

Next, we were told to park in one particular section and walk to a permit building to obtain papers to cross. We did so, but finding the building proved to be a frustrating task, and it took us a while to locate the right office. The staff was leisurely hovering outside, enjoying the sun and chattering away in Spanish. When we arrived, they took our passports and proceeded inside to process the paperwork we would need to have stamped at yet another building. It was all so bizarre. We loaded back into the Canary and proceeded to the next parking area, right beside the security checkpoint office. Apparently, that wasn't the right parking area, even though it was directly in front of the building, so we were told to get back into the Jeep and move it to another parking lot much further away. I stayed behind, entered the building and waited for Michael, passports in hand. A short time later, my slightly-winded and sweaty husband joined me in the cool, air-conditioned building. We took our place in line to have the entry documents and passports stamped. Once we had completed that, we were told that *I* would have to exit out of a different door, while Michael collected the Canary and then went through the vehicle pick-up line to collect me on the other side. *Wow,* I thought. *Was this Ft. Knox?*

Nearly half an hour passed before I could see the shiny Canary in the line-up, but I wasn't allowed to proceed to the vehicle until Michael had parked in yet another designated pick-up area. I waited until he found a space, and got into the vehicle. From there, it was an easy line to exit the security checkpoint, and it even bore a large sign overhead displaying the words "To Chetumal." Finally, a clear direction! The road to Chetumal was abreast the highway and spread out deep instead of wide on either side, so there wasn't too much to see from our vantage point, just a few homes and a couple of shops on the way past. We decided not to stop in Chetumal at this time, as we took longer at the border crossing than anticipated and wanted to arrive at our resort before the dinner bell that evening. We had a 5-hour drive ahead of us, and it was already mid-morning.

We proceeded rather quietly, me noting the bizarre Adventureland we had struggled to get through so that we would remember the procedures and the buildings for next time. I made several notes such as these during our travels to Belize, from how long it took to get from one village to another, to where we could find the cheapest supplies in stores around Belmopan and Spanish Lookout. I compiled a binder of information, both for our purposes and those of our future guests staying in the cabanas in later years. I had plans to create "things to do and places to see" brochures for guests and provide a basket of goodies, with handmade soaps, lotions and moringa tea, all made on our property.

I was doing all that I could to make things easier for Michael, keeping his mind and supply needs straight while I loosely planned for a potential Airbnb resort, healing retreats and the like. I proceeded with seeing hypnotherapy clients via Zoom as much as possible, but my business was still fledgling, as virtual sessions aren't as popular as in-person, even though they are just as effective. It was difficult to comprehend building my practice into anything locally. My services would be far more than what the locals could afford or what the expats would require, and I felt a bit lost in my purpose, but I never shared this with Michael. I just carried on, taking my notes and making future plans. Plan A, stay in Belize; or Plan B, move back to Canada. I lived day-to-day the best my heart could muster, the future a blank slate, a mystery.

I was truly looking forward to our stay at our Cancun resort, and even more so, my trip back to Canada, eager to see the bundle my grandbaby was growing into. Secretly, I knew – felt through my entire being – that I would likely not return to Belize once I reached Canadian soil. I knew I couldn't ignore the pull to be with my family once again, but the feeling went deeper than that, coming from somewhere I couldn't explain. I relaxed and released the feeling, the Canary's windows rolled down with sun shining on my face, arm loosely holding the window frame, as I took in the local scenery for the first time. As you now well know, dear reader, we never did arrive or get to celebrate our incredible 12 years together; instead, three days before our 12th anniversary, my life went in a completely different, unreal direction.

CHAPTER 9

Tap My Heels

March 5-12, 2019, Mexico

The day after Katrina and Casey broke me out of the hospital was a bright and sunny one, not just outside, but in my heart as well. I was one step closer to going home to Canada, my family and friends. In the meantime, I would attempt to enjoy the time in Bacalar in grateful comfort, despite my limited understanding of the work and processes we still had to endure before going home could become a reality. Bacalar is a beautiful town, located on Lake Bacalar, near the east coast of Mexico. The colorful shops and amazing aromas from the local restaurants were enticing, and the narrow, quaint, cobblestone streets reminded me of the quick trip Michael and I enjoyed to Seville, Spain, during our trip to Portugal a few years previous.

Strolling leisurely was about all I could handle, and not without the constant support of my little team. The dizziness was still substantial. My concussed head, sore neck and bruising were one thing, but the sheer exhaustion I felt even walking from the hotel bed to the bathroom was tremendous.

Despite this, I still had absolutely no choice but to get up and get moving so that we could get the necessary documentation signed to release Michael's body to the funeral home for cremation, and set me on a course home for Canada.

Adam and Vera arrived early the next morning to pick us up and take us for our first of several trips into Chetumal, to the one and only police station in the district of Quintara Roo that dealt with all "expat-related" wrongdoings. The drive to Chetumal from Bacalar took approximately an hour, but each trip there and back felt like an eternity. I had vertigo and headaches, and driving made me more nauseated than I had ever felt before. We would frequently have to pull over so that I could be sick on the side of the road. I didn't think I would ever feel normal again. I dreaded every ride we had to take but persisted because I wanted to get everything done and leave.

When we arrived, Adam and Vera escorted us into the station. The building looked like an abandoned, 2-story, small apartment complex, rather than an official police station. As we made our way to the stairwell, we noticed a dirty white toilet sitting just inside an alcove under the stairs. It was funny and bizarre, and we wondered what the story was behind it. The cobwebs and dust indicated it wasn't in use or even connected to anything, just a unique piece of sculpture for all to enjoy. Kat, Casey and I exchanged looks. *Where the hell were we? What kind of "professional" office were we entering?* We slowly climbed the stairs to the 2nd-floor office. When we finally made it, the girls and I sat in plastic lawn chairs, another questionable furniture piece in an equally questionable office. We had no choice but to push the trepidation aside and wait as Adam spoke to the officer in charge of taking my statement. While Adam was conversing, the girls and I watched a bit of Cockroach Speedway as one or two raced across the office to hide under the copier machine. We exchanged glances as the secretary got up from her desk and approached the copier, wondering with bated breath if one of the roaches would leave its shady resting spot and run over her toes and, more importantly, what her reaction would be to said cockroach being so near to her person. Disappointingly, however, the roaches stayed put.

When the exchange of information between Adam and the robust Mexican plainclothes officer was complete, I was called upon to give my statement. Vera introduced me to "Pablo" and explained that I would have to attest to the events as best I could to my recollection. Pablo, the dark-haired Mexican police officer, who looked as though he rarely missed an opportunity to delightfully partake in a chimichanga, seemed to be a pleasant enough fellow. With Vera's interpretation, he read off the contents of the official report. This was the first piece of the accident puzzle that I received. Immediately, I chimed in with a few required changes before I would sign off. The police report stated that we had been traveling in excess speeds of at least 120 kmph, and our boat trailer must have come off the vehicle and ran into us, causing the accident.

Firstly, the Canary was not the "speed demon" Michael wished it had been. It couldn't do speeds over 90 kmph, as much as Michael willed it to do so any time he got behind the wheel. It was a small point of fact, but it mattered to me just the same. We were the only vehicle in the accident, and neither Mexican nor Belizean vehicle insurance covered the cost of vehicle replacement anyways, but it was one fact I knew for certain; therefore, I spoke up. The next matter of contention was the boat trailer. We did not own – and never *had* owned – a boat trailer, let alone a boat. A trailer was involved in the accident, however, and this was my first clue as to what caused it in the first place. The trailer had Belizean plates, was resting near our overturned vehicle (also with Belizean plates), and no one who stopped at the accident claimed the trailer, so it was presumably ours. This was noted and would have to be investigated further. Until that interview, I was unaware of a trailer being involved or causing the accident, as I still had no memory of the accident itself.

I gave the rest of my statement of the events as I remembered them. Michael and I had left Chetumal at approximately 10:00 a.m. on February 28, after we had made our way through the Mexico/Belize checkpoint, which was also documented, if they chose to look into it. It was a few miles past Bacalar when the accident occurred, so it must have been close to 11:30 a.m. at that time. That checked out in accordance with the ambulance and clinic's records as well. After I corrected the officer in regard to the speed in which we were traveling, this also checked out as per the timing of the accident. The rest of the statement was a simple matter of fact that was proven by the records that I had left with Nicole in October 2018; copies of our marriage license, passports, driver's licenses and so on. I was so grateful for intuition leading me to this coincidental gathering of estate documents prior to our winter arrival in Belize. Things would have been much more complicated if Nicole wasn't able to send the documents to Katrina or Adam for proof.

Adam had the forethought to print all of the documents he knew would be required, prior to our visit to the station and subsequent 3-hour interview with Captain Chimichanga. What should have been a simple statement had turned into a much bigger ordeal. Once I finished providing my details, Pablo said he would now have to make adjustments, discuss some of the details with the officers on scene and so on. We would have to return the next day to complete the required paperwork. My spidey senses were tingling, but what he said made perfect sense. I was anxious to be done and book flights home, but I understood this was still an eventuality.

That evening back at our hotel, we decided to venture out for some food and a chance to breathe in the glorious ocean air. Like moving through molasses, we made our way down the narrow street. Passing restaurants and shops, individuals would stop us and give condolences, at times even offering food from their menus. I was touched and grateful for the kindness of strangers, at first unsure of how they could even know I was recently in an accident, but how could they not? Our accident was still today's headline, splashed all over the Caribbean news. It was all people could talk about in their small-town gatherings.

We didn't venture far at first, as my legs couldn't carry me for long. We took frequent rests, plopping me into a chair or leaning me against a pillar, while the girls would run into shops and grab water, juice, fruit and other supplies we would later need at the hotel room. We even found a small clothing store and were able to secure a few more articles. Nothing too sparkly; I didn't require sparkle for attention to be drawn to me, merely needed a change or two of clothing for the next few days. We found a lovely restaurant near the water, close to our hotel, and settled in for a decent meal. Suddenly feeling ravenous, as if my body was truly awake for the first time since my arrival at the Bacalar hospital, I reached for a menu. Previous thoughts and indications from Michael that "I could be a Vegan now" were dashed when I ordered a heaping order of chicken wings. Kat and Casey giggled, ordering their own Mexican favorites and refreshing drinks. We took our time eating, relaxing, discussing the day and guessing at when we could book tickets home, but that was a pointless exercise at this juncture. There was still a lot to do in the coming days.

The next morning, trusty Adam and his assistant Vera were waiting outside the hotel for our second trip to Chetumal's police station and morning visit with Pablo. We made the trip in relative silence, the girls catching up on messages from family and friends. I was trying not to look out the windows for fear of blasting the car with fruity chunks of breakfast. Travel sickness was suddenly a real thing, something I'd never experienced until now. We arrived at the police station and parked, and I considered leaving the remainder of my breakfast in the lonesome toilet, giving it some purpose in its seemingly useless existence, before trudging up the stairs. Officer Pablo, however, was nowhere to be found. The secretary was apparently the only person in charge today, stating he should arrive soon. I didn't take her for a liar until hours later, when there was still no sign of Pablo. We waited, and waited, and waited some more.

Almost four hours after our arrival, he finally sauntered in, unapologetically. He and Adam exchanged slightly heated Spanish chatter, in which Adam discovered that Pablo was missing some pieces of required paperwork from the main office, as they were not ready. Apparently, we could not complete the process until he had obtained said papers for me to sign off on. In my blurry, concussed state, neck and body aching after sitting erect in the flimsy, plastic lawn chairs for almost four hours, I couldn't focus or comprehend what was going on, so I just agreed to everything that was said – a dangerous practice, I knew – and we were on our way back to Bacalar. Adam was more than a little upset, voicing his concerns to our little group. He was highly suspicious of the officer and didn't truly believe his story.

On our way back to Bacalar, resting in the comfortable backseat of Adam's car, I suddenly said that I wanted to see the scene of the accident, if it wasn't too far out of our way to do so. Katrina and Casey were not sure this was the best idea, but I insisted. I needed to see where it had occurred and if it would jog my memory even the slightest. I watched all the buildings, signs, trees, plants and so on, recognizing everything until we got to about 300 meters from the accident scene. There, I couldn't recognize anything. My mind had blocked the memory a significant distance away from the point of impact, and the subsequent 75-meter roll to the spot where the Canary landed.

That was where we stopped. Adam did a quick U-turn, parking on the opposite side of the narrow highway, and we got out of the vehicle and crossed over to the area of the accident rubble. The grey shoes Michael had been wearing were still there, along with a shirt he had purchased in Palm Springs several honeymoons before. It must have flown out of the same bag they had retrieved and brought to the hospital. I collected the shirt but left the shoes; a slight recall of the shoe to clog an argument we had days before whispered to me. The entire right side of the Canary was lying in the ditch, hardly a scratch on it, the striped yellow paint marking the spot. The hardtop and roll bars had been completely stripped off in our tumble, shards of metal, glass and plastic lay scattered along the highway and the wide, grassy ditch beside it. Eerie red reflectors from the brake lights were scattered in bits, like blood smatters from the vehicle itself.

I viewed the scene as a spectator in the stands, not as the woman who'd escaped the deadly crash. My face was rigid, void of expression as I took it all in quickly, one step ahead of the bubbling grief and pain. With some assistance, I took meter-length strides from the point of the accident to the apparent point of impact and counted 75. We had rolled incessantly by all appearances, obliterating not just my husband's beloved Canary, but also ending our beautiful life together. My heart felt so heavy, my body numb. Gratitude and grief swept through me as we made our way back to Adam's vehicle and set off for our hotel in Bacalar. I held Michael's shirt close to me, tears trickling down my face. I could barely breathe, barely see, and I could only try to hold it together a little longer. Katrina and Casey rested their hands on me or held mine, their energy a much needed support I was so incredibly grateful for in that moment.

After seeing the accident scene, knowing the contents of the police report and seeing all of the pictures of the accident, we were able to piece together the most likely scenario for what took place. We had been heading north toward Cancun, the narrow highway fairly void of vehicles from my recollection, but with at least one vehicle either in front of us or in the on-coming lane, hauling the boat trailer that was involved in the crash. The trailer must have come free of its hitch and hit us, or Michael swerved so hard to avoid it that we ended up in the 75-meter roll. Based on the extent of Michael's injuries that I had witnessed the day of the accident and verified by Adam, it was assumed that the hitch of the boat trailer was actually the cause of his death.

It was completely possible that, if the boat trailer had released from an on-coming vehicle, it could have bounced up, smashing through the Jeep window and striking Michael, killing him instantly. It was all making sense but did not jog my memory in the slightest, and as we had no medical or forensic examiner assigned to our case, it would remain forever unknown for certain. I felt sick to my stomach as we traveled back to Bacalar, the rest of the trip in silence. Once we were back at the hotel, I told the girls I wanted to go live on Facebook.

"Are you sure, honey?" Katrina asked.

"I think it's necessary. I think I should let everyone know I'm ok and update them on what's going on." I knew people had been asking, messaging Nicole, Casey and Katrina like mad. Friends and acquaintances were looking for updates on my condition and when I could come home. The girls agreed, and Casey started the live video.

"Hi, everyone," I started. "I just wanted to let you all know that I'm out of the hospital and doing okay, and that we are making some progress toward getting me home." This is where I would look to Kat for answers. I was in attendance for all of the discussions and appointments we'd had thus far, but in body only. My mind could not put the words together to explain what we'd done so far and what still needed to be done before coming home. Katrina jumped in with a full update. Once she was done, this time it was I who was crying.

"We could not have done everything that needed to be done without Kat being here," I continued. "I know I have a family that would have gladly come to my rescue, but *it just had to be* Katrina." It was true. I still believe she was the perfect person for a nearly impossible job.

After we had finished recording, I felt at ease, cathartic. I was able to release my fears, anxiety, gratitude and emotions in a fury, even though I could barely find the words. The reality of all that we still had to accomplish before leaving was somewhat astounding. Hearing Katrina update the status of the process to everyone was confusing and unreal to me. There was still so much to do! And as I had no mental capacity to take it all on, I could only go along for the ride, trusting every part of the process and the people responsible for me.

The next day, we set on our way, yet again, for Chetumal, and waited hours, yet again, for the elusive Pablo. Adam had the secretary call Pablo, and she returned to say he wouldn't be on duty that day. By this time, we were more than aggravated. I asked Adam if Pablo was trying to make us sweat, in the proverbial sense, so that we would offer a bribe for him to complete his task. Adam agreed, but when I said to "pay him whatever he wants – we need to get home," Adam refused, saying he wouldn't allow such behavior on the part of his own countrymen to continue. He was embarrassed and regretful that there were people such as Pablo in such an important position of authority, who would stoop to such degrading levels. It wasn't the picture of Mexico or its people that Adam wanted to paint. He excused himself and made a few calls while we sat in the same uncomfortable chairs and waited. By this time, a lone, lowly cockroach, one who had been tracking back and forth across the office days earlier, had given up waiting for whatever morsel was thrust upon him and died, mid-trek. Perhaps he had met the bottom of the secretary's shoe. Hard to tell, as cockroaches are, thankfully, not "squishy," so there was no evidence of the "how."

Adam returned several minutes later to announce that he had called the office in charge of this one and talked to the superior ranking officer. He, apparently, was appalled at his subordinate's behavior and insisted we come to his office in Chetumal to complete the paperwork, gather my belongings (that were located at his office) and be on our way. Finally, we were nearing completion of the pieces of documentation that would release Michael's body to Adam and allow me to apply for my temporary visa, should mine be gone for good. We were all silently hoping that the belongings located in the office included my passport, laptop, purse and so on, but chances were slim.

The office was only a few blocks away. Once we arrived, we were escorted to a waiting area bench, while Adam met with the senior officer in charge and relayed our experience. The senior officer walked directly over to me and personally apologized for the behavior of his staff and for our tragedy. From what we were told, the subordinate who was holding out for the bribe was fired on the spot, as was his supervisor, both from the same office. We were then taken to a separate room for me to claim my baggage. Seeing my suitcases in their office was so odd, but a massive relief. They were in great shape, despite the tumble they took, but they had also been stripped of their contents, except for the clothes I was planning to wear to Canada when Michael and I parted after our anniversary trip. My backpack containing our laptops, iPads, cell phones and passports was also completely emptied of its contents. We now knew for certain that we would have to make a trip to

Playa del Carmen to the Canadian Consulate and obtain a temporary visa in order to get me home. It was a devastating moment. I was so hopeful that my passport would be there, and if it had been, we would have booked flights to leave Cancun within a day. Now, it would potentially add another full week to our stay.

Not only had our personal belongings, wallets and money been stripped from our bodies at the accident scene, but our suitcases had been rummaged through and several articles stolen. The rum, hot sauces and cigarettes we had purchased for friends back in Canada were gone. Personal care items, clothing, hoodies and our evening wear was also taken. The only articles left were my leggings, socks and shoes for me to change into before bracing the cold in the still-snowy Canada. The people who participated in this criminal activity had not only stripped our personal belongings, but they'd also stripped what little I had remaining of my own identity. In the months leading up to the accident, I had been questioning my role in our marriage, our life together in Belize and how I could adapt to remain a loyal, loving partner. It may not have been blatantly obvious to me at that moment, but in the weeks and months to come, I would feel both abhorrent and elated at the stripping of my identity. I was, all at once, shedding the person I once was and finding out who I now wanted to become.

I was disgusted and shocked at the lack of respect given to us as accident victims on the side of a Mexican highway, lying in a ditch, crying beside my dead husband. It would be some time before I could find forgiveness for many things that transpired during those weeks, including how some of our own, disreputable acquaintances from Canada judged us for the choices we had made along the way. My children bore the brunt of this particular bunch thinking that we were "taking a vacation" at Michael's expense. That the funds from the Go-Fund-Me were being used for our "holiday," that we should've chosen cheaper accommodations, and they couldn't under-stand why both Katrina *and* Casey were even taking the trip to begin with. I'd like those insignificant morons, for just one minute, to walk in our bloody shoes, live with our physical, mental and emotional pain, and see how well they'd fare.

I know that Michael would have been absolutely horrified at the behavior of some of the people he knew personally and their treatment of us, both in Mexico and Canada during our Mexican "holiday." He could be a very patient man when he needed to be, but if there was a blatant injustice to be found, he would drop his deep baritone voice one more octave lower, look the perpetrator directly in the eye and let him or her have it. He would barely need to speak before the person in front of him was quivering. I asked Michael once I was home, safe and sound, and things had settled to a new normal, why we had been "attacked" by so many when we were in the crux of the most difficult time of our lives.

He simply stated that, "*Fear, guilt and shame rule their lives, and from that place, they claim no self-responsibility and can find no peace and harmony within themselves or with others. They have no recognition of their place in the thread of life, and that we are all part of this thread is a disillusion to them. What one person does in this thread affects all.*" It made sense and was true to the belief I held in regard to most people, my clients included. Although I no longer speak to these people, having no real relationship with them to begin with, I was finally able to forgive them their transgressions and move on.

The day was long and exhausting, but this excruciating step was now complete. Even though criminal activity and theft was evident, we had avoided blackmail. I noticed Katrina crying once again. It seemed that at the completion of every step, Kat cried. It was like she held her breath through each piece of the process, and when each painful step was complete, she could finally release her breath – and her tears – and relax.

We were all so grateful to the Federales Commander-in-Chief for his participation in pushing the necessary documents through, but we just wanted to get back to the hotel and crash. It was late by the time we arrived, found some food and slipped into deep, exhausted sleep.

The very next day, Adam and Vera picked us up yet again. Part of the requirement for me to travel was to have a thorough examination by a physician, as dictated by the Canadian Consulate. Adam took us to Chetumal to meet with the physician, located in a rather simple clinic. As gracious as the good doctor was, I hesitated to give him the total truth of my condition, as I wanted to go home so badly, and I didn't want anyone to prevent me from doing so. He gave me a simple check-up and asked how I was doing. I downplayed the dizziness I felt, which would occasionally make it impossible to walk in a straight line. The headaches were tremendous at times, but this I also downplayed. I did admit to *some* dizziness, however, which resulted in an appointment with a local otolaryngologist (ear, nose and throat doctor) to ensure that I didn't have any inner-ear issues prior to flying.

We would have to make yet another doctor visit that day, later in the afternoon. In the meantime, Adam dropped myself, Vera, Kat and Casey at a restaurant for lunch and to kill some time between appointments while he went back to his office to take care of his other demands. Adam picked us up a couple hours later and brought us all to the otolaryngologist. Once we arrived, I was more than ready for a rest from the lengthy day. My head hurt, my body ached, and I was so nauseous that I worried I would throw up on the good doctor. As I was ushered into his office, I was greeted by a man who'd surely just walked off the set of a Mexican soap opera. He was tall and suave, with grey slicked-back hair and sporting multiple diamond rings. He was wearing a fitted lab coat and was, in fact, the doctor I was there to see. His office was elegant, resplendent with white and grey marble and solid brass fixtures – and it all looked incredibly expensive. I worried about the cost of the visit, grateful again for the Go-Fund-Me money we'd received. It had gotten us through so much of the trip thus far and would be needed for so much more to come.

Vera interpreted my condition and reason for the visit, to which he "tsk-tsked" and gawked, uttering apologies in Spanish for losing my husband. He not only looked the part of the typical Mexican soap star, he was also a bit over-dramatic, albeit gracious. He stood up, grabbed his otoscope and moved around his desk to stand beside me on my right. He bent down, placing the otoscope into my right ear. Murmuring something before moving on to my left – seemingly everything looking good on the right – when he placed the otoscope into my left ear, he gasped.

"Aye-aye-aye!" He exclaimed, sucking in air.

It was apparently bad, unless the good Mexican soap opera doctor was being over-dramatic. As it turned out, he wasn't. The otoscope felt like it was made of shards of glass as he slid it into my ear canal, but it was, in actuality, pressing against an ear full of it. This would prove to have much to do with the dizziness I felt and the discomfort in my left ear. He had me move from the chair at the front of his desk to his patient table and began to remove the shards one-by-one, placing them in a small, stainless steel kidney dish. They each made a soft "clink" sound as they hit the dish. He pulled out shard after shard, wiping blood as he went. As he completed the process, I felt a great weight lifting off of me with every shard removed. I could also hear out of that ear again, previously feeling like I was underwater, or better yet, under sand, not knowing the extent or real reason why.

It was a huge relief. He explained to Vera that he was unable to remove the pieces that were further down the ear canal, as they were encapsulated in bloody scabs growing around them and were too close to the eardrum. He advised that it would be best for my ear to heal some more and potentially push those pieces out on their own, or be removed by my own doctor once I arrived home. He indicated that the remaining pieces were quite large and would cause a bigger issue for me now than they would later, after my ear had time to heal from his manipulations. He had done the best he could and was happy to sign a letter clearing me for travel. Hurrah! The doctor's bill turned out to be quite an expense, just as I imagined it would, based on the office and surroundings. Being a specialist in Mexico was, apparently, quite lucrative. I could only imagine what a doctor on a Mexican soap opera would make. Katrina graciously paid it before shedding her usual emotional tears at being another step closer to our return to Canada. Crying had become her "thing," and we knew if Kat was crying, another step had been completed.

Avocados

We were finally able to head back to our hotel in Bacalar and rest for the evening, readying ourselves for the day ahead, which would involve a trip to the funeral home. Adam was finally able to bring Michael's body there, after ten days of resting in the local morgue, completely unattended to. Adam was distressed the entire time he had been assisting us in our endeavors to have his body released, and he now needed us to come and make cremation arrangements and choose an urn. He already knew that I had no desire to view Michael's body, and at that point, it wasn't necessary or advisory for anyone to view him anyway, as his remains were in an advancing state of decomposition. I was thankful Michael's body would now be in Adam's care to prepare him for cremation.

My reasons for cremating Michael's body, rather than transport him back to Canada, were three-fold. First, he'd already told me he wished to be cremated and his ashes spread over our property in Belize. Second, regardless of decomposition, his body had taken such a terrible beating that the funeral would have to be a closed coffin anyway. Third, the expense of shipping his body back to Canada was mountainous, and I knew Michael would definitely not want us to spend that kind of money on him. He was a very humble, simple man who had absolutely no problem whatsoever spending money on his wife or kids, but he never had any desire to spend it on himself. He wore the same, ratty work clothes, the same clogs and the same work boots for years. It was worse than pulling teeth to get him to go shopping or spend any money on himself. I learned of Michael's wish to be cremated when we had updated our wills the year before.

When we had discussed it originally, he said, "Dig a hole on the property, and push me into it. Then plant an avocado tree over the spot!" He always had such a weird sense of humor, but this did make me laugh.

"Why on Earth would I do such a thing?" I asked.

"Then, when you and your new husband are on the property, you can feed him the avocados!" He replied, his denim blue eyes sparkling with mischief. That was Michael. Full of mischief and smartass remarks that would have everyone in the room exploding in laughter.

Adam had several pieces of paperwork for me to sign and asked me to choose an urn to transport Michael's remains home in. I saw a bio urn, the type of urn you could bury so it would later grow into a tree, and knew that was exactly what Michael would want. Unfortunately, a bio urn wasn't acceptable transport for the ashes, so I would have to choose a proper urn, one that could be sealed shut for the trip home. I chose a very simple brown rectangular cube, one that would sit beautifully on the table at the Celebration of Life we would eventually have back home. I also purchased the bio urn and would ask our hometown funeral director to transfer some of Michael's ashes into it after the ceremony, so I could plant it at a later time.

Once everything was complete, Adam said he would prepare Michael's body for cremation and, once they were ready, deliver the ashes to whichever hotel we were staying at in Playa del Carmen. We said a bittersweet goodbye to Adam and Vera, unable to put into words the gratitude we felt for all of their assistance during this process. If it wasn't for them immediately coming to the hospital to help me after I woke, it would have been so much harder to connect with family back home, and I would have felt much more lonely during my stay. We also would have had to pay off the officer and supervisor in charge at the Chetumal police station. I remain forever grateful to them for their time and attention to my case. They are truly magnificent people. Upon leaving the funeral home, as with each completed step, Katrina cried. I wasn't always sure of where we were in the process, so I would look to Kat. If she was crying, I knew we had finished another step. It was endearing yet funny as hell, and we thankfully found humor in the smallest things.

PLAYA DEL CARMEN

For the next step of our journey, Katrina connected with Leo, our Canadian Consulate agent in Playa del Carmen. We were now able to obtain the documents needed to bring myself and Michael's ashes home! Because of the timing, we knew we would make it to the Consulate on Friday, March 8, just before they would close for the weekend, and we'd have to wait until Monday before receiving my temporary visa and Certificate of Clearance to bring Michael's ashes home. Knowing this, Katrina began researching hotels in the area close to the

Consulate, but staying at a hotel also meant going out and searching for meals and so on.

It was a tremendous effort either to bring me to food, or to bring food to me. No restaurants in Bacalar or Playa did "take-out" like we do in North America. Most restaurants were not equipped with styrofoam containers, so every time the girls would order "to-go," the staff would have to dig up yogurt containers or food boxes, clean them out and pack them with food, sometimes just giving them the food in bowls or on plates to return later. Plastic bags could be found in markets and shops, making it easier to pack fruit. The girls would have to cut them up in the hotel room, then pack the cut pieces into some kind of creative container to bring to me during my stay at the hospital. Not only was the food transportation difficult, but moving me from place-to-place in my woozy condition was, at times, monumental. Going up and down the steps of the Bacalar hotel was a huge effort, due to the dizziness and total exhaustion my body was fighting. Not only was there a flight of stairs to climb to our hotel room – they were spiral! This added even more stress to my system and took us even more time to walk up or down, pausing often to allow the nausea to pass.

Taking it all into consideration, I suggested we wait out the weekend at an all-inclusive resort instead of a hotel. We could spend the weekend relaxing after our busy, difficult week, with meals only steps away. It made the most sense, given the situation, so Katrina called her travel agent friend, who then booked us into the best-priced, all-inclusive hotel she could find: the Hotel Riu Palace, only a short distance from the Canadian Consulate. We knew this would definitely give the "haters" back in Canada something to talk about, and indeed it did, but I didn't care. I was in a living hell, moving through it like the thick, bloody sludge that covered my eye that fateful day when I peered through it to view my beautiful, lifeless husband. We packed our things, said goodbye to our wonderful hosts in Bacalar and took a cab to Playa del Carmen.

Racing against the clock to make it before the weekend closure, we had the cab take us directly to the Consulate, as we were cutting close. Once we arrived, we asked the cab driver to wait for us and hold our luggage, explaining we were unsure how long we would be. Our cab driver was truly wonderful. Once Katrina explained our circumstances for being there – that it was NOT for an enjoyable vacation, but was rather a port of necessity – he took total responsibility for us and remained our cab to call, should we need anything in the days ahead. He was a gracious and lovely man. Inside, we met with Leo, the Canadian Consulate representative, previously from Quebec. Leo had moved 18 years beforehand to take his current position, and who could blame him? Playa del Carmen is absolutely beautiful! It was such a pleasure to meet Leo at last and to thank him for all of his hard work and assistance in connecting Adam with me at the hospital.

"How did you figure out I am Canadian and find my family?" I asked. I may have been privy to this information previously, but my recollection not being what it should be, I couldn't recall and felt clear-headed enough to ask.

"Really, it was all through social media," he replied. "Facebook, in particular."

He went on to tell us his story. He had seen the pictures of the accident on the news and noticed that the couple from Belize were caucasian; he then considered the possibility that they may be Canadian. He connected with Adam, as he was the Consulate's closest contact to the accident and had worked with the Consulate on several similar occasions. Adam found out where they had taken me and made the initial trip to see me. As there were no documents with me, they had to either start their own investigation or wait for me to wake up.

They obtained the insurance papers from the Canary and started there.

"You weren't listed on the ROCA database," Leo continued, "so we had to turn to Facebook for answers."

"What's ROCA?" I asked.

"Registration of Canadians Abroad," he explained. "It's a database where you can register your travel documents, the dates of planned travel and emergency contacts, should anything go wrong." I had never heard of the database, but now, I wished I had. It would have made the process much quicker and easier for all involved.

Leo narrowed his search on Facebook, finding Michael's profile first. He could verify that it was Michael through pictures and posts of us in Belize, unloading the Canary from the sea can upon its arrival and so on. He then alerted the RCMP in our hometown, who made the initial visit to Michael's mother to bring her the news. In the meantime, I had woken up enough to provide mine and Nicole's names to the hospital staff, who relayed the information to Adam and the Consulate, confirming the connections. The entire process took approximately three hours, and I was truly amazed at the detective work they did to bring it all together.

Once again racing against the clock, we signed the required documents and hopped back into our cab, en route to a nearby photography studio to have my picture taken for the temporary visa. Again, I was thankful that I had given Nicole the binder with copies of our IDs and passports, as this was instrumental in obtaining the permits to fly Michael's ashes home. It wasn't as simple as placing the urn in a carry-on. There were documents to go along with it so that airport security wouldn't question the contents and have to open the urn, documents we would most certainly need, as you will see later. Passport photo now in hand, we sped back to the Consulate to deliver it to Leo before the weekend closure. The paperwork would be ready sometime on Monday, which meant we could book flights to head home on Tuesday. At last! The end of this nightmare was in sight. Katrina cried as we left the Consulate, another incredibly vital step complete, her tears proof of fact. We could now head to the resort and relax.

DECOMPRESSING

The Riu family of resorts are all quite outstanding, and this one, in particular, truly lived up to its name with beautiful marble floors, tall pillars, pools and simple but elegant rooms. It was a resort fit for a queen, and I knew instantly that Michael would have approved of the choice, as he always wanted nothing but the best for his wife and would choose our vacations and hotels accordingly. He insisted upon the best of the best, and it was usually me who would balk at the price tag. I wasn't balking today. I could feel Michael's arms around me, escorting me through the grand entrance, pleased that we had made such an exceptional choice after such an intense couple of weeks.

Upon our arrival, we were accosted by the overly-friendly and handsome concierge. I was still in the neck brace with a noticeable indication of bruising, now turning a green-yellow up the left side of my face and neck. This garnered unwanted attention from both the staff and other guests that, frankly, made me very uncomfortable. For a moment, I thought perhaps the all-inclusive resort idea was a mistake. I was hoping to be oblivious, but in a resort with several hundred other people, that would be impossible. Katrina and Casey pulled a few key staff members aside and explained our reason for being there. After that, we were shown to more private dining tables and seated a little out of the way by the pools. We purchased a large, floppy hat and dark sunglasses for me at the gift shop, and I could manage a few minutes to a few hours without my tell-a-tale neck brace, until one of my personal mother hens would insist I put it back on.

The sun, normally something I would bask in unadulterated by sunscreen, was far too hot and too much in my current state; a pounding headache would ensue. A large umbrella was placed over my chaise lounger by the pool so I could lounge in peace and protection, until I would retreat to our room for a long, peaceful nap in a dark, cool environment. The girls were finally able to decompress, the worst part of the trip now over. It was time to just chill and be thankful for the place we were in. For me, it was a time to reconnect with Michael and start the process of journaling his messages to the best of my ability, with the somewhat limited use of my hands. They were no longer curled into fists, but they weren't exactly springing to life either, and long writing sessions were a chore.

Laying by the pool, Michael would give me messages for family and friends. In the early hours of each morning, he would wake me up with his locomotive snore – although, at times, he and Katrina battled for first place in the Epic Snore Division – and the messages would start pouring in again. I would write in the light of my cell phone or on the deck of our room. I would write everything I was able to in short spurts, until my hands became so cramped and uncomfortable I would have to ask him to stop for now. Most of the time, he restricted the messages to what he knew would provide me with comfort, that he was ok and that I would be.

The bulk of his messages were for family and friends, which he had previously told me in the hospital but helped me now to recall. As I wrote, slowly and haltingly due to the aches in my hands, he also halted, giving me time to process the information like a secretary taking dictation. I realized that both during the writing and afterward, once every message was written and the paper was folded and put away, I had no recollection of what it said. This felt like more than just my concussed mind and memory gap at work – this was an ethereal disconnect. I was merely the messenger, so the contents of the message were none of my business. I wasn't yet ready to hear the stuff I knew would be "heavy," the messages for the world. That, Michael would reserve... for later.

I napped frequently, propped up on my lounger under the shade umbrella, and as I drifted, I would be gifted with incredible images of my family and our future. The visions would come like rainbow waves, appearing as though through an auric kaleidoscope. One such image was of Casey, standing in front of a very tall, handsome man, both of them in their bathing suits by the ocean, and I sensed it was in Italy. I knew at once this was her future husband, and her life path was revealed to me in an instant. I gasped, sitting up quickly. Casey, lounging beside me, was at my side, full attention.

"Mama, what's wrong?" She asked, seeing the tears streaming down my cheeks.

"Oh, Casey, I saw him! I saw the man you will marry, I saw your life. Oh, it's incredible!" I was so in awe of the images swimming before me.

"Tell me more!" Casey exclaimed.

I gave her a few details but felt a warning creep up my spine. *"Don't give away too much, this is still her journey,"* Michael's voice floated through me. I stopped and laid back down to rest again.

Ashes

The rest of that day and the next were much the same. Michael woke me around 3:00 or 4:00 in the morning to give me messages, and I wrote out as much as I could manage before drifting off again, doing the same during the day as I lay convalescing, either by the pool or in our room. Sunday afternoon, Katrina received a WhatsApp message from Adam's staff that they had arrived at the resort to deliver Michael's ashes. We walked slowly to the enormous reception area near the main entrance, Kat on one side of me and Casey on the other. Two gentlemen arrived, one rather large and burly, the other short and slender. Neither one was wearing the telltale funeral home emblem on their shirts. They were "incognito."

We found a vacant seating area far enough away from the reception traffic, so as not to bring additional unwanted attention to our party. The larger of the two men – a rather gruff looking fellow who you wouldn't want to be caught in a back alley with – presented us with the box containing the urn. He placed the box on the marble coffee table in front of me. I immediately started to giggle, then giggled some more. My giggles soon turned into full on belly laughter, until tears started rolling down my cheeks. All eyes turned to me, questioning my deplorable activity. The box containing my dear husband's ashes was that of a 42-cup coffee urn. I giggled some more. Burly Man must have thought that he needed to explain why my husband's ashes were hidden inside a coffee urn box.

"To maintain your privacy and not to draw attention," he explained.

I had, without a doubt, drawn more than enough attention to our little group activity with my outburst. But the group, not quite getting the joke, required further explanation.

"My husband was a coffee addict," I began. "I would constantly have to remind him to drink more water, less coffee. I hear him in my head, enjoying the ultimate irony. His ashes have been presented to me in a 42-cup coffee urn box, and he is fully enjoying a 'take that, wife' moment."

Katrina used her special app to translate my story to the two men, and I laughed even harder, but this time, everyone joined in. Then, I sensed Michael's presence standing in the corner of the room, leaning against a pillar, legs crossed, smoking his cigarette and giving me a look of sheer enjoyment at my expense, he himself chuckling. What would have been an incredibly difficult moment of accepting my husband's ashes turned into one of the funniest I had ever shared with him in all our lives together. He gifted me this moment, and for that, I was truly thankful. He had, once again, softened my 3rd-dimensional reality. We thanked the gentlemen and took the box with the urn safely tucked inside back up to our room. I placed the box on the credenza, smiling.

"Thank you, honey, for this amazing experience," I whispered. "Now you can enjoy all of the coffee you want, in peace."

The three days spent at the resort were incredibly healing, with some joy and laughter and relaxation. The previous days had been harrowing, frightening and painful, and we were grateful for this time to catch our breath. I felt like we had run a gauntlet through fire, nails and lava, past the naysayers, the gossipers, the thieving and the disreputable. However, for as much as there were awful people in Mexico and Canada to deal with on this journey, there were also so many people we met and who took care of us throughout our experience, showing kindness, compassion and love, and we owe them an eternal debt of love and gratitude in return. We learned a saying as we trekked back and forth from Bacalar and Chetumal, taking in the culture as much as we could between our painful excursions. "*La vida es preciosa.*" Life is precious.

Monday morning arrived, and we made our way to the Consulate, completed the documentation required to bring Michael's ashes home and obtained my temporary passport. It was a simple sheet of paper with my new passport picture (looking rather gaunt and bruised; a scary version of my former self) and personal information. The paperwork for Michael was a little more involved and would have to be kept on our person, in the event that the staff at airport security needed to open the suitcase and questioned the contents of the urn. Once we had all of the documents in hand, we left the Consulate, elated. We could finally pack to go home, and again, Katrina cried.

COMING HOME

We said goodbye to Playa del Carmen, wistfully promising to return and enjoy the beautiful beaches and salty sea under better circumstances sometime in the future. We hired a transport to take us to the Cancun airport, Michael's ashes tucked safely away in Casey's carry-on suitcase. We had to do some clever rearranging of all of our suitcases to accommodate not just the lovely brown urn that contained the remains of my dearly departed, but also the coffee box his urn had arrived in. The 42-cup coffee joke just had to be shared with those who knew Michael back home, and I intended to have the coffee urn box present at his Celebration of Life. We carefully collapsed the coffee box and tucked it into the biggest suitcase.

The drive from Playa del Carmen to the airport took about an hour. The three of us sat quietly in the backseat of the hired shuttle, pondering the previous ten days and the road to recovery that lay ahead. I was still nauseous, dizzy and headachy, assuming that wouldn't pass anytime soon. Nicole had already pre-arranged appointments with my doctor, a massage therapist, physiotherapist and chiropractor back home. I was, once again, grateful for my family and for all of the amazing people who donated to the Go-Fund-Me. The funds that remained after this devastating adventure would pay for my rehabilitation and Michael's Celebration of Life.

We arrived at the airport with plenty of time to work through security. I was promptly placed in a wheelchair, as walking through the airport, waiting in line and walking to our gate would be far too much for me to bear. We strolled to the check-in and presented our passports. I pushed the piece of paper the Consulate had provided in front of the clerk. She was immediately confused by this and handed it back, asking for my passport.

"This *is* my passport. ***Look***." I was immediately frustrated. *Please, Lord, don't let anything else fall into the path home.*

Luckily, the passport was accepted, but I no longer had my departure paper that I would have received when Michael and I entered Mexico two weeks earlier. The small stub of paper that was ripped off of the larger declaration you must submit when you enter, was, of course, missing, along with my original passport. We were shuttled to another counter separate from the main check-in to obtain a new document. It cost $100 US to obtain this meager little stub, along with a full explanation of the reason why I had lost mine in the first place. Stub in hand, we went back to the check-in, obtained our boarding passes and then headed to security. Thankfully, we didn't have to wait in line (priority boarding – thank you, wheelchair) and were waved through. An airport attendant shuttled me through first, the girls placing the precious carry-on on the belt for an X-ray and taking their turns going through security themselves. That's when things got a little dicey.

Katrina seems to attract a pat-down whenever she goes through a security line-up. The tattoos on her upper arms and back may be part of the reason, her large boobs the other. One could hide a lot of goodies in a large bra, after all. She was immediately pulled to the side for a wand search. Casey made it through security, but the carry-on containing Michael's ashes was opened. She watched in horror as the security staff took the urn out of the small suitcase, looking it over. She was sure they were about to open the urn and inspect the contents and started shouting at them to stop and not to open the urn.

Katrina could hear Casey's shouting while her pat-down continued and shouted for them to stop and look at the paperwork she had in her carry-on.

Meanwhile, my escort was wheeling me past security toward the boarding gate. I could hear the shouting but couldn't turn to see what the commotion was all about. The security staff were looking at the two of them like they had just tumbled off the looney bus and were suddenly on high alert to investigate whether or not they were smuggling narcotics in the urn. The guard holding the urn told the girls to relax, they just need to scan the urn through the X-ray on its own, sans suitcase, and review the paperwork. Katrina's happy security officer finally released her from his thorough pat-down and retrieved the Consulate documents, proving the contents of the urn. This satisfied the security staff, and they zipped the urn back into the suitcase without a second glance, as if a cremation urn was a boring, everyday occurrence.

By the time Katrina and Casey had gathered their belongings and joined me outside of the security area, Katrina was crying. We had made it through! We were on our way home, at last. This time, Casey and I cried with her. We felt like we had run a long marathon of hurdles, except the hurdles were, at times, downright evil. We were exhausted and elated, the finish line only a mere day away. We would fly straight to Calgary, Canada, and would have to stay overnight at the airport hotel, as our flight home wouldn't be until the next morning. We were so close, yet still so far.

By this time, I was able to spend a little more time with my neck brace off without feeling like my head was going to fall off my shoulders. For this flight, however, I was happy to keep it firmly in place, wrapped around my neck and supporting my head while I dozed through the flight. Once we arrived at Calgary, a wheelchair was waiting for me, and we were shuttled to the comfortable airport hotel for the night. We were so grateful to be back on Canadian soil, despite the chill in the air and the sight of snow outside. The next day, I could see my children, grand-baby and the rest of my family. Sleep was nearly impossible; we were all too excited.

We woke early the next day and called the bellman to help us with our luggage. He was a man of many bellman talents, wheeling both me and the cart full of luggage straight to the check-in kiosk and then to the security lineup. He stayed with us until I was shuttled through the X-ray, waving goodbye on the other end. This was it. We were finally on the very last leg of our journey, and, you guessed it, Kat cried.

CHAPTER 10

Reunion

March - April 2019, Canada

The flight from Calgary, which normally took only 45 minutes, ended up taking hours. We were unable to land, due to fog, so the pilot had to circle the airport, waiting for it to lift. After two hours, he was forced to turn our plane back, and we ended up in Edmonton! The three of us died a little inside, again being so close, yet so far from home. It was madness! We were delayed in Edmonton another few hours before taking off once again. We alerted the family who were waiting for us at the airport that we were turning back, and several even texted, "The fog really isn't that bad. We can basically see everything." So frustrating.

Once we were en route again, we texted everyone and let them know we were on our way. This time, we kept all of our fingers and toes crossed and prayed the entire 50-minute flight. We landed much later than planned, but we had finally made it! I was greeted by a flight crew member with a wheelchair at the door, waiting somewhat impatiently to disembark. We walked in an all-too-slow procession down the long, endless hallways, until we finally reached the doors of the arrivals area, where my family was waiting. When Kat and Casey pushed the doors adjoining the hallway to the meet-n-greet reception area, my heart was bursting. There was my family, at last!

I had only a few seconds to take in the reception party before the first person to greet me, my oldest brother Rick, had me up out of the wheelchair and into his embrace. He cried and cried, holding me tight, whispering, "I thought I'd lost you. I was so scared." It must have been awful for everyone, realizing how close they'd come to losing someone they loved, now knowing with full, terrifying clarity that our relationship should never be taken for granted. Rick and I have grown much closer since.

The next few minutes were all about hugs, tears and love. It was a bittersweet reunion, seeing my other children for the first time since losing their beloved step-father. I could feel their pain reflecting mine in the tears streaming down their faces. Our best friend Linda was also there. She, who'd had the longest relationship with Michael out of all of us, would truly be left with a large hole in her life, an impossible void to fill. My heart hurt so hard for her while we embraced, her tears wet upon my cheek, mingling with my own.

"I'm glad you made it, girl," she said, and could barely say any more.

Next was my youngest daughter, Carrie. Normally a vibrant, happy young lady, in this moment, she seemed so small and frail, bursting into tears the moment we embraced. There were no words, just gratitude for being able to see my baby girl again and hold her so close. I could feel her heartbeat, her tears mingling with mine. I could see her brother over her shoulder, waiting for his turn, so I moved to hug him. I completely lost it then – as did he – and I still do every time I think of that reunion, even writing this now. There is just something about my baby boy that brings out all of my emotions, pride and love. We have been through many tough times together and have always been each other's rocks. He broke down sobbing, his much taller frame completely engulfing me as he held his momma close.

Everyone around me was hugging and embracing Casey and Katrina and each other while I made my way from person to person. The tears flowed, some laughter mixed among the tears, with some talk about the flight, the fog and the frustration we'd all collectively felt. When I got to hug Nicole, she was holding my granddaughter. Just 3-months-old, she was still so little and squishy. There was no way I could pick her up with my hands still being weak, but I could kiss her and hug her while her mommy held her close. I took a step and settled into one of the reception area chairs, holding my arms out to Nicole. She laid the baby in the cradle of my arms, ensuring she was supported.

"This is what I've been waiting for," I bawled, tears dropping onto the sleeping baby's blanket. I had come so close to watching her grow up from a vantage point up above, a ghostly presence checking in on her from time to time, and she never knowing who I was.

The entirety of the past two weeks came crashing around me as I held the baby as close to me as the strength in my hands and arms would allow. I was grateful for all the "coincidences" that had brought Michael home at the beginning of February, enabling him to see his granddaughter for the first and only time. The understanding of the pathways we create as spiritual beings, long before our human existence, the intricacies of our life map and the times, places and events within it, all became so very clear. Michael would have made an exceptional grandfather, except that he really wouldn't have had the chance to bond with his grandchildren, as his insistence on staying in Belize permanently was his priority. As you now know, dear reader, it was not a priority I shared. At last, I could breathe, finally close to my children, grandchild and the rest of my family again, where I belonged.

Reunion over and eyes wet with tears, Katrina, Casey and I had a moment to embrace once again in gratitude and love, bonded together forever for the experience, then we made our way to our separate vehicles. My son and Casey were going back to their shared apartment in the city for the night but planned to make the trip to our hometown the next day for a long visit. Katrina left for her home in the same city, and me, home with Carrie, Nicole and the baby. It was an incredibly difficult separation from Katrina and Casey after the time we spent together. I felt like a part of me was being cut off, leaving an even bigger gap in my life after losing Michael. It was all so surreal.

SANCTUARY

On the 2-hour drive to Nicole's, I went over as many of the details of the past two weeks that I could recall. Nicole had been in constant contact with Katrina and Casey during the entire ordeal and knew far more than I did, but she let me talk just the same. By the time we arrived home, it was late and dark, and I was incredibly exhausted. Nicole showed me to "Nana's room," the small spare bedroom that was furnished with a queen-sized bed, bookcase and nightstand. Nicole and Carrie had gone to my last remaining storage unit – everything else we owned had been shipped to Belize the year before – and gathered my metaphysical and spiritual books for the bookshelf. They made my room a sanctuary, with candles, an essential oil diffuser, fluffy pillows and a TV, a room for healing, Netflix and chill. I rested well and fully, feeling the pressure of Michael's body by my side, the sound of his snoring softly in my ears.

The next day, Nicole showed me hundreds of messages

received from friends and family through Facebook. I read through many of them, unable to get to them all but no less astounded by all the love, support and concern. Nicole had given up trying to respond to them. It was just too much to bear, and she had so many other things to attend to, my grand-daughter being the main priority. For the first couple of weeks after my return, I was unable to pick up or properly hold the baby without help. My hands didn't have the strength to grasp the robust, wiggly little bundle. I spent many hours with her resting on my chest, feeling her beautiful life-force energy between us. I couldn't help but think about how "lucky" I was to have the opportunity to watch her grow. This, over all else, was the greatest blessing. Baby and I created an everlasting bond during those months of convalescing that has only grown deeper as she's bloomed into toddlerhood.

Nicole unpacked my belongings and hung what little clothes I had in the small closet in my bedroom. She unpacked the tan and creamsicle blood-splattered beach bag and held up the empty bag to me, horrified.

"Oh my God, Mom. This is blood?"

"Yes, not sure whose," I replied, somewhat distracted by my wriggly grand-baby.

"What would you like me to do with it? I could try to get the blood stains out but..." She turned the bag over and peered inside. "It's kind of everywhere."

"Maybe a bit of bleach?" I asked, suddenly unsure on the process of getting blood stains out of fabrics or doing laundry in general.

"Bleach would ruin the fabrics. I'll try Dawn dish deter-gent instead." Nicole set about the task of soaking the bag in a sink full of Dawn. (Turns out it cuts grease AND blood!) The results were not a 100% improvement, but it was infinitely better than it was. Once the bag was dry, Nicole tucked it into my closet with the now empty suitcases.

BITTERSWEET

I was so thankful I had no memory of the accident, and I was also thankful that people didn't press for more details, but there came a time shortly after arriving at Nicole's place to convalesce that we decided to keep visitors away. So many people wanted to come by and see me, but it was all a bit too much, so we reserved visitation for the five people closest to me. Being anywhere near friends of mine or Mike's, talking about what happened over and over again was cathartic but exhausting. It hurt a lot, physically, mentally and emotionally, but it also helped me to begin the next phase of the healing process. Talking about life with Michael brought back so many joyous memories, along with questions about what may have happened, or how things could have been different. It takes a long time to accept a tragedy, understanding that you will never again see or hold the person so close to you and having no choice in the decision of their death. I tried to be so strong for everyone else; it was only in my private time with Michael's spirit that I allowed myself to fully feel.

Our friends Paul and Lisa were among the group of five who were able to visit. I was delighted to present Paul with the boxes of Jamie Oliver cookbooks, as Mike had requested when I was in the Bacalar hospital, along with a message I had written from Michael. I knew that part of the message that came through me was also from Paul's father who had passed a couple of years previous, but, as with all messages I channeled, I couldn't recall what he had said. As expected, Paul broke down while reading the message, the bittersweetness spilling over onto the page. Other close friends who visited were somewhat at a loss as to what to say. I could sense the hollowness they were experiencing over losing their wonderful friend. Our embraces were long, tearful and also full of joyful amazement that I was even alive to enjoy the love and hugs.

I attempted to tell people about my experiences in the Bacalar hospital, about the messages, and I relayed Mike's words to them all during this time. It wasn't easy. I was now faced with fully accepting, stepping into and owning the person I had become. I could channel the dead and I now understood, perhaps for the first time ever, how life after death truly works, how we all come to be, how we all eventually end up when we cross the veil between life and death, and how it was now my responsibility to tell the world the truth. I wasn't sure I was ready but decided to do it anyway, fully realizing the task before me. If people thought I was crazy, so be it. If I lost friends, then they weren't truly friends to begin with.

For the first time in years, I faced the possibility of persecution once again, of being "burned at the stake." I had to stop caring how others might react and evolve into the person I was truly meant to be, once and for all. And, to my absolute delight, I was relieved when the friends and family who were presented with Michael's messages were all very supportive, loving and emotional at receiving his gifts. I hoped his visits and messages would continue and that he would also continue to encourage, support and comfort me. We, as a family, had already faced persecution from people one degree separated from us, and I knew this part of our journey would not be over just yet. There was still Mike's Celebration of Life to get through, but I could feel a dark cloud overshadow what was supposed to be a joyous celebration of Michael's life. We made plans to hold the celebration at the end of March 2019. That would give us enough time to meet with our local funeral home director, plan the ceremony and alert friends and acquaintances who would want to attend. In the meantime, I focused on healing.

HEALING

Amidst the physiotherapy, chiropractic and doctor visits, I went for a Holy Fire Reiki session that the practitioner, an acquaintance of mine, had gifted me. Being a Reiki Master myself, I knew that turning to energy healing was probably the most fundamental and important piece I could do to facilitate physical, mental and emotional healing. I had never experienced Holy Fire Reiki, so I was eager to try it. Nicole dropped me off at the practitioner's office, a lovely healing space inside a metaphysical shop in our hometown. The room was small but comfortable. As I lay face up on the massage table, listening to the soft music and enjoying the scent of the various candles lit around the room, I immediately relaxed.

The practitioner started the session, first cupping her hands under my head. I felt the fiery heat of the practitioner's hands on me as she moved around the table, placing her hands on my left shoulder, then my left hip. The intense warmth and weight of the practitioner's hands laid at my hip for several minutes. Then, I felt the pressure of her hands move to the *right* side of me *and* on my left! My eyes flew open to see that no one was on my left side, but the pressure and heat was still there, heavy and intense. I knew immediately that it was Michael, assisting the practitioner in her task to heal my injuries and soothe my soul. I closed my eyes, grateful for his presence. As the practitioner moved her hands up the right side of my body, I also felt Michael's hands on my left, moving in tandem with the practitioner's on my right. The pressure and heat was just as intense as the practitioner's. I was absolutely thrilled at this connection and settled in to enjoy the process.

Afterwards, the practitioner, who was silent throughout the session, said, "Michael came into the room as soon as we got started. He wanted to help and was on your left side the entire time I was on your right." I smiled and told her that I knew, that I'd felt his large, heavy hands on me, just as if he were physically there. I was so grateful for this session and the experience, and I felt the subsequent shift in my own energy centers.

After that, I felt his presence on the edge of my bed every night those first few weeks at Nicole's, even heavier than before. The bulk of his weight pressed upon the bed as he sat there, night after night, keeping me company and watching me as I slept, fully aware of his presence. Scared, but not scared. At times, I would feel his weight shift from the end of the bed to lay right beside me, the bed itself releasing upward. Occasionally, he'd wake me up with his locomotive snore or to deliver a heap of new messages. I would take in all of the wonderful messages he gave me, and sometimes, we just sat in silence until I felt comforted enough to fall asleep. A mutual friend told me they felt Michael was visiting regularly, that he was with me every night, curled up beside me, watching me sleep and comforting me in my dreams.

Indeed, he was.

MESSAGES FROM MICHAEL

A couple of weeks later, I met with a dear friend and Reiki Master, Caroline, for a healing session in her home. My darling friend also has the ability to channel and receive messages from spirit guides or the departed during sessions, and she free-writes the messages afterward. The session itself was so intense that she had to sit down, unable to continue. The energy transference proved to be just too much for her to take and was making her physically weak. We talked about what she saw and was told; Michael had been in the room, curled up by my side. She knew Michael personally, her ex-husband having worked with him years before we got together, so she knew who she was seeing, and the energy she was feeling from him was larger than life. She managed a few pages of notes at the end of the session:

"Tammy, I felt Mike come in right away," she began. "It's like he went right through me to you. I was shown a medallion. A large medal, given by a government agency. A permit to operate or some type of approval marker."

What she saw was a survey marker that is assigned to a project and implanted in the concrete, asphalt or, in our case, a Mayan ruin. Michael and I used to have such fun finding the various survey markers on our numerous ruin tours around Belize, and, as you might recall, dear reader, it was a kind of "competition" between us that I always won, irking Michael to no end.

Caroline continued, "For today, he wants you to know – to confirm your knowing – that he is with you. This happened immediately. He cuddled up on your right side. When I questioned if that's what he did, he then hopped over to the left, and I heard, '*There's no wrong side to my girl. All sides are beautiful.*' I sense he is very supportive in organizing. I hear, '*getting things done.*' He's with you, and I hear '*making lists.*' He says it's a good idea... there's so much more to say, but for today, this is all."

Everything she told me made perfect sense. Michael used to sleep on my left side, so I had to silently chuckle a bit knowing he had hopped over to my left side when Caroline questioned him about being on the right. What he said next about all of my sides being beautiful made me smile; even in death, Michael was so sweet. It also made perfect sense that he was "getting things done" – his favorite saying and catch-phrase was "get shit done." And of course, he was constantly making lists of just what "shit," exactly, needed to be done. Everything Caroline shared so far was spot on.

Then she asked, "Did Mike smoke? Michael, or someone close to you?"

When I told her he did and that he had stopped when we first got together but later progressed to almost a pack a day in the final years of his life, she said, "It must have been Michael that visited me earlier today in preparation for today's session." She had been in a yoga class before our session and stayed behind to meditate and rest, when she suddenly smelled cigarette smoke. The last remaining person in the room, she was quite confused, as the smell was incredibly strong, yet she was totally alone, and there was no smoking allowed in the building anyway. At that time, she'd brushed it off as just an odd, random "coincidence," but when the same smell came to her during our healing session, it all made sense, and the effects of his presence were incredibly powerful.

Lastly, she said, "I feel him very close to you, Tammy. I hear '*Heaven is full of help*'."

That was the last of the messages he gave to her to share, but then she was shown a lion with a flowing, golden mane. I explained how I had always told Michael that he was my big, beautiful lion with a beautiful golden mane of hair, so this didn't surprise me. Caroline went on to say, "In the realm of spirit animals, the lion wins the prize for most relentless fighter in the face of life's challenges. The Lion Spirit represents courage and strength in overcoming difficulties. He's so with you."

She then drew three tarot cards: card number 9 for Solitude, card number 3 for Heartache and card number 2, The Waiting Game. The Solitude card's message is a reminder of how important it is to pause, still the mind, meditate, reflect, rejuvenate and discover the wisdom and answers within the very soul of your being. The Heartache card revolves around disappointment, sorrow and separation, which can cause upheaval and distress. The Waiting Game card indicates that you've worked hard to set things in motion in certain areas of your life, and you're now waiting for the results to come to fruition. As I reviewed the full messages and meaning of the cards with Caroline, I was astonished at how incredibly on point they were and thankful for the guidance provided by the Universe through these cards.

In yet another session, this time with another dear friend and Reiki Master, Michelle, I received an incredibly effective healing and nine pages of messages from Michael, channeled through my friend, about what I would experience and accomplish now, moving forward in my life. Michelle was aware of the accident and the fact that I had lost my husband, but she had never met Michael personally, had never seen a picture of him and didn't follow us on Facebook, nor had she seen pictures or details of the accident itself. Knowing all this made the reading even more profound. The pages read:

April 16, 2019

Client: Tammy Tyree

Reiki/inner guidance/higher sense perception

I am asking for guides/ancestors/loved ones connected to Tammy, to come in and assist and guide her on her journey at this moment of time. I access Tammy's energy field, and I notice how powerful and strong her energy field is. She is seeding new beginnings in my vision, gently and slowly, taking in every moment and being still, for this stillness provides Tammy with messages from the spirit world.

As I work with Tammy's energy field/balancing, I see a vision of Tammy's husband, blond, with long hair and glasses. He's wearing yellow clogs, shorts and a flowery shirt. He has a bracelet on his wrist, and I see a necklace around his neck. *"Bittersweet,"* he says. *"Bittersweet. Tammy, my Soul Mate, the* strongest person I have ever known. I would not have done what we did, together, without Tammy. She has always been my rock."

He helps me somehow with this energy balance, as he stands across the

table from me. He says: "*What was so ironic about that particular day, is that we had said to each other 'we will be there before the evening falls.' We had planned everything. Well, Tammy was my planner. Tammy is very good at planning. Just some relaxation for the two of us, a celebration of being together. I now know why I had to go, Tammy. I now know. You belong with your children, Tammy, everything is changing now. You belong with your children.*"

He says: "*When I met Tammy, I knew we were meant for each other, true Soul Mates. Candles, music and most of all, laughter and so much love. She, my wife Tammy, can give great massages, strong healing hands.*" He says: "*My father, I have seen. My brother, I have seen. Tammy's father, I have seen, and you know what, Tammy, look at this...*" I see a medium-sized dog, dark brown or black, with him in spirit."

(This was our dog, D'fer, who passed away the year before. She used to go on Michael's work trips with him when she was a pup, and she was his "baby.")

The male spirit says: "*Tammy knows I am not dead.*" He shows me

a small glass with alcohol in it, and he shows me a cigar, and he shows me big plants, very big plants, and he says: "*Tammy will continue the dream that we have set out, but in a different way. Tammy is going to help people just like you. Tammy will heal with her hands, and her mind will receive messages, and this is her purpose in this lifetime. Her true purpose.*"

(Michael would often pour a drink of our favorite Old Master's Coconut Rum and smoke a cigar on the deck of our cabana, and he was very proud of the large, tropical plants and flowers he had planted on the property).

"*Tammy knows about a healthy diet. She knows about how everything is*

from the stomach, created in the stomach – dis-ease. Tammy is now ready and will be ready whenever she opens her new door and will help people in many ways. I now know Tammy." He says: "*I did not like snow and cold weather anymore. I had enough of the cold.*" He shows me a waterfall and a small pool of water. He says: "*There are so many amazing places to discover, and that's what we did; we discovered things in nature.*"

Then the male spirit says: "*I still sleep with my wife at night, her legs over*

my body." He says: "*I will stay with her until she is healed completely, and then I will come back, part of my soul will be back. Tammy's daughter, my daughter, will have another baby. I will be that baby. Tammy, I will be part of that baby. My soul will be part of that baby.*" Then he says: "*You know that I have had such an amazing life. It was so beautiful with my wife, Tammy. We worked hard together, always, we were a team.*" Then he says: "*I will show you much more.*" He shows himself holding a baby. "*I fell in love with this child, a connection so strong, like falling in love all over again.*"

(This image was of Michael and our granddaughter, the only time they met).

"*My mother is getting older. She has a hard time walking. Her body is*

sore. She is the one that would always say: 'You have to do what you want to do in life.' Tammy, she does not have much time left. She is the one that will recognize that life is getting harder and harder for her. Her back is sore, and she is not a complainer. We spend so much time together." He shows me a bundle of keys, many keys in one bundle. He also shows me a safe, and there are papers in this safe and money in this safe.

(There was a safe in our cabana in Belize with our marriage certificate and money. Tony immediately took possession of the safe and the keys for it the day the accident happened and brought the contents to me in the hospital in Bacalar).

He says: "*I know Tammy is looked after financially. We did our*

homework." Then he sits down at the table. He shows me a small toothpick, and he uses this to clean his teeth. He says: "*Tammy knows how quiet it was in nature. So quiet, I love the quietness. Tammy, everything went the way it was supposed to go. We were looked after in so many ways.*" He shows me a "For Sale" sign. "*It will sell, Tammy. It will sell, and the people that will buy this will have a dream like we had.*" Then he shows me a cat, and he says: "*Wouldn't it have been funny if that cat went missing. I loved that cat, you know.*"

(We had two adopted cats on our property, and the little one would follow Michael throughout the property but then get distracted and lost, unable to figure out how to get back to the cabana. Michael would have to go out searching for her before dark. He would mutter and huff and puff about the silly cat, but deep down, he absolutely adored his little pal).

Then he says: "*What I like the most is that we are never apart. Never,*

Tammy, we are always together." He shows me that he likes sleeping naked, that he is not shy. He says: "*Who wants to wear clothes in bed?*" He says: "*When it rained, it poured, and the sound on the roof was powerful.*" Then the male spirit says: "*Tammy will help many people, you know. That is her true purpose. Many healing modalities are her future.*" He shows me a pool table with so many people surrounding it, and he says: "*We know so many people, and everyone is part of our journey.*"

Then he says: "*Tell Tammy that when she lies in bed, I kiss her forehead, and I stroke her hair. I loved wearing my yellow clogs, and what I really liked was watching the sun go under.*" Then he says: "*Tammy knows what she needs to do, she knows.*" Then he steps away, and he says: "*Forever, remember Tammy, forever.*" He leaves roses behind, many of them. He stands there and waits for me to be finished. He says: "*Thank you.*" Then it becomes still. He is fading away. I wrap Tammy in love, harmony, peace and good health. Then he comes back one more time. "*Sell everything there, Tammy. Do not bring the heavy things back. Sell it all.*" Then he fades away again. That was all.

Michelle finished her writing and shared it with me, looking partially confused as to the contents. She, naturally, wouldn't know what many of the images and messages would mean, such as the part about our cat or the weird clogs, or even the drink and cigar. I explained it all to her, and we enjoyed the personal jokes and stories she was now privy to. The session and reading left me feeling so elated, peaceful and full of wonder. What was my path now? Michael had told Michelle that I knew what my path was, but did I really?

FINAL SHARD

After the session with Michelle and hearing all that Michael had to say, I was satisfied with his insistence on selling the property in Belize, as I truly didn't want to continue with the project on my own and no longer had any desire to live there without him. Shortly after this session, I connected with our friend Wanda, the realtor in Belize, and had her list the property. As for the tools and equipment, our dear friend Troy would be able to deal with all of that for me, as he had taken most of the valuable tools from our sea cans for storage and use on his property anyway. He promised to sell what he could and utilize those funds to maintain the property. He was also gathering enough funds together so he himself could purchase as many tools as possible, but I felt that, because of his enormous generosity to date, he should be given something in return. He wouldn't accept any money for the maintenance and security he provided, so I gifted him the mini-excavator, forcing him to accept the offering. It was the least I could do, and it would be useless if left on the property, whereas Troy would put it to great use. He was honored and excited to accept.

I continued with my weekly physiotherapy and chiropractic visits and was so grateful for the care and concern that each doctor or practitioner took with me, even though there were definitely things that I could not do, like movements or adjustments that couldn't be done just yet, for fear of further injury to my neck, head and spine. I had a minimum of four appointments per week between my doctor, chiropractor, physiotherapist and massage therapist. Each appointment was painful and thoroughly exhausted me. The time I spent at Nicole's recovering was all about resting, holding the baby and being no use to anyone whatsoever. Ever so slowly as the weeks progressed, I was able to move a little more and walk a little further, still with some dizziness, and we would attempt short walks around Nicole's neighborhood or downtown after my appointments. I would have to hold on to my grand-baby's stroller to steady myself, otherwise the world was one big, dizzy, spinning merry-go-round that I couldn't jump off of. The progression to normalcy took months. The biggest thrill for me was finally being able to pick up my granddaughter – with some assistance – and give her proper cuddles. She was such a wonderful light in the darkness of my world, and I was truly grateful.

It was almost two months after the accident that my doctor was finally able to retrieve the final piece of glass from my left ear, the one the otolaryngologist in Bacalar was unable to get to and had left behind for me to expel... later. It was painful, as she had to hold the otoscope and the tweezers in my ear at the same time, digging rather deep, so close to my eardrum that I could hear the clip of the tweezers as they gripped and extracted the shard. My ear bled profusely at its removal. It was about a 1mm cube, clear with the reddish tint of blood. She dropped it into my hand. The final piece of the Canary, the only piece to come home to Canada, had finally been released.

This was such a bittersweet moment. A finality to the tragedy, the loss of my love. I cried at that moment, partly because its extraction hurt so bloody much, and partly because of the depth of reality this tiny piece of glass represented. My doctor passed me a tissue and held me while I wept. She knew, as a doctor and as a woman, what a broken heart looked like. I kept the shard of glass, carefully taping it into my journal. For the size of it – such a small, seemingly insignificant, tiny little shard – it was truly a monumental piece of symbolism, for what it represented was larger than life.

My life until now, the loss of my love and our time together here on Earth, was truly over.

CELEBRATION

As I continued to heal, we made plans for Michael's Celebration of Life with the assistance of our incredible local funeral director. It was held at the local Catholic Church Hall, a rather informal gathering with large round tables set up all over the room and a buffet of snacks to be offered post-memorial. There would be no graveside burial, as I planned to bring Michael's ashes back to Belize to be spread over the property he loved so dearly. The evening before, we decorated the tables with the staggering amount of baseball caps Michael had collected over the years, which had been left behind in our Canadian storage container with other household items intended for later shipment to Belize. I also carefully unpacked all of his antique survey levels and equipment and placed a piece at the center of each table. After the ceremony, the pieces were handed over to one of Michael's closest friends and a fellow surveyor for listing on eBay. I kept a piece for myself, and Michael's son chose one to keep as well.

The urn containing Michael's ashes was showcased on a single table at the front of the room, with a huge arrangement of tropical flowers – all of Michael's favorites – to brighten the space. He would have loved the massive arrangement, containing mostly heliconia, the flower he most admired and grew copious amounts of on our property. Prior to the ceremony, our funeral director was able to arrange for memorial glass-blown pieces for myself and anyone else in the family who wished to have one. They were swirled with clear glass, colored glass and bits of Michael's ashes. Each piece is a beautiful memento for the members of our family who chose to have one. Mine is bright orange, the color of our Kubota tractor, Michael's pride and joy that he spent endless hours on, pushing dirt around from place-to-place on our tropical estate. The glass globe is showcased in an antique china cabinet his mother gave me when I was finally able to make a home for myself a few months after the Celebration.

Casey purchased a beautiful, cylindrical silver necklace with one diamond at the top meant for holding the ashes of a loved one. Our funeral director sealed a tiny bit of ash inside, and she wears it often. Some of the ashes were given to Michael's son in a vial of his choosing that he could keep or spread in the places around our town that meant the most to him. Some of his ashes were buried with a lemon tree and a lime tree in my new apartment, some remained in the urn we had brought them home in, and the rest returned to Belize, months later, with me and three of my children, where we spread them around Michael's favorite Ceiba tree.

There were over 250 people in attendance at Michael's Celebration of Life, which touched my heart deeply. Many of Michael's co-workers made the trek from as far away as Winnipeg, Manitoba. What was the most poignant, however, were the men that Michael mentored throughout his career, first as a surveyor and then as a construction manager. These young men had, in turn, gone off to start their own businesses or climb to major heights in their individual careers, and they all attributed their success to Michael's encouragement, support and urging. Their stories of his intelligence, care and management brought everyone in the room to tears. Hearing these stories was such a blessing and gave us all just a little more insight into the incredible man Michael was. Many of them referred to Michael as "Dad," a label he was most proud of. He was a humble man and refused to take credit, even when it was due, but secretly, he would tell me how proud he was of "his boys" and allow himself some time to boast. Knowing there were several men who wanted to follow in "Daddy's" footsteps meant the world to him.

Casey gave an amazing eulogy. At one point, as she was standing there in front of the throng of people talking about her precious step-father, she broke down. I rose from my seat and approached her, slipping an arm around her waist, offering as much support as I could muster. She read a passage from one of her favorite books and spoke of Mike's love:

I had such a hard time picking and choosing between stories to share about Mike,
 while at the same time keeping it short and sweet. So, I

decided to make this about Mike's love. Mike came into my life when I was 11. I soon found out, as we all did upon meeting Mike, that he is many things; he is a smartass, he is hard working, the KING of overkill, devoted, fun, kind, and he LOVES to make fun of me. He's secretly a big softy, but above all, he is love. I have learned this over and over again about my dad. From the first time he lectured me about drinking wine from his cellar, to bonding over it pretty quickly and, eventually, planning a Napa Valley wine trip together. Or when he was teaching me to drive standard and let me plow through a field and stall continuously in his first Jeep, knowing absolutely that the clutch would never be the same again, and he would pretty much have to call this one a loss. Yet, as we drove around town, he never complained, only explained, and at the same time, he let me figure it out for myself. I was happy and free, which made him happy (and twitch). Mike was able to look past the details, the material, the frivolous, and focus on the important, undeniable powerful energy that is love. Everything is love. Mike is, was and will always be, love.

Mike has taught us all many things in this lifetime; one of the most valuable to me

is how important it is to enjoy ourselves while we are here. There is no reason to fear any part of our journey; the experiences we have are simply reminders that we are all strong enough to survive anything. So often we focus on the mundane, negative or, truthfully, unimportant parts of our lives. We move through life waiting, stagnating, believing that we can't have or don't deserve everything we want right here and now. Really though, it should be so simple. I mean, look back at Mike's life, the memories you have with him, the experience he has had, the accomplishments he has made, the fun and adventure. He was truly a light for us to follow and learn from. So, I implore you all, in Mike's honor, to show love always, to everyone, all of the time. "Get shit done," make your journey enjoyable and always value your past.

La vida es preciosa.

To Mike

The rest of the afternoon was a blur of condolences and endless hugs. People ate, shared stories and drank coffee, some moving outside to share a cigar or cigarette in Michael's honor. I made the rounds, thanking everyone for being there, not taking any sustenance for myself; just letting everyone enjoy the day and the stories as much as they could. We had a large table at the back of the room with photo albums and pictures for everyone to look through. I had purchased a beautiful journal with a gold-gilded cross on the front that was passed around the room, allowing people to write their appreciation and connection they had with Michael. It was the best memorial gift of the day.

They say it takes a long time to comprehend a tragedy. I understood I would never see him again, never hold him again. I understood it was all final, no reprieve. I stayed strong through the ceremony, offering comfort to everyone else, plastering a smile on my face. Many well-meaning friends offered the usual cliches, but please, don't tell me, "I'm young," that it "will get better," or, "I'm lucky to have known such a love." And don't offer condolences. None of it is comforting. You only end up staring at the person offering such niceties, wondering how life could have taken such a sudden, abrupt turn, and what did that mean for me now?

In fact, you should *never* offer condolences to a person who has just lost their love. I know this may sound insane, because what else can you do? But, in offering an apology for their loss, you are merely anchoring their pain, and the more often they hear it (which you do, endlessly, sometimes for weeks or even years) you further emphasize that they should be sad and grieving. Instead, offer up a celebration of the wonderful life he or she lived, what an incredible impact they made on the world and what a great friend they were to you, your family or whatever the case may be.

Having fully experienced this for myself, and with my background in hypnotherapy, I understand how the subconscious mind anchors emotional events, and hearing the apologies from people over and over, that emotional adjunct is anchored so deep, it actually gives the griever no relief from their personal anguish. When people would offer apologies, which they still do when they realize I'm a widow, I merely say, "Please don't be. I was granted the opportunity to live an amazing life with an amazing man, and I celebrate him daily."

When I have been in a position to offer someone else an apology for their grief, I never do. Instead, I offer a joyous tidbit, noting what an amazing life they led and what an amazing person their spouse/child/father/mother was. Try this the next time you are tempted to offer sympathies, perhaps on someone's Facebook feed, and you will see that yours is the only offering that gets a thankful comment from the person in grief. People want to be reminded of how amazing their significant person was, not feel sorry for their loss in perpetuity.

All in all, the day was a success. The issues with the "haters" we'd braced ourselves to face did not manifest, much to our relief. I could smell Michael's cigarette smoke, alerting me to his presence in the back corner of the room throughout the day. I had an image of him leaning against the wall, legs in their usual crossed position, smoking his cigarettes. At times, I would sense him in the side kitchen window, the ladies of the Catholic Hall serving team oblivious to his spiritual presence as they bustled about the kitchen, moving through him. I could sense him milling around the men who he had mentored and coached, so incredibly proud of them and the lives and careers they had created for themselves. I wasn't surprised by his presence. He wouldn't have missed his own Celebration for the world. Myself and the few others in attendance who were able to see him there witnessed his quiet, humble pleasure, feeling the bountiful love of everyone in the room.

CHAPTER 11

New Normal

2019, Canada

A bout a month after Michael's Celebration of Life, we decided it was probably time for me to start driving myself to my appointments, first using Nicole's car, then my own vehicle. We had sold my car to an auction house in Manitoba prior to leaving the province and moving to Belize for the winter in 2018, so the only other vehicle I had to use was Michael's Ford Platinum. We'd stored at Linda's farm, and it was time to transfer the title into my name. Michael had purchased the one-ton truck three years previous and still had a few payments left, but thankfully, there was enough in our savings to cover the loan.

Nicole wasn't too thrilled to allow me to venture out on my own, still concerned for the unexpected dizzy spells that would occasionally occur, but I promised to take it slow and call a friend if I ended up on the side of a road, unable to continue. I managed just fine, and although I was grateful for Nicole's care and concern, I was also anxious to move forward in my own healing and life's purpose. I also felt like I must have been somewhat of a burden, although Nicole would tell me time and again that I was not, and that I could stay with them for as long as I needed to. I felt so loved and looked after, but I was also itching to set off on my own.

Nicole and Shawn's place was a rather small 3-bedroom and felt a little cramped. By this time, I knew I didn't want to move back into the family home Michael and I shared, nor remain in our hometown; I just couldn't handle the long winters under looming grey clouds, and the annual promise of five to six feet of snow didn't hold any attraction for me, as I'd grown accustomed to spending Canada's winter months in Belizean summers. Nicole and Shawn, on the other hand, wanted to raise my granddaughter in the place where Nicole grew up. The small, quaint town was attractive, to be sure. Nicole had a couple of friends from school who were also in the stages of raising a young family, and Shawn wanted his daughter to learn to ski so they'd be able to go together.

One morning, as we were driving back from an appointment in town, I said to Nicole, "Why don't you guys buy my house?" My tenant had given his notice, so it seemed like the perfect time for all of us to make the transition. Nicole began crying immediately. I was a little surprised, but, clearly, it had been on her mind; she just wasn't able to bring it up, allowing me the time to make some decisions about my own life. The thought of living in the home where she had grown up, the home Michael had lovingly renovated and built beautiful gardens around, was exactly what she was hoping for.

We started making plans. Once my tenant moved out, we cleaned, painted and started moving their things over. Then we cleaned and prepped their own small home for their new tenants. At the same time, I started making plans to move to the Sunny Okanagan, where I knew I wanted to be. It was close to amazing lakes, an airport, close to friends and my brother Richard and, of course, my son and Casey, who had been living there for a few years already. This was definitely the place I'd rather call home, even though it meant a 2-hour separation from my oldest daughter and granddaughter. I found a beautiful apartment on the 4th-floor of the same building that my son and Casey were living in. It had a great view of the city from the small deck and the lake in the distance. It was a 2-bedroom, perfect for Carrie to make the move as well, later that summer. She wanted to start University, feeling stagnant in our small hometown. Here, I would be surrounded by my children, with the exception of my oldest and my grand-baby, but I was secretly hopeful that they would one day move closer to Nana.

I had one storage unit of belongings left in Canada. The rest of my home and previous life's belongings had been shipped to Belize the year before. This 10x10 foot storage unit contained one queen-sized bed, my mother's cedar blanket chest, given to her and my father as a wedding gift, my collection of books, all of my kitchen things, some random knick-knacks, paintings and a couple of televisions. It was mainly kitchen goods, which was incredibly helpful. However, the little unit was sorely lacking any other pieces of furniture, so I started shopping on Facebook Marketplace for affordable, eclectic items that suited my boho taste. I spent little and treasured every piece I found, most of which were vintage or antique.

While exploring my new town one weekend, I found a round, antique table with a beautifully carved pillar leg for $40. I Immediately connected with the seller and arranged to pick it up. Casey came with me, and once we arrived and saw the table in the driveway, ready for pick-up, I was shocked. The table had a couple of water rings on the top, but otherwise, it was an incredible, heavy oak piece, approximately 60-80 years old and worth far more than the $40 I paid for it. We had a "quick, get it into the truck and go" moment, giggling as we did so. I didn't want the owner to suddenly come to his senses and realize he had priced it far too low. I stored it at Linda's farm in one of her small sheds, until such time that my new apartment was available and ready for me to move into.

Michael's half of the storage unit was somewhat of a revelation. There were VCRs and DVD players, and plenty of VHS tapes and DVD discs, which I knew Michael had wanted to keep and bring to the property in Belize to utilize in the "communal recreation room" he planned to build at the center of the cabanas, close to the pool and communal kitchen. I truly didn't see myself using the VCRs or DVDs, having most of the movies and TV shows I cared to watch available on Netflix and my Apple TV, which had also been packed and stored. There were other items, too, that I knew I would no longer require, such as saddles and tack for the horses we no longer had, also something we thought we may eventually have again in Belize, so we kept them.

Among the bins of Michael's odds and ends were bins of his work clothes. Jeans, boots, jackets and work shirts, most of them shockingly clean and intact, unlike so many of his farm clothes he lived in while working on our property. I decided to keep the work shirts, one for myself to wear as a smock when I would paint, and the others to cut into squares and work into a quilt. I knew I would want to include Michael's dress shirts that were still in our cabana in Belize, so I tucked the shirts away in a separate box and kept them with his other personal belongings. Next, we planned and executed a storage unit sale. One of my sisters came to visit and assist with the sale, a rather bittersweet day. To see some of the items that Michael had held onto leaving with new owners gave me pause. "*Sell it all*," was what he had told me during my Reiki session with Michelle, and his words gave me the comfort I needed to proceed.

When my apartment was ready, I moved one truckload at a

time from the storage unit. My bed was first, along with all the kitchen items. I started painting the living room and the kitchen bright, sunny colors, went shopping for a couch, found a lovely vintage trunk for a coffee table, an old suitcase on legs for a side table and an antique bookcase, which would also serve as a TV stand. Things were starting to take shape. I found a headboard and night table for my bedroom and a small desk to hold a new laptop. I wouldn't be able to see clients at the apartment, but I could continue to offer virtual sessions from my own bedroom office.

Summer clothes were something that I had none of, having only winter clothes in storage, in the event that I returned to Canada to visit during the chilly season. My summer clothes were in our cabana back in Belize, where they would remain until I could travel back to deal with the contents of our home there. I went shopping on occasion, mostly to Value Village, finding a few pieces here and there, or deals at Walmart and, sometimes – when they were having a great sale – my favorite store, Le Chateau, where I'd purchased my wedding dress. Shopping without Michael meant shopping was boring and uneventful, but it gave me the opportunity to decide what my new look might be, starting from nothing.

When I thought about it, I missed certain aspects of our life in Belize; our little cabana we'd modeled with our own hands, the property and its ever-evolving growth, all the foliage, flowers and trees we'd planted and the friends we'd made over multiple years of honeymooning and, eventually, purchasing and building our tropical estate. It's so odd to embrace your new life and miss your old one at the same moment. It brings on many emotions, both joyful and painful, like the Belizean clouds bursting, their bellies full of the tears from another life, soaking you to the bone within seconds. I had come to love the random showers of rain, and I still do, in my new home. They coexist with my random shower of tears, as if God and the angels want to help wash away the pain.

One particularly fine Saturday morning – the morning of my first birthday in 12 years without Michael – I found myself standing in my new apartment's bathroom, the lid of Michael's cologne bottle in my left hand, the bottle in my right. I could feel the cool, soft, triangular lines of the bottle in my palm. I didn't need to spritz any of the precious liquid. I only needed to breathe in the heady scent emanating from the spray nozzle. This cologne, "Tribute" by Mary Kay, had been discontinued; thus, the last one-third of the bottle had to be savored. How the bottle managed to survive the accident, I do not know, but there it was, at the bottom of the tan and orange creamsicle beach bag I had packed for our final honeymoon trip, fully intact and presented to me by the nurses at the Bacalar hospital.

Other random articles had survived the massive blowout and had been collected and placed in the bag along with the cologne. But nothing held any greater significance than that bottle and its last remaining liquid. Blue-green like the sea, the triangular black cap with gold edging worn and faded from all the times he had grasped the lid and pulled it off, before generously pumping the nozzle, distributing the scent over the skin I would happily nuzzle later. That scent has always comforted me, so delicious and masculine, but not overwhelming. Breathing it in deeply, I could feel the familiar longing in my abdomen. The subtle stirring. My favorite place to be was at the base of his neck, the place where this scent often settled. I'd press my face against the long lines of his thick, tanned neck, where it reached the crest of his clavicle and stretched out to his shoulders.

This was the place to be. I would trace my fingers up and down, softly following every line of muscle, memorizing every freckle, breathing in the beautiful mixture of fresh mountain air and that cologne. It soothed me, keeping me calm and relaxed, while at the same time transforming me into a wanton, lustful goddess. I breathed in the delicious scent again from the bottle, taking it fully into my lungs, my heart and my soul. On more difficult nights, I would spritz one quick tap onto my décolletage so that the scent would fill my senses all night long, and I could dream of happier days.

I placed the cap back onto the bottle with a snap, sealing it to await my next fix. I tucked the bottle back onto its bathroom perch, where I could see it clearly every time I walked into the room and imagine him doused in the blue-green mist, knowing the effect it had on me. That bottle contained more than a carefully-measured mix of perfumed ingredients. It contained spectacular memories. All of the times we made mad love after he had applied it, drawing me into his arms, hearing my breath deepen, then quicken as the stirring deepened. The times we went out on the town, dressy casual, talking long into the evening, planning, sharing and loving each other. Although I would never smell that perfection on his body again, I was ever so grateful to the person who retrieved that beach bag and returned it to me.

I celebrated my birthday with a small family gathering and Thai takeout on the rooftop deck of my new apartment building. Now, in my 51st year, I was starting over from scratch, with a few pots and pans, a handful of clothes and a bed. It was as surreal as it was exciting, stepping into my new life, trying to settle into a new normal and decide who I was without my husband. After leaving Nicole's place and moving into my own, I no longer *felt* Michael sitting on the edge of my bed or laying beside me as I had at first. Although I know he never left me, he remained quiet in the background, an unseen visitor, just scoping out the new digs.

I continued with my virtual hypnotherapy clients from

around the world, and even though I had completed my studies, I kept active in the College of Professional Hypnotherapy classes, assisting and providing help to the other students, all via Zoom. Prior to the accident (and non-coincidentally), I had gone deep enough into myself, my studies and my work with clients and other students, that I began to experience the presence of entities attached to either my clients or a few of the students. Michael, however, was the first "entity" I ever actually channeled. I believe this was all part of the greater "plan" Michael had mentioned at various times through his channellings, and it was essential that I develop the ability to sense, speak with and understand these entities, providing counseling to those who did not understand they'd passed on, as well as the people they had attached themselves to. If I didn't have my internal belief in Source (what we might also call "God"), if I hadn't had the experiences I'd had with other entities leading up to the moment I discovered that I could channel Michael, I don't think I would have been open to receiving the messages that Michael gave me, nor would I be able to pass them on to you, dear reader. Now, I have enough case studies documenting these interactions with my clients, other hypnotherapy students and the entities that have come through to fill a whole book – and I shall, after this one.

I had finally come full circle. It was time to start *this* book, and my classmates were the first ones, besides my own children, to know. When I declared to my class group that I set an intention to write my memoir, that afternoon sitting out on my patio, I could smell Michael's cigarette smoke wafting through the air. I looked behind me at the neighboring 4th-floor apartment patio and saw no one there. I looked down at the street, 4-floors below, and examined the other patios – all unoccupied. The apartment building was very new, and not even half of the apartments had been rented. The cigarette smoke smell lingered on my tiny deck – no actual smoke in sight, but the scent was definitely there. I knew what that meant, and I was finally ready. I went inside, pulled my laptop onto my bed and opened it to start writing. I felt the weight of him sitting on my bed once again.

"Ok, Michael," I said. "Let's begin."

DEAD MEN STILL SPEAK

His voice filled my mind, comforting and soft, yet firm: *"I'm with you. Right next to you. I'm smoking my cigarettes and smiling at you and your silliness. I'm with you at night, under the covers, your leg over mine. I'll be with you for as long as you need to heal. We have always been inseparable, and we always will be. I know, at times, I drove you a little nuts with my crusty ways, but despite our individual quirks, our love was deep and true and always will be. We have a book to write, and we will do it together. Me in your head, my hands on yours, feeling the words flowing from your fingertips to the keyboard.*

I know your pain is deep and real. It's ok to want to love again, to want to be close to someone. I'm ok with that and am still with you through everything. We are still experiencing life together, you and I, and even though it's not the life we dreamed of living together, we're still living it. There's much work to do. You have so much to accomplish, and you'll do it. Spread love and joy and blessings to everyone on Earth, and show them how love continues. No matter what happens to us in body, our spirit carries on, loving, living and laughing. You're my baby. You'll always be my baby. We'll always be together, forever. Our love will never die."

Tears blurred my vision as I typed his words flowing through me. "You said I have to write a book. What do you want me to say?" I asked.

"The point of the book you will write is to show proof beyond the 'life after death' rhetoric. To show, by way of your personal

story, that we have a direct connection to a vastly higher Source, to each other, and that death is not to be feared – it is simply the gateway to our true existence, once we have completed our mission on Earth," he explained. *"Assuredly, you are all human, in need of scientific reasoning, and I am delighted to share that with you, to the extent of my knowing and understanding through my own experiences."*

"Okay. What is it that you want me to do?" I asked.

"Spread love and joy and blessings to everyone on Earth, and show them how love continues. No matter what happens to us in body, our spirit carries on, loving, living and laughing," he continued. *"It's time for a great awakening. It's time to remember our BE-ING, who we are, why we are here and to create mass, global change. Know bigger and better things are available to you; you only need to ask. The Universe will provide the rest."*

"And how am I supposed to do that?" I asked.

"Be open and ready to receive your requests from the Universe. Everything is coming to you. Reveal your true nature with no fear. You are a light for this world. Shine. Invite change and growth and be ok with letting things go that you no longer require. The more who know how to channel and trust their abilities, the better the world will become. You are a powerful being. Spread the message. The work is easy. You only need to be still long enough to receive the message."

"Michael, what is the message?" I urged.

"Everything is energy. Your thoughts are energy. Energy, combined with matter, brings creation to your being. You have the ability to form energy into matter and create. Do that. You are but one silver cord within the universal grid line. You all dream. Desires you wish to fulfill. The greater the dream, and the more energy put toward it, causes creation. If, right now, with everything that is happening in the world, you feel fearful, judgmental, angry, disillusioned – you are OUT of alignment

with Source energy. We Source Energy Beings are all here on Earth to stimulate experiences and situations. All Energy Beings choose their roles. Those who've chosen murder are most disconnected from the truth of their being [Source]."

"Many people would argue against this," I replied. "They would say they never 'asked' to be victimized. How would you explain that?" I could sense the incredulity from the masses with the information he was providing and needed clarification.

"Law of Attraction brings together the murderer and the victim," he continued. *"The word 'victim' here is simply used for the purpose of explaining how murder can happen. You have made a prior agreement [before incarnating into your human body]. We each have the option to focus on the positive or the negative end of something. It is necessary to experience the negative in order to then experience the positive. Most people beat the drum of negativity and fear and activate the victimized end. The fearful and the murderer still play a positive role. Together, they launch intense rockets of desire to stimulate profound, positive change in their homeland [with Source]. Source is gathering much information about the emotions related to the experience. This is the purpose of humanity – experience. Some individuals beat the drum of positivism. They are not really victims. They know they are deliberate creators and know that nothing can happen to them without their permission."*

"How are we supposed to live?" I asked. "There is so much negativity in the world."

"Being joyful, positive, having freedom, love and empowerment means being IN alignment with what you know is true. Being fearful, angry, disillusioned and reactionary is being OUT of alignment with what you know is true and means you are out of alignment with Source!!! The Enlightened know that death is meaningless because there really is no death," he explained. *"Funerals are for the living. They are a ridiculous*

tradition. You don't really die. If they choose to 'die,' by whatever means, they do so willingly, knowing that this is all a game. And remember that we have laid these plans for the series of events far before our birth in this life. Either way, we – Source Energy Beings – have recorded a great amount of data in our memories and DNA as part of our evolutionary process.

Source now knows what extreme fear and isolation from knowing [Source] feels like, and what human beings will do under many given circumstances. Where is the learning, you ask? Well, that memory of separation [from Source] helps us to determine what we [Source Energy Beings] want for ourselves in the next evolution on this planet – as individuals and as a race of people. Remember who you really ARE: a Source Energy Being, capable of altering the universal fabric. Keep it positive! Stay in alignment! Love is the strongest, deepest emotion. Choose Love!"

These words gave me so much comfort, and they were very much in alignment with what I'd known since I was very young, too young to articulate what I knew and felt in my heart, unable to follow in my brother's footsteps and take Christianity, Heaven and Hell seriously. I wanted to ask about his own demise, so I continued.

"What is death?" I asked.

"Death is never by accident and is never an ending. Every eventuality is planned from before our inception, and death is merely the passageway to completing the task that was laid before us, to living a life outside our current cellular structure, in our true form," he explained. *"It is not something to be feared. Quite the opposite, in fact; death is a glorious reunion of our souls to the One Source. That Source (which many of us call God), lies within each of us – **not** outside of us, as I was raised to believe – and ties us together in a beautiful web of coexistence."*

"Were you in pain when you died? What was it like?" I recalled the coroner telling Adam that he believed Michael's blow to his head meant instantaneous death, but who could know for sure?

"I was spared any pain, my love. Not to worry, and the details of the accident are not important," he reassured me. *"It was all meant to be. There were three plans of manifestation at work here. I was given the choice as to my Earthly demise, and I chose the path that would bring you the least amount of pain or discomfort."*

This intrigued me.

"What do you mean? What were the other paths? Who gave you the choice?" I was almost giddy, anticipating his reply, butterflies running amok in my belly.

"We have free will to choose," he replied. *"This is something you have known since you were young. One path would mean that I would still live; however, I would be in such a state that you would have had to care for me the rest of your life. I didn't wish to put that burden upon you. The other path would have meant you would have been hurt and would have possibly died from a bullet in the crossfire of a random shooting outside of our intended destination."*

I was absolutely gobsmacked by this information. Immediately, I flicked open Chrome and did a Google search of shootings outside of Cancun on the day of our accident. It took a lot of research through various news sources and articles to find it, but there it was, a small notation on a reputable news website. In a neighborhood that we would have passed through in order to get to our resort, a shooting occurred. The lives of two individuals were lost that day, but thankfully, not mine, as we never arrived at that location in the moment in time when the bullets flew. I could barely breathe. This information was so incredible, so monumental – an even deeper peek into our original life plan.

I slammed the laptop shut and went out to the small deck to breathe in the fresh air. Tears streamed in droves down my face, feeling a huge weight pressed upon me, yet lifted off of me at the same time. I repeated "thank you," over and over again. I didn't want to experience either of the potential manifestations Michael had described. It was hard enough to get through losing him, but to have him an invalid or both of us greatly injured or dead was just too much to process. I spent the remainder of the day in quiet contemplation, journalling, walking and absorbing the day. Questions flowed through me that I still wanted to ask, and, hopefully, Michael would answer... later.

LATER

After I had some time to process the bombshell of information Michael had given me, I returned to my laptop and felt into his presence. "I have some questions. Is it ok to ask you?" The request seemed so surreal; his reply was immediate.

"*You can go ahead and ask your questions,*" he said. "*Lay your concerns and worries out for me to see. There is no judgment, only love. There is nothing in this world to be fearful of, and everything that is happening in your present existence is merely your human experience. It has no hold on you, and the experiences are not YOU. They are merely put in place for the purpose of the experience itself. If you remember, you are in complete control of your entire existence. You are **not** the product of your environment, but you **are** the product of your choices on how you handle your environment. Choose love, choose forgiveness and choose wisely who and what it is that you wish to experience.*"

"Ok, thank you. First, I believe that what I'm doing here is channeling you. What is channeling, exactly?" I asked.

"*Channeling is merely a communication between yourself and Spirit or Source energy,*" he explained. (Spirit, Source and each and every one of us being one and the same – remember, all things are connected.) *"It is as simple as having a conversation with someone across the table from you. If it helps, simply close your eyes, and listen. Truly listen. Not with your ears, but with your heart, mind and soul. What can you feel coming through you? What messages can you hear?"*

Not quite certain I was fully understanding, I asked again for guidance on how to explain channeling and the process.

He continued, *"Learning or re-learning how to communicate with Source energy is really like learning how to breathe for the very first time. You just have to DO it, and you will KNOW."*

"Is it really that simple?" I replied. "A kind of a 'get over yourself' situation?"

"That is correct," he confirmed. *"You think you don't have the ability to channel from the other side, but when you were first born, you didn't think you could breathe, either. In fact, you screamed your insistence to be put BACK into the warm waters of your mother's womb, and it was in that moment that you remembered: 'Oh yes, this again. I did this in my last life too – ok, right, this is normal.' Yes, as normal as breathing, and so is channeling. You are one with Source energy, so really, the conversation you are having is with yourself, your intuition, your guides, angels, God, Jesus and whomever else you choose to have present. Call them all in, they are with you all the time anyway."*

Satisfied with his explanation, I moved on to my next question. "People are so afraid of death, dying and what's waiting for them on the other side. So many believe in the concept of Heaven and Hell, or they are afraid of 'damnation.' First, explain fear, please." I knew this could potentially be a big one, so I relaxed, my fingers on the keyboard, ready to go with the flow.

"Fear is a man-made, man-taught reaction to something that is not otherwise understood or accepted," he began. *"There is*

NO fear in your spiritual form. When you are being your true nature [Source], there is only Love."

I waited for him to continue, but he was silent. "That's it? That was easy," I scoffed. "So, if I hadn't been brought up to 'fear God' or with threats that I would 'burn in Hell' if I didn't accept Jesus, I may not have learned fear at all?"

"That's a tale as old as... well, time," he replied. *"You know that you had previous lives and what those were, one of them being a natural healer in the 14th century. You were hung and burned. Do you remember? The masses were told by the darker forces buried deep within the souls of men that all healers should be considered witches and burned. They laid such fear in people's hearts, people who would take the word of the authority at the time – the church – that there was no other option for them but to comply. You may or may not recall, but your brother in this lifetime played a large role in that life as well, as the clergyman who called you blasphemous and evil and 'kicked the bucket' so you would hang."*

Here, I had to stop, once again completely gobsmacked. Everything, my entire life this far, my on-again-off-again relationship with my fear-mongering Holy Roller brother, now made complete and total sense. We'd been down this path before. I wasn't strong enough to do "battle" with him then, so we were again contracted to go the distance in this lifetime. This time, however, I remained strong and stood my ground, happy with my own beliefs. I had to ask...

"I think I understand now why we are in this life together again. In essence, I'm reliving that previous one, until I can find the strength to 'defeat' him. Is that right? Does this happen for everyone?"

"Yes," he confirmed, *"depending on their own free will and the choices made during the planning phase [before we are born into our human bodies]."*

"Explain the 'planning phase,' please," I asked.

"When you are in the life between lives, during the period of time when you cross over from your 3rd-dimensional reality back to your other dimension, you have a time for review of your life and a time to plan for the next one," he explained.

"How long does that take?" I asked, thoroughly intrigued. "And do you plan this alone? Are there teachers or guides?"

"It takes as long as it takes, and yes, you have your own set of guides to assist you," he began. *"They are accessible at any time in your life, whether living or passed. There are angels, archangels and ascended masters, and even past loved ones. We are all available to you, anytime you need us. You just have to ask. We cannot interfere in your life, but we can help if asked."*

"Good to know, thank you. A lot of times, people can feel the presence of someone they loved who has passed over. What would you call this presence, and what about entities or ghosts? I have worked with a lot of them but would like to know, from your perspective, what the presence really is."

"Everything is energy. When you sense a presence or even see a ghost, you are seeing a form of high vibration," he explained. *"Humans are all molecules formed into matter. It takes an incredible amount of energy to form into a human, to grow, to expand, to develop a brain, heart and so on. But it is still YOU, forming your vibrational energy into that human to begin with! It's not some being or object or alien that creates humans, as we all come from the same Source, and we are all vibrational energy. If you can create you, in matter [material form – the body] there on Earth – think what else you are capable of!"*

"Excellent point!" I replied. "Nothing outside of ourselves is responsible for our creation or our demise, you say. So, if we have participated in the planning of our lives and in the creation of our human form, then it would be reasonable to say that we are solely RESPONSIBLE for anything and everything that happens to us while we are on Earth, yes?"

"YES! You're getting it. But remember that YOU are part of

SOURCE, and therefore, we are all ONE, which means we all share in the responsibility of each other <u>AND</u> what is happening in the world around us." He continued, *"There should be NO BLAME, only responsibility; for actions, for words, for thoughts, for wars, for murder – we are all ONE and, collectively, we are responsible for everything that happens within ourselves and each other."*

I took a breath. "Okay, that's heavy, and that understanding would naturally lead to a lot of guilt in people. Blame, victimization and guilt. How can we overcome that?"

"With love," he replied. *"Love for yourself, love for your neighbor and love for every creature, plant, animal and human. If everyone on Earth in human form would take responsibility, what a different world it would be."*

His words moved through me. *Love for your neighbor.* The Bible, it turns out, didn't get that part wrong, but that's for another discussion, at another time, and maybe even another book. Sensing our channeling session was nearing its end, I asked my final question for now.

"If you could tell everyone in the world ONE thing, what would that be?"

"There is truth and a universal flow of words, thoughts, prayers and an abundance of love for you on the other side," he began. *"My beloved Tammy and I are just here to provide you with an understanding of the immense love that is here for you NOW, and, hopefully, some humor, relief and enlightenment to bring ease to your current loss, and prior to your departure from this world."*

CHAPTER 12
Full Circle

October 2019 - Spring 2021
Belize & Canada

In October 2019, I made the last trip I would make to Belize for quite some time. With the world-wide pandemic lockdown commencing a few months afterward, I was grateful to have taken the opportunity to return, gather a few of my belongings and spread Michael's ashes over our property. I took three of my kids with me – my son, Casey and Carrie – as they had never been. As you'll recall, Nicole and Shawn had visited in Spring 2018, plus they now had a young baby at home, who was not at a good age for traveling to a hot, sticky country.

I was happy to take the kids on a tour of the country Michael had loved so deeply. We spent ten days going to several of our favorite places, hiking, swimming, river tubing and enjoying plenty of beach time. They all had an absolute blast. We didn't stay at the cabana on our property; that would have been too difficult for me. Instead, we stayed at a friend's guesthouse in Hopkins. We traveled to the property for only one day to clean out the cabana and prep it for renters. Troy was there to assist in any way he could, but it was just me and my trio of angels who helped me pack – ten suitcases in all – the things I wanted back in Canada and couldn't bear to leave for strangers to use.

The most important items packed with our personal belongings were Michael's dress shirts. Most of the time, they were hardly worn, except for when I could convince him to dress up for a dinner out, or if we were traveling to Cancun for our anniversary trips. Otherwise, they were kept in my closet, protected and out of reach of Michael's red-clay farmer's fingers. I had plans to turn all of Michael's dress and still-decent work shirts into a quilt to wrap around myself when camping with our mutual friends. That way, a little piece of Michael would always be in our company.

Once we had finished packing, the kids left me alone in the cabana to do another walk-through and say my final goodbyes. Pausing in our bedroom, I ran my fingers along the handmade headboard, carved with a hummingbird pattern. I had been so touched to receive this precious piece of artwork from Michael, and it saddened me that I couldn't take it with me. The cost to transport it to Canada would be far too great, and I wanted once again to respect Michael's wishes to "sell everything," the cabana furnishings included. I said a silent goodbye to the cabana, locking the door behind me one last time.

Troy, his wife Anne and the four of us gathered around Michael's favorite tree – the Ceiba – said a few words and shared a moment of silence before I scattered Michael's ashes around the base of the tree. My attempts at staying stoic and strong were thwarted by both relief and bittersweet goodbyes. I felt the separation from the property for the final time, with no interest or expectation to step foot on it again. Canada is and will always be my home. My place is beside my children, just as Michael had said. The future, now mine to create.

FAREWELL

Sometime around December 2019, Michael let me know that he was about to ascend to the 6th dimension. He was, for lack of deeper understanding, "leaving me" to continue his good work in the higher realms. Around this same time, I also realized that, quite organically, I had been led toward my purpose. People and objects and programs started to fall into place, and I woke up to knowing and understanding what I was meant to do. Michael told me that everything and everyone that needed to come into my life was either already here or on their way.

He also told me (through a mutual friend and psychic) that he had been getting into some deep caca from the "Elders" because he had given away so much information during his time roaming between the dimensions and being with me the last few months. Apparently, he had to be "reigned in" a few times, so as not to give away too much and to let me have my own experiences as they unfolded before me and make my own choices. I had to laugh at that, as Michael, in life, continually had to be "reigned in." He was stubborn and strong and had an incredible mind, but all too often, he became obsessed with antique survey equipment collections on eBay or went on seed-buying sprees on Amazon, to the point of ridiculousness.

The day I felt him leave, the apartment was suddenly empty and lonely and cold. I pushed forward in developing the skills that I needed to bring his messages forward and complete the writing of this book. About a month after Michael made his "exit stage right," I thought I would try to channel him, a "check-in" of sorts. I didn't know if it was possible to really touch base with him after he said he had to go, but I missed our connection. I missed feeling the weight of him on the edge of the bed, and I still had a few questions.

I went into a deep meditative state, asking for his guidance. What I got was quite a surprise! Instead of "just Mike," a *whole group* of beings made themselves known to me. They showed up as large streaks of beautiful, bright, brilliant colors, mainly yellow, gold and turquoise. They told me that the spirit of my husband was deeply involved in the preparation of continued life on our planet, as well as his eventual reincarnation in a few years time. They let me know that they would make themselves available to me anytime I required something. I asked them what I should call them, and they replied:

"You can call us... Michael."

MEMORY

To this day, the accident itself is a single period of time in my life that I have no complete recollection of, and I hope to never fully recover it. Blocking the memory of the accident in its entirety was paramount to my healing process, and I greatly appreciated the Universe in its infinite wisdom for that small grace. I simply didn't need to know. It would be well over a year later that I actually had a hypnotherapy session in which I *would* remember some of the details, as I started showing signs of PTSD at passing ambulances and went into sheer panic mode while driving my car.

One sunny spring morning in 2021, I was driving from my apartment to the gym, and in order to get there, I had to travel a short distance on the busy main highway through the city. I kept to the inside lane, as my left turn would be just ahead, about three or four traffic lights later. Suddenly, I saw ambulance lights up ahead in the oncoming traffic, then a second set close behind the first. I couldn't hear the wail of the siren with my radio on, but I didn't need to. Triggered from the subconscious memory of the trauma, my body went completely numb as I crept along then sped up, following the flow of the other cars on the road. My breath shifted, hitching, and I began to gasp.

I quickly reached for the window's auto roll button, welcoming fresh air onto my face. Dark, fuzzy dots crept into my vision. I knew I would pass out soon, and if I didn't get off the highway, I'd be in another world of hurt, potentially taking several others with me. I could barely see through the fuzzy, blackening vision, not behind me nor in my sideview mirrors, before quickly crossing in front of a semi-truck then into another lane, the far right, unable to see if anyone was speeding up behind me. I turned abruptly, pulled into a parking lot and slammed my car into park. Opening all of the windows with quivering fingers, I waited for the shaking to subside and my vision to clear. It took several minutes for my body to calm down, and I knew I was having a post-traumatic stress episode.

It was time. I needed to unlock the trauma and release it, or take a chance that there would be more episodes like this one, potentially causing injury to myself or others. Once I was home again, I contacted my mentor and friend Jasmine, owner of the College of Professional Hypnotherapy, which I attended to earn my degree. We had become good friends immediately after connecting and attending the classes, both online and virtual, in the years I took to complete my degree. We had been through a lot together as friends, and we would call upon each other anytime one of us was in a state of crisis or needed advice, or just to chat. I called her as soon as I got home that day, and we set a time to meet for a virtual session.

When we met, I explained the event that had truly shaken me, and Jasmine then invited me to relax and allow the hypnosis to unlock the event and trauma, in whatever way was right for me. Hypnosis has taken a lot of flack in recent years as something that is more "quackery" than a real, thera-peutic method of healing, but I have witnessed clients who have been in psychotherapy or counseling for the better part of 10-20 years, who are finally able to heal within three to six sessions of hypnotherapy, utilizing the work that we do. I usually work with people who have suffered loss or have anxiety, stress and depression, but, as you now know, I've also helped clients who've had entity attachments and have cleared them and their homes, working both with the individual and with the connected spirit. Part of the reason I attract such clients is because of my deeper understanding of life and death and the process of transition, which I will cover in my upcoming book, *Entity Case Files*, to be published in 2022.

Jasmine and I had previously worked to clear her own demons, entities that had attached themselves to her during her first pregnancy. Prior to the clearing, she had no interest in participating in the life of the child growing inside her, nor did she have any real desire to be a mother. After the clearing, she was able to fully embrace the joy and excitement of her pregnancy, and a deep connection between her and her baby flourished in her final weeks before his birth. Now, working with my friend and colleague in my own hypnotherapy session, we asked my spirit guides and angels, Archangels Michael, Gabriel, Uriel, Haniel and Jesus – and, of course, my Michael – to wrap me in a coat of protection and take me back to the earlier incident (spotting the ambulances on my drive to the gym) and the ensuing panic attack. I was there immediately and felt my body go cold, shaking.

"What is happening to you now? What is going through your mind?" Jasmine asked.

"Nothing," I managed. "I see spots... I can't breathe. Everything is numb."

Jasmine immediately reassured me and helped me calm my body. "You're protected by the angels," she reminded me. "Go to the ambulances. Follow them... where are they going?"

"They are going to assist an older couple whose husband had a heart-attack or stroke," I explained.

"What do you want to do? How can you help them?" She prompted.

"I wrap them in a coat of protection, the ambulances, the workers. I'm helping them get to where they need to go safely, so they can do their good work."

"Good," she said. "Now, have your angels protect you as they guide you over to your own accident in Mexico. What do you see?"

I paused for a few moments, drifting over the continents, viewing the beautiful landscapes and countrysides with my guides, until I arrived at that place in time when and where the accident occurred. I could feel Archangel Michael's intense presence right beside me, blue cloak flapping behind him as his enormous wings carried us. His strong right arm was wrapped around me, and his hand gripped my shoulders. His left hand held mine, leading me to the scene in time where the accident occurred. I felt safe, protected and ready to face my fears. We floated above the scene.

"I'm there," I said.

"What's happening?" Jasmine asked.

"There's a vehicle in front of us. It's large, like a Suburban. The boat trailer has detached itself from the vehicle. I'm not even aware of this happening at all. I've been looking out the passenger window at the views. Then I blacked out." My voice cracked.

"You are safe and protected by the angels," Jasmine reminded me. "Go on, what happened next?"

I calmed myself and continued. "Michael didn't even yell or scream; he just tried to get out of the way. He swerved hard to the right. The boat trailer bounced up and hit him – right through the driver's window – into the side of his face, killing him instantly. He's gone, and we are rolling at full-speed down the highway. I'm not even aware that I'm hanging on to the 'oh shit' handles of the Jeep, one on the glove box in front of me, one on the right roll-bar. My hands are clenched so very tightly and sustaining cuts and scratches as we roll. Michael and I butt heads at one point, breaking the flesh on the left of my skull. Blood is already seeping into my eyes. The rolling stops, but my fists remain clenched. That's when I open one eye slightly and see that Michael has passed over." I finished relaying the memory, my heart racing but still feeling protected and safe with the distance between myself and the scene below.

"What do your angels or guides want you to know about this time?" Jasmine asked.

"They are showing me that there is really no reason for me to remember the full details of the accident. It serves no purpose, but they are happy to oblige. My guides and angels were all there at my silent beckoning to protect me, and in fact, they moved me out of my body as the car rolled and rolled over 75 meters." I was astounded at this revelation.

The fact that I had an intense grip on the "oh shit" handles of the Jeep answered the question as to why my hands were so unwilling to unwind afterwards. The rest of my body was shielded and protected as it was being tossed like a rag-doll, and I suffered very little bodily damage. I rose higher above the scene, completely serene and at peace. Jasmine then took me back to my car, to the PTSD event I had experienced earlier.

"Picture yourself on that drive, happy and relaxed," she instructed. "Where are you heading?"

"I'm driving to the hospital with a few copies of my book, *Dead Men Still Snore*, in the seat beside me. I'm going to donate them to the palliative care wing of the hospital. They will bring peace and ease to the people who are facing death and to their families."

"Good," Jasmine replied. "Now, you see the ambulances in the on-coming lane. What are you thinking now?"

"I am sending them love and light, wrapping the ambulances, the workers and the people who they are going to assist in a coat of love and protection."

"Do you feel any anxiety about seeing them?" She asked.

"No, just peace, love and using my ability to help them brings me comfort."

"Good," she said, satisfied with the progress I'd already made in comparison to the beginning of our session. The traumatic imprint lingering in my body and energetic field had been cleared. "Whenever you're ready, open your eyes."

Afterward, we went over the details of the session. Traveling over the accident scene in Mexico brought tears to my eyes and a softening to my heart, which I desperately needed. It solidified my understanding of my purpose in the world, my mark on the Universe, and it quantified the direction of my life. And that was it. The shattering end of our love story and the beginning of my new life, the moment when my world was altered in one single, cataclysmic event that shook me to my very core, until I could establish a foot-hold in a new life, a life of *my* design and choosing, fulfilling my purpose and sharing our story of love and the journey of the soul with the world.

BORN AGAIN

In Summer 2020, after about a year of being on my own and attempting to live up to the responsibility that was tasked upon me, writing, researching and finding my way, I felt a "shedding" of my old self and former life beginning to take place. A ceremonial "in with the new" was in order, a baptism of sorts in celebration of a new life. I drove myself down to the local lake, where I performed my simple but powerful little ceremony. Slowly, I walked into the cool, welcoming waters. I paused, clasping my hands in front of my heart, thanking the Universe for its divine wisdom and glory, for my life, my future and my family. I made a promise to live the rest of my days with full intention, thought and devotion to healing myself and others.

I moved my praying hands up to clasp my nostrils on either side and fell backward into the water, baptizing myself anew and washing away the past few months, accepting who I was now and allowing myself to be spiritually "dedicated" in the manner in which I truly believed in my heart. Unlike the baptism I had received as a teenager, I had no conflicting emotions, thoughts or feelings. This time, it didn't feel forced, and this time, I baptized *myself* in my own beliefs, not those of others that had been pushed upon me. I had come full circle, and this time, I allowed my own beliefs, faith and wisdom to wash over me with the gentle waves. In the cool waters of the lake on that summer day, I committed to moving forward into the rest of my life with gratitude, wisdom and love, until it is time, once again, for me to cross the barrier of the 3rd dimension, and to be born, again, into my next life.

If there is only one thing you take away from this book, let it be this: call it God, Source or the Divine, as I do, but remember – we are all part of the same, One Source, and there is *never*, even for a moment, any separation. For each and every single, individual part affects the Whole. Last, but not least...

La vida es preciosa.

Epilogue

The thing about grief when the person you've lost is your love and soulmate, is that the desperation you feel for bringing them back is equally matched with your need to be held and comforted by any other warm body. This is why we tend to throw ourselves into a new relationship so quickly after loss, whether we have loved and lost through death, or through separation and divorce. We miss the closeness, the feel of their body next to ours, the talking late into the night and the planning for the future. We grasp for this when our beloved is gone. Many months after Michael's passing, my work with hypnotherapy clients – both living and departed – for surviving loss and grief, anxiety, stress and depression, opened me up for further expansion. Eventually, a new list emerged for finding a partner who was absolutely into the same spiritual and metaphysical things as I am, and I found myself ready to attract the man who fit the new description.

On the Monday morning of an August long weekend, I woke up groggy and reached for my phone. That wasn't exactly an uncommon thing for me to do, but I'd usually wait for the sleep to creep out of my eyes, or, at the very least, leave the gadgets alone until I got up out of bed and had a good pee and my daily meditation. Not this day, however. On this day, I slid my finger directly over to the App Store and typed "Bumble" into the search bar. The app came up, and I downloaded it. Sitting up straighter in bed, wiping the sleepy sludge from my eyes and thinking, *what the F?* – I logged in with my Facebook profile and updated a few key points about my likes, then hesitated.

What was I doing? I didn't have any reason to start dating again, least of all this soon. But in thinking that, the gnawing itch at the back of my brain said, "*He should love to do all of the things you do, be outdoorsy and physically fit and healthy. He should like hiking and camping and love the water and hockey, and he should be completely accepting of who you truly are and what your purpose is.*" These happened to be the things I had been missing in a partner in the final years of Michael's life. That, and physical intimacy, as you already know.

After a quick tutorial on the Bumble app's swipe method, I was relieved to learn that it's only women who can initiate any type of conversation. I began a brief search, not truly giving any credence to what I may find there. *Left, left, left – HELLO! John, age 47.* John was super good-looking, with dark hair, dark eyes, a brilliant smile and a fit, tanned body. His profile indicated his "likes" were hiking, camping, water sports and hockey. *Be careful what you wish for...*

I swiped right, and BOOM! "You're a match!"

No kidding.

I was then given the opportunity to send him a message.

Hmmm... what should I say?

As it was the long weekend, that seemed like a decent opener. "Hi, John!" I typed. "How's your weekend going so far?" It took him only an hour or so to message me back.

"Hi, Tammy! My weekend has been great so far! How's yours?"

Somewhat unsure but also excited, I responded, "Good! All the usual things, soaking up the sun. I managed to get some paddle boarding in."

"Sounds amazing!" He replied. "I've never tried paddle boarding. Maybe we could go sometime?" He gave me his number, asking me to text him if I'd like to go for a walk or a coffee. I left it alone for a while but continued to swipe left, left, left, then another right, but there was no instant fanfare "You're a match!" with any other fella' now on my radar.

I sent messages to four other guys, and they all replied, but nothing gave me the "feels" like John did. Later that day, I received another message from him on the app. "Would you be available to go for a walk later?" He asked. "If so, you have my number!"

I saved his number on my phone, adding the contact name as "John - Bumble," and texted him directly. "Yes, I do have your number. :-)"

He texted back immediately, and we made tentative plans to meet for a walk later that day on the walking trail near my apartment. After numerous outfit changes before settling on a simple pair walking shorts and T-shirt, I arrived at the parking lot by the trail. He was already waiting for me, just as handsome as his profile pictures, and at 5'11", he was 3/4" shorter than me. I decided I could live with that if it meant seeing that beautiful smile and tanned, fit body every day. He greeted me with a warm hug. My nerves, stomach and throat were in an uproar. *What was I doing? Was I truly ready for this? How did this happen? Where did he come from?*

We started on our walk and casual conversation. When I got to the part about being a recent widow, he immediately said, "You're not ready to date!" So, it seemed, he was also astute. I gave it some thought, feeling the question through my entire body.

"You have a connection here, don't let it go," the voices from beyond flowed through me.

"Well..." I started. "I come from a place, a belief, that there are no coincidences in life and that everything is meant to be, that everything has a reason. Although I'm not necessarily looking for a new relationship, I would enjoy being with someone who is like-minded, who can show me the hiking trails, go to hockey games with me, enjoy the beach and the weather and be good company, then we can see where it may go from there."

Seemingly satisfied with my answer, we continued a light conversation, walking and chatting. At one point, an incredibly strong feeling came over me, an essence washing over my entire body. Warmth flooded in. I had to focus on one spot in the distance and keep my eyes trained on that spot or I'd surely faint. The shivering, amazing flood of feelings was heady. I lost my breath, stopping at a small bridge, pretending to take in the view of the babbling creek flowing underneath it. I instantly smelled Michael's cigarette smoke and slowly looked around. No one else was there. But Michael was, his energy flowing through me, palpable and thick. I could feel his excitement mingling with my own, and I knew he was giving me his blessing. I pushed through the rest of the walk, feeling stronger and more relaxed, but still not completely understanding how it was I came to be here. I followed my feet in the direction only they seemed to know I must go.

Back in the parking lot, John gave me another hug, and we made loose plans to meet again later that week, and we did. I texted him a couple days later and asked if he'd like to try paddle boarding. Naturally, he said yes. We agreed to meet at my apartment building that afternoon and take my car to the beach. I packed my tan and orange creamsicle beach bag with a towel, sunblock, water and a couple of coolers, pausing for a moment to brush my fingers across the now-faint blood stains on the bag.

"I hope this is ok..." I asked Michael. A whiff of his cigarette smoke filled the air. Smiling, I finished packing the bag and headed to the parking garage. I waited around the exterior of the building for John to pull up in his grey Ford truck. As he parked, I pulled my car up beside his vehicle. He leaned out the driver's door, sunglasses protecting his eyes, and he smiled a dazzling, brilliant smile, giving me a thumbs up.

"Ok to park here?" He asked through my open car window.

"Yes, great! I'll pull ahead and wait for you," I replied, my heart involuntarily in my throat. "Oh my God, oh my God, oh my God," I said under my breath as I pulled my car ahead. "He's sooooo good looking! Holy hell!"

I was cut short as John opened the back door, tossing in a small cooler and beach towel. He closed the back door and opened the front one, sliding into the passenger seat. My heart was about to explode.

"Hi!" He said, grabbing me to give me a quick hug and flashing that incredible smile.

"Hi yourself! You ready for this?" And that was it. I took him paddle boarding. My full expectation was that he would fall in, hopefully several times, as a newbie often does, but he did not. He remained steady and sure.

During our paddle boarding adventure, we paused for a while to dive in and cool off. Lounging on the boards, we chatted for what seemed like hours. I was open and honest with John about my beliefs and shared how deeply spiritual I am. He admitted to not questioning his own spirituality, but was happy just to be who he was and leave the bigger plans to the unknown. He was definitely grounded in the 3rd dimension, but that was good enough for me, and I let go, allowing the future to write its own tale and feeling grateful to have someone to keep me grounded and steady at the times I've needed it most. Later that evening, I texted John and asked how he enjoyed his first paddle boarding adventure.

"I don't know, I was too busy admiring the view," was his reply.

Daftly, I texted back, "Yes, it's a beautiful place to board," thinking of the lake and the beauty of the surrounding hills.

"That's not the view I meant," John replied with a smiley-winking-face emoji. I blushed and sputtered, my heart throbbing like a teenager with her first crush.

"What are you doing tomorrow evening?" I texted back. And so, it began.

It was refreshing to be so honest and open about myself, and he continues to make me feel safe, loved and respected. He's even curious, at times, about my spiritual experiences, and he's become my greatest cheerleader. He often boasts to new and old friends about me writing this book, and, on occasion, has asked if I could communicate with a few dearly departed friends, a true acknowledgment of who I am at my very core, and I couldn't ask for more or be happier.

As hard as I've tried to "see" if he would be my steady and sure for the rest of my life, the Universe has kept this mystery from me to relax and enjoy its unfolding. In the meantime, we enjoy the simplest things that life has to offer; nature, gardening, hiking and each other, with grateful and full hearts. When we go camping, I'm often found sitting by the fire, wrapped in the quilt of Michael's shirts I made shortly after bringing them all back from Belize. John, accepting and appreciating the work that went into the quilt, the love I had for the man who wore the shirts, and the story of our life together, gratefully snuggles under it with me in the camper, as we drift off in peaceful sleep together.

Oh, and in case you were wondering... *he doesn't snore.*

Acknowledgments

I always read a book's acknowledgements written by the author. To me, they represent the work as a whole, so it's only proper to credit the family, friends and vast team involved in the writing, because truly, writing isn't all about the author. Without the supportive team behind the scenes, there would be no book! It gives me the deepest pleasure to be able to acknowledge the following:

My rockstar, badass editor, Kenzie Templeton. We have built an incredible relationship based on the solid foundation of this book, and I look forward to developing many more books with you by my side. (P.S. You had me at "woo-woo.")

To my cover designer Larch Gallagher, for your tiring efforts in creating and re-creating everything to absolute perfection, thank you for seeing the vision. You are incredibly talented.

To my accountability team, Mike, Roman and Christy, thank you for your unwavering support and weekly cheering squad. Special thanks to Christy for knowing what I needed in a book cover before I did. You're the best!

To my boyfriend DJL, thank you for your unconditional love, support and excitement at seeing this work being written. ("This is my girlfriend – she's writing a book!") I know it took much longer than anticipated, but it's so worth the wait! Remind me to get you an autographed copy – heehee. ;-)

To KK, thank you for dropping your life so that you could pick up mine. Forever family, I love you so much. What the heck more can I say to you? LOVE YOU!

To my family, what would my life be without all of you in it? Thank you so much for your love, support, encouragement, emotions, care, concern and being the greatest people a Mom and Nana could ever ask for. You are my purpose, my life, my love. I am forever grateful you chose me to be your Mama and that you are all in this dimension, by my side.

Did You Enjoy This Memoir?

If you enjoyed reading this work as much as I did writing it, please leave a review on Amazon (or whichever book retailer you purchased it from), or email me tammy@ tammytyree.com! Reviews help my work be "seen" and spread the word!

An Invitation

As incredible as my story may seem, I know that I'm not alone in its expression. I would like to invite any and all women who have experienced similar loss, grief and communication with their loved ones to share their stories with me for publication in this book's forthcoming sequel, *Dead Men Still Speak*. Please send your submissions to: tammy@tammytyree.com with "Submission" in the subject line.

PLEASE NOTE**: By way of your submission, you are agreeing to publication in my book and understand that not all stories may be suitable for publication.

A Gift for You

To receive my list of the "Top 5 Books that Changed My Life" for free, please go to: https://tammytyree.com/

For more information on the author, other titles, programs and offerings, please visit https://tammytyree.com/

Manufactured by Amazon.ca
Bolton, ON

24541608R00210